The
Power
of
One

THE SOLO PLAY FOR PLAYWRIGHTS, ACTORS, AND DIRECTORS

Louis E. Catron

The College of William and Mary

WAVELAND
PRESS, INC.
Long Grove, Illinois

For information about this book, contact:
Waveland Press, Inc.
4180 IL Route 83, Suite 101
Long Grove, IL 60047-9580
(847) 634-0081
info@waveland.com
www.waveland.com

The author and publisher wish to thank those who have generously given permission
to reprint borrowed material:

"Nice Shoes" from *The Essential Bogosian: Talk Radio, Drinking in America, Fun-house and Men Inside* by Eric Bogosian, © 1994 by Eric Bogosian. Published by Theatre Communications Group. Used by permission of Theatre Communications Group.

"A Poster of the Cosmos" by Lanford Wilson reprinted by permission of International Creative Management, Inc. © 1988 by Lanford Wilson as an unpublished dramatic composition. © 1991 by Lanford Wilson.

"Lousy Language" from *Fires in the Mirror* by Anna Deavere Smith. © 1993 by Anna Deavere Smith. Used by permission of Doubleday, a division of Random House, Inc.

Acknowledgments for borrowed material continue on page 234.

10-digit ISBN 1-57766-620-8
13-digit ISBN 978-1-57766-620-2

Printed in the United States of America

7   6   5   4   3   2   1

For Markwood Lincoln

CONTENTS

ACKNOWLEDGMENTS

I owe deep gratitude to a number of people and institutions who helped shape this book. Among them are

Jon Jory, Artistic Director of the Actors Theatre of Louisville (Kentucky), who has been a dominant leader in showing the power of the solo play and has shown remarkable support of new plays. Jon graciously shared his insights into the monodrama. His staff guided me to scripts of countless monodramas in the theatre's archives.

Richard Palmer, Professor of Theatre at the College of William and Mary, who patiently read versions of the manuscript and made insightful comments and helpful suggestions.

The College of William and Mary for a grant to enable me to research the monodrama.

The editors of *Dramatics* and *Writers Digest* magazines, who published my articles on the solo play, leading to this book.

Lisa A. Barnett, whose consistent support, good will, and collegiality made the entire process smooth, efficient, and enjoyable.

And most of all, my students, who helped create these materials, asked penetrating questions about the essentials of the monodrama, and through their scripts and productions showed what the monodrama could be.

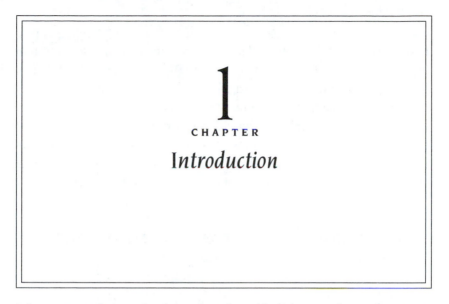

1

CHAPTER

Introduction

It is necessary to have a point of view about the world which surrounds you, the society in which you live; a point of view as to how your art can reflect your judgment.

To rebel or revolt against the status quo is in the very nature of an artist. A point of view can result from the desire to change the social scene, the family scene, the political life, the state of the ecology, the conditions of the theater itself. Rebellion or revolt does not necessarily find its expression in violence. To portray things the way they are, to hold a mirror up to the society, can also be a statement of rebellion. You must ask yourself, "How can I bring all of this to the statement I wish to make in the theatre?"   —Uta Hagen

THE SOLO PERFORMER SITS AT A DESK ON A NEW YORK STAGE, framed by a simple setting—ordinary black stage curtains, minimal stage lights, and on the desk a glass of water and a box holding a manuscript. He creates an intimate one-to-one theatrical relationship with his audience as he weaves an autobiographical tale that is loosely based on writing his novel, which he calls a "monster in a box." Alone, he holds the stage for a full evening's production, as long as the traditional multicharacter, full-length play. (Later we'll discuss in detail this performance and others mentioned below.)

This solo production illustrates *the power of one*—a solitary performer presenting a theatrical experience as richly vibrant and varied as multicharacter plays. It has a carefully honed script with a beginning, middle, and end and an actor impersonating a character; it may bring to life a historical or totally fictional character or even an autobiographical story; it may be a drama or comedy; and it may be a story of one person or it may involve a number of other characters that the actor evokes in the audience's imagination—*but there is only one actor.* As we discuss shortly, you'll find that these one-person productions are popular in theatres all over the country, offering challenges and rewards to beginning and advanced playwrights, actors, and directors while simultaneously entertaining audiences with insights into individual humans, statements the theatrical artists decide best reflects their point of view about their own corner of the universe.

SOLO PERFORMANCES: THE POWER OF ONE ON STAGE

On Broadway and off-Broadway professional stages, you find solo performers demonstrating *the power of one* in captivating theatrical productions as they share with audiences what playwright Thornton Wilder calls theatre's power to express "the sense of what it is to be a human being." These solitary actors may represent well-known figures, bring a novel to life, blend extracts from plays, or move boldly to new forms. For example, an actress becomes the poet Emily Dickinson in a performance that wins theatre's highest awards. An actor is President Harry Truman. A former musical comedy star acts presents novelist Truman Capote and tours the production following a successful New York run. A well-known television and Shakespearean dramatic star plays dozens of characters from a Charles Dickens novel. The daughter of a famous acting dynasty weaves a solo performance using extracts from Shakespeare's plays, her homage to her father, and receives standing ovations on tour around the country, while her New York production results in a nomination for a Tony Award. A playwright and actor uses the metaphor of a caveman to create a wryly comic exploration of the traditional "battle between the sexes," setting records as Broadway's longest running solo play, even prompting New York's mayor to proclaim a special day to honor the play. On tour, it performs to sold-out audiences in major cities.

A *Personal Expression*

Solo performers often may echo actress Uta Hagen's statement, quoted earlier, to use their art to reflect a personal point of view in a "statement of rebellion" to "portray things the way they are." For instance, a skillful television comedienne plays a number of women coping with the pressures of being female in the modern world. A college theatre professor writes solo plays for herself to perform, transforming actual events into a compelling stage event, in one playing two dozen enraged and spiritually damaged people victimized by a bitter racial riot in New York. An internationally respected playwright creates a young man in conflict with police who, invisible and silent, surround him in an interrogation room; the young man's friend died of AIDS. In Chicago an actor creates one-person dramas like half-remembered dreams that are performed with original music; an actress in San Francisco performs a one-woman tribute to her mother, a victim of Alzheimer's disease. The Joseph Papp Public Theater in New York later presents both solo plays.

Educational, Amateur, and Professional Productions

The art of solo performance is alive not only in New York but across the nation. Established educational, amateur, and professional theatres often present one-person plays, and from time to time you also find them in coffeehouses, lofts, church basements, libraries—any space that can be converted into a place for an actor and audience.

For example, in a Virginia college's studio theatre the student playwrights, actors, and directors work closely together to present an evening of half a dozen original short one-person comedies and dramas. Each script is a personal vision of an aspect of the theatre artist's world, examining such topics as family relationships, peer pressures, personal choices, death of a family member or close friend, and the delightful or bewildering aspects of love.

In a Kentucky professional regional theatre eleven talented actresses appear in an equal number of short solo plays, each different yet all linked by the vision of an unusually gifted playwright. One character is an old woman who wants to live in a fast-food restaurant, another is a baton twirler who transmutes twirling into a religious ceremony that is bizarre but somehow frighteningly familiar, a third is a young girl coming to grips with the death of her mother who never appears on stage but is nonetheless distinctly present in the audience's imagination. Later they perform the solo plays in New York to popular and critical acclaim.

The solo play can be an entry to a theatrical career. For example, a college actor, eager to develop his skills so he can carve out a career as an actor, writes a one-man play about a famous American humorist. He tries out pieces of the script in small clubs and schools, seeking to learn what works through experience. He learns well, ultimately performing his solo play on Broadway and receiving professional theatre's highest awards, leading to a highly successful career as a film, television, and stage actor.

The one-person play often expands a theatre's regular bill. In a central Illinois town, for instance, a theatrical company that specializes in historical outdoor summer theatre productions decides to venture into new areas. It includes solo dramas about Eleanor Roosevelt and John F. Kennedy in its season's bill along with its multicharacter biographical play about a former president. For the actors and directors, the result is a deeply satisfying artistic experience; for the theatre, the productions are a new source of income for relatively small costs; and for local residents and tourists, the one-person shows are journeys into the essences of significant Americans.

Solo performances are often labors of love, stimulated by a hunger to use talents for which there are few outlets. For example, an amateur actress in a small western town where there is no theatre persuades a local church to allow her to transform its basement meeting room into a stage for her one-woman show that she's written, staged, and produced. Virtually all local citizens attend her play.

Solo plays can allow writers and actors to venture into new areas. A Hollywood screenwriter and movie biographer turns playwright to create full-length solo plays of legendary Hollywood actors such as Clara Bow, Orson Welles, Carole Lombard, and Clark Gable. Soon he has a collection of eight one-person plays that are performed around the country.

The one-person play can be a tool to teach theatrical concepts. A college theatre faculty develops an innovative hands-on Introduction to Theatre class in which the students combine a study of theatrical history, literature, and theory with actually writing and staging short-short solo plays. Even though the students are not theatre majors and initially resist the possible embarrassment of artistic self-expression, they find that the short plays are *doable* projects, less complicated than multicharacter plays but nonetheless containing the essential storytelling quality of the theatrical experience. At the end of the semester students collaborate to become a miniproduction company that brings the solo plays to life in front of the class and an appreciative audience of interested friends. The process helps them apply abstract concepts to the concrete realities of production, and they learn, through first-hand involvement, how theatre is created. The experience helps them discover answers to the question, What is theatre?

The solo play is also an educational tool for advanced artists. A prominent regional theatre requires interns in acting to write one-person plays for themselves to perform. The interns find that writing solo plays makes them better actors because it improves their understanding of theatre as a story-telling art, and creating solo pieces designed for themselves to play forces them to evaluate their performance strengths and weaknesses. The act of writing, they discover, allows them to encounter their private selves. The creative exercise stimulates additional creativity, and the experience leads some to continue developing one-person plays at other theatres.

EARLY SOLO PRODUCTIONS

From the present we travel backward in time to primitive societies, discovering that the solo performer predates recorded history. Over its history, the one-person show made numerous contributions to theatre, even helping the art overcome attacks from legislative bodies or survive adversity and prejudice. We also discover that the solo performer has a long and honorable tradition.

A prehistoric tribe gathers around a flickering fire to watch a shaman who becomes, alternately, god, hunter, and savage beast of prey. His ritual is, in a very real sense, a one-person performance that incorporates an organized story, characterization, theme, gesture, magic, impersonation, dance-pantomime, and costume—the ingredients of theatre—in a traditional ceremony that teaches members of the tribe how to deal with the mysterious and often frightening unknown world that haunts the shadows beyond the fire's light.

In Greece, long before the formal beginning of the classical theatre, solo performers called *rhapsodists* (oral readers) present legends and history, awakening interest in theatre and setting a pattern that years later would be developed by well-known playwrights such as Aristophanes, Sophocles, and Euripides. In Rome, *histriones*, also solo performers, enact a variety of characters, and their works create interest in what will later become the formalized theatre led by playwrights such as Plautus and Seneca. These solo artists-historians-entertainers are chroniclers of their times, impersonating significant leaders and events of the past to captivate audiences in the present, an enjoyable and enriching imaginary journey through history that makes theatre an important force in their societies.

Despite the rich birth of the art in Greece, Western theatre virtually disappears after the advent of Christianity—virtually, but not totally. During the Middle Ages, when formal theatre does not exist, solo performers keep the theatrical spirit alive as they travel Europe. In outdoor courtyards, in inns and taverns, and at feudal lords' banquet halls, the medieval *scôps*, *gleemen*, *goliards*, and *jongleurs* use stories and music to tell stories of their times and bring heroic figures to life.

An eighteenth-century English political leader named Walpole, angered by theatrical political satires, sharply restricts most theatre through a sweeping Licensing Act. However, he does not succeed in limiting theatre. George Alexander Stevens, an enterprising actor and playwright, ingeniously circumvents the law by presenting entertaining one-person productions that he labels "lectures." Because Stevens's plays aren't "plays" according to the legal definition, the authorities can't stop him. Others imitate Stevens's success. As a result, a lively form of theatre continues despite antitheatre regulations.

In eighteenth-century America the southern states, founded primarily by a cultured class from England, are delighted to welcome theatre, but the puritanical religious settlers in the north are suspicious that the art is somehow immoral and they pass legislation to ban the art. Again, presentations of lectures—actually one-person performances—cleverly make end runs around antitheatre regulations.

A century later the stratagem works yet again in small rural towns throughout the new American western states. In the late 1800s, the Lyceum and Chautauqua organizations, seeking to offer American citizens cultural and moral education, begin presenting highly reputable intellectuals, politicians, and clergy who travel across America in high-caliber tent shows, giving educational and morally uplifting speeches. Soon solo performers appear in the same circuits to present *platform readings*, primarily readings from novels. Those evolve into solo actors becoming the various characters in the novels and then into solo performers presenting theatrical works. From that it is but a short step to performances of multi-character plays. Those citizens who suspect theatre may be immoral, even the devil's work (Why else would one put on makeup and costumes except to disguise one's evil nature? And we all know, of course, that theatre folks are merely lazy layabouts who never do an honest day's work.) find these solo performances to be morally acceptable because they are presented in the same tents in which the nation's educational, religious, and political leaders appear. They also discover that the theatre isn't so evil or disreputable, after all, and even—surprise!—can be entertaining and uplifting. The solo actor becomes acceptable, thus creating audiences for multicharacter, full-scale theatrical performances that soon play in the tents. Interest in theatre grows as a result of those initial solo performances, and educational and community theatres spring up in small towns. Theatre gains strength in areas that had been hostile to the stage.

Eighteenth-century literary figures present readings from their novels. For example, Charles Dickens, a theatre buff of the first caliber, tours the world acting dozens of characters from his novels, attracting large audiences and popular acclaim. So, too, do other writers such as Mark Twain and Edgar Allan Poe. They are followed by actors who present lectures in which they impersonate characters. Again, despite some Victorian citizens' belief that theatre is morally unacceptable, the solo performers make theatre respectable.

THE MONODRAMA, SOLO PLAY, OR ONE-PERSON SHOW

In all the preceding instances the solo theatrical form is what some prefer to call the *monodrama*. But the form is so flexible that it also is called a *monologue* (sometimes prefaced by *dramatic* or *theatrical*), a *solo play*, or a *one-person show*. In an evocation of vaudeville, when a turn meant an individual specialty act, you may hear theatre veterans call it a *solo turn*. The monodrama at times may be called a *dramatic reading* or a *platform reading*, but those types of solo performances more typically refer to readings from literature without impersonation of the characters.

Certain postmodern monodramas fit within the larger category of *performance art*, a reference to a highly individualistic piece specifically designed for a particular actor's abilities and interests, most often written and performed by that performer. Performance art often is solo works. Content or style of some performance art may disturb certain audience members. Several such productions have been attacked by a few vocal political and religious figures, who admit they haven't seen such shows but oppose them anyway, reminding us of Pastor Manders, the sanctimonious variable-standard character in Henrik Ibsen's *Ghosts* who condemns various literary works he finds in Mrs. Alving's collection, not because he's actually read them but because he has heard *about* them. The attackers usually claim the content or style is immoral. Because a very few such controversial performance art pieces may have received some financial support from the National Endowment for the Arts, such critics even insist that all national funding for all arts should be eliminated, a sweeping condemnation that deeply concerns artists and audiences.

An Unheralded, Yet Powerful, Form

Strangely, although the monodrama is one of theatre's powerful artistic forms, with roots we can trace to prehistoric times well before the beginning of organized formal theatre, references to the monodrama are conspicuously absent in books on theatrical history, playwriting, acting, directing, or design. These are only a few anthologies of monodramas. The lack of scholarly attention to the solo play seems even more strange given its historical contributions, longevity, artistic values, popularity, and number of variations in style, content, form, and length that make it a significant contribution to theatrical art.

Audience Response

Although theatre scholars and historians may overlook the one-person performance, it has ardent supporters. Audiences enjoy the power of the solo performance, whether at professional and regional theatres, touring shows, or local amateur and educational organizations. For example, producers reported excellent attendance at monodramas during a recent New York season, which included a number of solo performances on Broadway or off-Broadway, such as Spalding Gray's *Sex and Death to the Age* 14, Lily Tomlin's Tony-winning *The Search for Intelligent Life in the Universe*, Dario Fo's *Mistero Buffo* (*Comic Mystery Play*), or Eric Bogosian's *Drinking in America*.

To cite another example, in 1991 Patrick Stewart discarded his *Star Trek* 24th century role as Captain Jean-Luc Picard of the Enterprise and warped back in time five centuries to perform his own one-man adaptation of Charles Dickens's *A Christmas Carol*. Stewart performed thirty-nine different roles in a two-hour solo performance that enchanted audiences at New York's Eugene O'Neill Theater. Warm critical response prompted Stewart to repeat his one-man show in following years.

In 1993 the Joseph Papp Public Theatre presented two monodramatists—Marga Gomez and David Cale—in repertory. Gomez presented autobiographical, one-woman shows such as *Memory Tricks*, an homage to her mother, and *Marga Gomez Is Pretty, Witty, and Gay*, on the subject of homosexuality. Cale combined music with what he called his "emotional autobiography" in *Deep in a Dream of You*, which he developed at the Goodman Theater in Chicago. It followed his earlier original one-man performances such as *Smooch Music* and *The Nature of Things*.

In 1994 the British actor Michael York toured with his *Rogues and Vagabonds*, a one-man play that included passages from William Congreve's *The Way of the World*, Shakespeare's plays, and Noel Coward's lyrics. York expanded his vision to honor performers, using his solo presentation to show performance techniques of such legendary actors as John Gielgud and Laurence Olivier.

Also in 1994, Eric Bogosian, an experienced monodramatic playwright and actor, attacked the "politically correct" society with *Pounding Nails in the Floor With My Forehead*, in which he played a number of characters. His one-person performance was presented at New York's Minetta Lane Theatre, directed by Jo Bonney. Scene designer John Arnone opened the stage area to the back walls, lighting designer Jan Kroeze used brilliant white light on Bogosian and colored the rest of the stage, and sound designer Raymond D. Schilke provided rock music for continuity between scenes.

More recently, Rob Becker's solo performance in *Defending the Caveman* set the record for the longest running Broadway one-person show. Becker also enjoyed successful national tours of his comedy about the perennial differences between males and females.

These are but a few examples that illustrate the power of the one-person performance. Countless others could be cited.

SPECIAL ADVANTAGES OF THE MONODRAMA

With expert writing, performing, and directing, the monodrama is an exciting one-to-one communication, actor to audience, with compelling insight into the solo character, powerful language, and opportunities for tour de force acting. The intimate contact of actor with audience creates the theatrical magic that theatre workers and audiences treasure. In one way monodramas are like soliloquies in that they offer a rare opportunity to explore a character's inner secrets that normally would be concealed from the others in a multicharacter play, but unlike the soliloquy the solo play is a full work that is complete in itself. For actors and playwrights, creating the hidden *inside* of a character can be an exciting challenge to create truths; for the audiences, discovering what lies beneath a human's public image can be an insightful and enriching experience.

The solo play welcomes both traditional and new forms, and its creators are determined to remain free to explore controversial issues, experiment artistically, or look at traditional subjects. The one-person play is open to variations, such as intense drama or delightful comedy, or lengths from perhaps ten minutes to more than two hours. Not insignificantly in our era of skyrocketing production expenses, the solo play also is markedly less expensive to produce than its multicharacter relatives, increasing its attractiveness to producers and—playwrights, directors, and actors, please note—thereby opening new opportunities for performance.

These factors, coupled with the monodrama's artistic values, make the one-person play attractive to professional regional theatres as well as to amateur, community, and educational organizations that necessarily worry about rising costs. It is ideal as a regular part of an annual season and especially for performances on nights the theatre is normally dark.

Performer Artistry

"She did that two-hour show alone!"

"He played a dozen different characters all by himself!"

One principal appeal for performers and audiences is the very fact that a monodrama is a solo, a tour de force. For actors, the monodrama is an artistic challenge with more opportunities than multicharacter plays to display talents. For audiences, the soloist shows remarkable abilities, and we can conjecture that the novelty of a single actor also is appealing. For both, the virtuoso performance is one of the monodrama's more attractive qualities, rather like the difference between twelve people each juggling one ball versus one person juggling twelve balls. Audiences are impressed with the actor's ability to memorize such a long work, although actors think of that as mere kitchen work and are more interested in developing and sustaining the character without assistance from other actors.

Theatrical Storytelling

The monodrama is theatrical storytelling at its best, both *to* and *with* the audience, a masterful weaving of a web to enchant its audience in a highly personalized, one-to-one relationship, much like our wondrous evening bedtime rituals when our parents read to us about mythical dragons, common rabbits, or uncommon flying children, awakening our imaginations to travel to the Emerald City or through a looking glass. Often the monodrama is presented in a small theatre, even a makeshift space, creating an intimate environment that brings audience and performer into close contact that increases the magical appeal of theatrical storytelling.

Movies and Television

The monodrama is a durable creature, able to exist in varying environments. Its flexibility is illustrated by stage monodramas that show up on movie or television screens. For instance, Willy Russell's one-person play, *Shirley Valentine*, recently revived on Broadway starring Ellen Burstyn and directed by actor-director Simon Callow, was made into a motion picture. Paradoxically, that version Hollywoodized the play—movies tend to "open up" a play by adding characters and environments, regardless of its artistic reasons to remain within specific confines—by increasing the number of characters in Russell's one-person script. Jane Wagner's *The Search for Intelligent Life in the Universe* fared better when made into a movie: Lily Tomlin alone played the many characters. PBS-TV has shown a number of monodramas, such as Spalding Gray's *Monster in a Box* (the solo production described at the beginning of this chapter) and *Swimming to Cambodia*, among others.

SOCIAL COMMENTARY

"It is necessary to have a point of view about the world which surrounds you," says actress Uta Hagen in the quotation that begins this chapter. "You must ask yourself, 'How can I bring all of this to the statement I wish to make in the theatre?'" Hagen's philosophy is especially applicable to the monodrama, and many theatre artists find the solo play is a lively artistic form that expresses their personal statement or vision of their world. For example, monodramas may contain biting, significant social commentary, illustrated by Anna Deavere Smith's 1992 production of *Fires in the Mirror* (part of her series of one-woman shows called *On the Road: A Search for American Character*), in which she portrays twenty-six different male and female real-life characters from black ministers and Jewish housewives to street kids and activist Angela Davis. *Fires in the Mirror* dramatized what Smith calls a "cycle of genocidal violence" that stemmed from racial riots in Brooklyn the year before. To prepare her production, Smith interviewed people involved in or concerned with the conflict between African Americans and Hasidic Jews, sparked by a tragic incident when a car driven by a member of the Hasidic community killed a seven-year-old boy. *Fires in the Mirror*, presented at the Joseph Papp Public Theatre in New York, achieves its power with minimal properties and costumes, focusing instead on the story and performer. Playwright. and actress Smith was praised in theatrical reviews, and news magazines published articles about her work.

A second example of the monodrama's powerful social commentary is *Masks and Mirrors*, a drama about childhood sexual abuse that British actress Roberta Nobleman wrote for herself to perform. She weaves a tapestry of stories of novelist Virginia Woolf and composer Gustav Mahler, both victims of sexual abuse when young, into a powerful monodrama that chronicles her struggles to overcome the trauma she suffered as a child. The writer and actress toured American college campuses in the late 1990s. Often her performances were followed by lively audience discussions.

SUPREMACY OF THE INDIVIDUAL

The monodrama has other advantages, less visible but no less impressive. In our world that increasingly encourages, even forces, group thinking, group consciousness, and group behavior, the solo play is the domain of the individual. No crowd inhabits the stage with the solo performer. There's no need to conform to other actors' needs. Like the solitary sailor who races other solo sailors over lonely oceans or the single climber who tests personal skills in a private encounter with a mountain, the monodrama is the province of the individual. Actress Pat Carroll, reflecting on her performance in the biographical monodrama *Gertrude Stein Gertrude Stein Gertrude Stein*, says that she finds the solo performance is a rebellion against mass: "Acting solo has an appeal to me because . . . it is not mandatory that groups make things happen. I think it's important in this time of mass everything to realize that one person can have an effect on something."

Risky? Yes, certainly. It is safer to sail stormy oceans when a crew can help you handle the boat, easier to climb a mountain when there are other climbers holding the safety rope, and comforting to know that you have the support of others on stage with you. As a solo performer, once you step on stage you alone are responsible for the entire production. No other actor is available to bail you out if you forget a line. There's no one to help you through a difficult scene. You haven't the rewarding stimulus-response interplay with other actors. Even the backstage Green Room before the show can seem remarkably empty without the camaraderie of a large cast.

Yet acceptance of risk has its rewards, too, and many monodramatists appreciate the challenge of a solo performance. For them, it is reward enough. After all, they reason, artists are required to take risks if they are to grow. Always present is that deeply satisfying feeling of power and self-fulfillment when one is personally responsible for one's own work.

FOR WHOM IS THIS BOOK INTENDED?

I regard the theatre as the greatest of all art forms, the most immediate way in which a human being can share with another the sense of what it is to be a human being.

—Thornton Wilder

Let me be up-front about my reasons for writing this book. I have become an unabashed fan of the solo play, although the first monodramas I saw (at a theatre convention) were dreadfully dreary. I felt they were self-pitying whimpers, tiny episodes about boring people who whined about life's inequities and were satisfied to do nothing else, mere stream-of-consciousness stuff that might be appropriate for personal diaries but certainly not for audiences. Veritable yawns, all. As a result of that sad experience, I resolved never to see another and never to allow my student playwrights and actors to be involved with what I thought was an inconsequential form. What changed my mind to make me so enthusiastic? Seeing *excellent* monodramas, professional and amateur, in New York, in regional theatres, in makeshift spaces like church basements or libraries. Jane Martin's *Talking With . . .*, Anna Deavere Smith's *Fires in the Mirror.* Artists such as Eric Bogosian and Spalding Gray, and so many others. Taking the solo play into my classes and watching my student writers, actors, and directors create monodramas that revealed truths. Those flashes of lightning sent me to study and research the form.

The Power of One is a result of that study. I hope it will help you discover the unique attributes of the solo play so you can be playwright, actor, or director as you create your own monodrama. To that end, you'll find scripts of monodramas and exercises to help you create your own script. This book has dual objectives, similar in intent although different in audiences:

☐ This is a text for theatre courses such as introduction to theatre, playwriting, acting, and directing. Creating a solo play helps students gain access to performance and production concepts through the avenue of this unique, intimate form of theatre.

☐ This is also a learn-to-create-it-yourself book for beginning and experienced playwrights, actors, and directors who are not enrolled in theatre classes but who seek artistic challenges and rewards through the creation of a monodrama.

The monodrama is ideally suited for these goals. Because certain aspects of the one-person play are less complex than multicharacter plays, the monodrama is the heart of theatre boiled down to its three most vital essentials—script, actor, audience. It is worth emphasizing, however, that *less complex* does not imply less artistic. On the contrary, the solo play often achieves the highest possible artistic qualities.

For Playwrights

If you are interested in playwriting, you'll find that the monodrama is a valid artistic statement in itself as well as an important educational tool that teaches what makes a play. As a monodramatist you focus on creating a dimensional, interesting, dynamic character who will come to life on stage. In the process you will discover significant insight into techniques of writing powerful theatrical humans, language for the stage, and structuring a story with a beginning, middle, and end. The "show, don't tell" admonition given playwrights has special application to the monodrama, where a direct statement of a theme, or message, cannot be disguised by hiding it in speeches given to various characters. Experience writing monodramas will help you create monologues in multicharacter, one-act or full-length plays.

For Actors

If you're interested in acting, you'll discover that monodramas present challenges similar to those of soliloquies in multicharacter plays, although of course the monodrama will be much longer. Solo plays give you special opportunities to bring characters to life, show flexibility by playing multiple characters, sustain emotions, build motivation, and develop vocal skills, all while holding the stage in the absence of other actors. Clearly, the actor who can handle a monodrama is well prepared to tackle any soliloquy. Unlike soliloquies, which typically are drawn from plays that are several centuries old, monodramas represent today's voices. Further, the monodrama is a complete work, in contrast to soliloquies, which must be seen in the context of the entire play. Not unimportantly, monodramas also provide actors with excellent audition material because there's no need to edit out other speakers.

For Directors

If you're a director, you'll see that directing solo plays requires making a number of choices, some similar to those faced in more traditional multi-character plays. However, monodramas give you special challenges, such as helping actors achieve depth of characterization, working out tempo and key, guiding the actor to use vocal dynamics, and using blocking with but one character. As a result, you'll find that directing a monodrama will help you learn new skills or adapt and polish known techniques, which will enhance your future directorial projects.

For Theatre Workshops and Classes

Inventive theatre classes avoid passive approaches such as lectures and instead seek to bring the art to life through direct participation, following the time-honored "learn by doing" concept popularized by educational theorists such as John Dewey. The monodrama has special advantages in such hands-on classes because solo plays allow students to deal with the totality of the theatrical experience, unlike complicated full-length, multicharacter plays that are more difficult to grasp. Significantly less complicated, the monodrama's accessibility allows students in introductory classes to write, act, and direct, discovering salient aspects of dramatic structure, characterization, and content. It helps students experience the theatrical creative processes, seeing how playwrights, actors, and directors collaborate to make theatre.

The monodrama is also a significant form for other theatre classes. It is a potent communicative art that challenges those studying playwriting, acting, play direction, and design. Whether you are enrolled in classes or pursuing a do-it-yourself education in the art, through the monodrama you can develop personal creative abilities to become more proficient in the arts and crafts of theatre.

Through numerous examples, exercises, and descriptions, *The Power of One* encourages you to create your own monodramas to take advantage of the solo play's challenges, joys, and rewards so you can participate directly in the living, changing, fluid, ancient yet always new theatre that expresses humanity's deepest emotional and intellectual feelings and questions.

HOW TO USE THIS BOOK

Naturally enough, you will want to read chapters that focus on your special interests. For example, actors will look first for sections on performing; playwrights, the information about writing; and directors, materials on directing.

The Power of One, however, seeks to show theatre workers that narrow specialization on one aspect of theatre cheats them of insight into the full dimension of our art. Actors learn about acting by studying the arts of the playwright and director; playwrights discover aspects of writing by understanding the arts of the actor and director; and directors increase their knowledge of directing as they become familiar with the arts of the playwright and actor. In this book we seek to show how each theatre artist—writer, director, actor, designer—has the same basic goals, often even the same techniques. This book focuses on the collaborative process to create the theatrical experience.

Because the monodrama strips away distracting nonessentials, it encourages a breadth of vision about our art and helps develop personal answers to the question, What is theatre? The one-person play encourages a wide scope of study, and you are urged to learn as much as you can about all theatrical activities, including those you may believe are outside your particular comfort zone. You may then discover you want to venture into new areas that you've not explored.

Examples of Monodramas. Few monodramas are published in easily available texts. Most are found only in acting editions. Therefore, this book includes examples of monodramas. These will show you the solo play's characteristics. You may want to make a personal collection by ordering additional solo plays from play publishers such as Samuel French, Inc., or Dramatists Play Service.

A Theatre in Your Head. As you read the examples of monodramas in this book, encourage yourself to "see" and "hear" them on stage. Challenge your imagination to bring the scripts to life, transforming them from the page to the stage. Create a theatre in your head and envision the play on stage.

Your imaginary theatre is free from economic or pragmatic restraints and the play can take immediate shape in your mind without long rehearsals. In your "theatre in your head" you're free to cast your favorite actor, and you can use lights, scenery, costume, makeup, sound, and props that best suit your vision of the play. Continue creating a theatre in your head when you turn to the exercises regarding writing, acting, and directing monodramas. These exercises are designed to sharpen your imagination and creativity.

Read Each Script Aloud. Plays are not literature but instead are blueprints for stage performance. Silent reading to yourself may be fine for novels or essays, but it can't bring a play to life. Reading the monodrama out loud will make you think of the script as a stage piece and you'll better understand the character's emotions, basic desires, and attitudes. Through such reading you'll force yourself to notice nuances that may not be apparent by silently reading the script. You'll become more sensitive to character development, the play's rhythm, content, and meaning, and the importance of words and phrases.

Exercises

Chapters conclude with exercises that will help you understand monodramas and encourage you to create your own. The exercises direct your attention to choices you face as a creative artist seeking to bring a monodrama to life. For maximum value, *write your responses to the exercises* (don't merely think about them) to develop ideas thoroughly, to give you enriched understanding of theatrical art, and to save notes for future development into creating your own monodrama. Approach the exercises in good faith, allowing yourself ample time to do them completely and thoughtfully.

Monodrama Notebook

Exercises in this book are accumulative, each designed to take you through a step-by-step process of discovering what makes a monodrama and, by extension, the nature of theatre. Keep your exercises in your personal *Monodrama Notebook*. Because you'll find that you will want to reorganize your notes and insert new ideas about the monodrama you will create, the flexibility of a three-ring, loose-leaf notebook makes it an excellent choice.

The notebook also is useful as a journal, much like the ones playwrights and actors keep to record their ideas, notes, comments, record of artistic growth, and self-evaluations of their work. Use tab dividers to organize exercises, notes, and ideas for monodramas you might want to write. Start a bibliography of monodramas that interest you as a playwright, actor, or director, keeping copies in your monodrama notebook. Actors may want to include a section of solo plays that appear especially valuable as audition pieces.

Quotations

Throughout *The Power of One* you'll find quotations by leading theatrical artists. You've already noted that this chapter contained quotations by actress Uta Hagen and playwright Thornton Wilder, and we conclude with a declaration of faith in theatre's power by a historian. Such materials expand the text and give you more insight into the nature of theatre. Many theatre workers compile their own lists of quotations about their art and you may wish to use a section of your Monodrama Notebook for opinions and ideas that you find most valuable for your own growth.

The Power of One encourages you to experiment with the monodrama, taking advantage of its strengths and avoiding its weaknesses. You'll find, I hope, that the monodrama will help you work in close collaboration with other theatre artists, improve your particular skills and add new ones, and participate in an exciting and rewarding creative process. This book seeks to show you that through the monodrama you can express your particular point of view about life as it is, or as you think it should be, and share with others the sense of what it is to be a human being.

Without quibbling over which is the greatest of the arts, let us remember that the theatre makes its appeal on two levels: the aesthetic and the intellectual. On the aesthetic level the theatre, like music, painting, and dancing, makes its contribution to the emotional needs of man and to his hunger for the beautiful. On the intellectual level a tremendous proportion of the greatest ideas ever conceived by man have been expressed in dramatic form. Students of philosophy study Aeschylus, Goethe, Ibsen, and Shaw, as well as Plato, Schopenhauer, Nietzsche, and Dewey. No other branch of human learning can point with pride to a more impressive list of great names. No other field of literature can quite equal the drama in the total extent of its contributions. —Frank M. Whiting

2

CHAPTER

Confrontation and Self-Revelation

The core of the theatre is an encounter. The [character] who makes an act of self-revelation is, so to speak, one who establishes contact with himself. That is to say, an extreme confrontation, sincere, disciplined, precise and total—not merely a confrontation with his thoughts, but one involving his whole being from his instincts and his unconscious right up to his most lucid state. —Jerzy Grotowski

WE'RE IN A SMALL THEATRE WATCHING A PLAY. ONE CHARACTER, an old woman, sits in a chair. Thick eyeglasses. Only a few lights on the solitary character. No scenery. No props except for several bundles of newspapers at her feet.

For the fifteen or twenty minutes we discover the old woman's private life as she talks *with* us but yet somehow not exactly *to* us, revealing her private inner self as she confronts her dreams. It is a curiously personal experience that seems to give us a special magical power to see into the woman's heart. Although she is alone on stage, she describes other people in her life in a way that makes us see and hear them as she brings us into her world, sparking our imaginations to touch her life, making us players in her environment. The character's dynamic changes and revelations are so strong and intriguing that we forget that this is a one-person play, different from multicharacter plays with which we're more familiar.

The old woman has an extraordinary view of a most ordinary place—a McDonald's fast-food restaurant. She says she likes to sit in McDonald's all day, the first to arrive and the last to leave. She is unnoticed, she says, "Just like some ol' french fry they forgot." No one is pushed out. "It's a sacred law in McDonald's, you can sit for a hundred years. Only place in this world."

We discover that her goal is to live in a McDonald's. Why? The place gives her a sense of security: death cannot come to McDonald's. "No sir. No way. Nobody has ever died in one. . . . Noooooooooo, you can't die in a McDonald's no matter how hard you try. It's the spices. Seals you safe in this life like it seals in the flavor. Yesssssss, yes!"

The old woman sees an unusual quality in McDonald's: permanence. "Tell you what I really like, though, is the plastic," she says. "God . . . gave us the idea of plastic so we'd know what the everlasting really was. See if there's plastic then there's surely eternity. It's God's hint."

A fast food place's spices seal us safely in life? Plastic proves the existence of eternity? We smile, admiring the clever irony.

The sensitive audience member notices what the old woman does *not* say. She doesn't explain what is happening in her life to make her need a home at McDonald's. Is she one of the homeless? She doesn't complain about her lack of a better home, her economic status, her position in life, or the absence of friends. Is she abandoned, alone in the world? She doesn't speak about her history. Does she have a family?

Despite what she doesn't say, we come to conclusions about her life. We believe we know answers to such questions.

Why? Because the character fulfills one of theatre's primary goals: She stimulates our imaginations. The playwright carefully crafts the play so we know a great deal about the character, but with remarkable skill the dramatist also carefully makes artistic choices what not to write. The combination of details and omitted materials makes us encounter the old woman through her self-revelation and confrontation with a dream, and that draws us into her world to become active participants in her life. This relatively brief moment is a theatrical experience so intense and captivating that we feel we have insight into much of the totality of the old woman's life.

As the play ends she confides that she hopes they'll let her live in McDonald's because she has to have a dream. "Just a beacon in the storm. But you got to have a dream. It's our dreams make us what we are."

After the play is over, many of us remain emotionally involved in the old woman. We find ourselves caring deeply about what appears to be her pathetic situation even though—or more likely *because*—she doesn't complain or whimper. She doesn't seem to sense there is something sad about her life or goals, but we do.

We think about her dreams. And our own.

Dreams, she says, make her who she is.

Her self-revelation stimulates us to think about ourselves. What, we wonder, do our dreams make us? Are our dreams comparable to living at a fast food restaurant where spices seal in life and plastic represents eternity? Do we dream of a life in something that parallels—of all things—a *McDonald's*? We ask ourselves what might have happened in the old woman's life to lead her to dream of nothing more than a fast-food restaurant to call home. What happens in our lives to give us our dreams?

Our reactions, we notice, are similar to those we experience when we attend more standard full-length, multicharacter plays. Yet this play awoke our interest with only one character and in only fifteen minutes or so. For many in the audience this appears to be a fascinating new form of theatrical art. But it's been in existence for centuries.

AN INTIMATE THEATRICAL REVELATION

We've just seen *French Fries*, a short, one-woman play by Jane Martin, one of the modern form's leading playwrights, whose plays are widely produced in America and other countries. *French Fries* is one of eleven Martin monodramas in a collection called *Talking With . . .*, an appropriate title that neatly describes the solo play's intimate audience-performer relationship. You'll find Martin's *French Fries*, as well as other solo plays, in the next chapters, where we'll discuss the acting, directing, and writing skills that illustrate unique aspects of the monodrama.

Because the monodrama is less well known than multicharacter plays, we start our discussion here by looking briefly at the basic characteristics of the solo play. Later chapters define it in more detail, and throughout this book you'll find examples that further demonstrate the monodrama's variations. The goal of this book is simple: to help—no, to *encourage*—you to write, act, and direct your own solo play.

BASIC CHARACTERISTICS

The Private Person Behind the Public Mask. The monodrama has a special ability to communicate with the audience because it is the essence of theatre: *script, performer, and audience.* The character is revealed so completely, honestly, and freely that there is an intimate communication, a one-to-one relationship of character and audience. We are able to slip inside the character's private self, where we see deeply into his or her mind and heart, aspects normally hidden behind a public mask. Those masks are familiar to all of us. After all, don't we all wear various masks according to situations—the dutiful child, the conscientious worker, the intense artist, the attentively listening friend? Aren't we aware of—and often put off by—the masks we see on friends, employers, and even those we love? So, too, characters in multicharacter plays wear public masks, according to the situation created by other characters. But when we are alone, privately confronting ourselves, we remove that facade. Equally, the character in the solo play is seen without a protective mask. The result is a fundamental honesty. For playwrights, actors, and directors, creating that honesty is a rewarding challenge; for audiences, observing it is a remarkable theatrical experience.

The monodrama is at its best when the solo character shows the truth and honesty behind that public mask. We can illustrate that concept by looking at specific moments in more familiar multicharacter works. Consider, for example, a recent popular musical, the Gershwin comedy *Crazy for You*. Early scenes establish Polly as a tough, no-nonsense person, boldly holding her own as the only woman in a town full of cowboys, so strong that the men in town are wary when dealing with her. Yet we see an entirely different aspect of Polly when she is alone and can let slip that mask she must wear in public. She then is able to disclose a yearning for love—a hunger that she could never express to others—as she sings the hauntingly poignant "Someone To Watch Over Me." Equally, soliloquies such as Hamlet's "To be or not to be" give us insight into the young prince's insecurities.

Monodramas also take us into the private person unburdened by public masks. However, instead of being a moment (such as Polly's song or a soliloquy such as "To be or not to be"), the whole of the one-person play shows that interior truth.

An Encounter and a Self-Revelation. The solo play reminds us of Grotowski's statements that begin this chapter: "The core of the theatre is an encounter" and the theatre shows a character's "act of self-revelation." For character and audience, the monodrama is an encounter with what it means to be a human. For the character it is an act of self-examination and discovery that leads to self-revelation. For the audience it is an intimate encounter with the old woman while she reveals herself and confronts her personal dreams. We see that McDonald's offers a special refuge to the old woman, and we participate vicariously with the character as she confronts her being, dreams, and beliefs.

The one-person play is as elusive as quicksilver, defying attempts to hold it to a single definition or within strict boundaries. Although it is important to define certain parameters, the following characteristics should be viewed as guides only, not dictates.

Similarities to Multicharacter Plays

You will find that the monodrama has certain characteristics that are also typical of multicharacter plays. We can list some of them briefly here and amplify them later throughout this book.

1. *Conflict*, direct or implied, sparks plays to life. The character facing a conflict, such as between an urgent either-or situation, is far more dramatic, dynamic, and interesting than one who simply relates an aspect of existence.

2. Plays happen *now*. The characters are *experiencing* a situation, not at all the same thing as *did* experience. Effective theatrical pieces are written in the present tense, not in the past tense, as are novels and short stories; the action *is taking place now* as the play unfolds.

3. To create a powerful sense of immediacy and to maintain a sense of present, the playwright answers the question Why now?—why *must* the action happen *now* instead of yesterday or tomorrow? What is special about this moment? What is the present situation that the character must face *now*?

4. To maintain a sense of the present, references to the past are sharply limited. The playwright uses information from the past only when it directly relates to the dilemma that affects the character in the present.

5. A strong sense of *future* creates dramatic tension. From the very beginning of the play, the action suggests questions about forthcoming events. How will the character handle the dilemma he or she is encountering? What will happen? What actions will the character take? What will this situation mean to the character?

6. Essays and sermons *tell*, but plays *show*. The play's thematic core—its "message," so to speak—is implied, never directly stated, by the action, the character's goal, the conflict, the dialogue, the structure, the situation.

7. Regardless of other elements of structural design, effective plays are carefully crafted with a beginning, middle, and end.

Differences from Multicharacter Plays

Although the solo play shares similarities with multicharacter plays, it has distinguishing characteristics. We list some briefly here, again saving amplification until later.

1. The solo play reveals an interesting character who is experiencing a situation that *compels* him or her to speak. The character has a goal, perhaps a choice he or she *must* make or a deeply held desire that the character *must* fulfill.

2. The character in a monodrama displays emotional and psychological truths, often deeply personal secrets or beliefs that would be impossible to express if other characters were present in his or her world.

3. The solo character directly or indirectly *discovers* an idea or value that is significant to his or her future. That discovery is an essential part of the play's meaning and the dimensional characterization. It also helps audiences better perceive their own values.

4. The short solo play tells a single basic story woven around one central idea that typically is introduced in the play's first moments. Full-length monodramas, like full-length, multicharacter plays, have a more complex structure with added incidents, obstacles, conflicts, and complications to sustain the action.

5. Short monodramas, like one-acts, are highly compressed experiences. The experience is severely damaged, even destroyed, by pauses to indicate passage of time or a change in locale. If changes in time or place are absolutely essential, the playwright invents a way to make the shift with language and action, not with blackouts or by moving scenic units.

6. Only one character is on stage at a time, although the script can call for the single actor to play a variety of other characters. The monodrama also may imply the influence or physical presence of others,

either (unseen) on stage or in a nearby location.

7. Effective monodramas frequently are *dramas of language*, using imagery and poetic diction to enlarge the theatrical effect. Language is always a direct reflection of the character.

8. Careful editing and pruning is essential. Each word, phrase, and sentence should propel the action and develop the character.

9. Actors use a number of techniques to create a dynamic performance. The character's objective and emotions must be clear, reactions to obstacles and comparable stimuli should be played to add dimensions, and the inner truth of the character should be illuminated. The actor must use vocal variations—rate, pitch, volume, and timbre—to overcome the danger of a single voice becoming a mere drone of sound.

10. Directors design changes in tempo and key to maintain theatrical intensity through variety. Blocking carefully balances a need for visual variety with the demands of enhancing characterization.

11. Monodramas, especially shorter ones, most often use little or no scenery and only few properties or other production devices.

A COMPARISON WITH OTHER FORMS

Whether comic or dramatic, the solo play's prime attribute is compelling characterization with focus on internal truth. Monodramas often can be more free-wheeling than multicharacter plays. For example, solo plays may be tightly plotted or loosely structured, and they may experiment with style, language, and structure. Like their multicharacter relatives, effective one-person plays are complete in themselves and communicate fully without outside information such as introductions or program notes, and they are carefully constructed with building action that rises to an ultimate climax.

Conflict and Tension

Many monodramas are built with the conflict and rising action that is typical of multicharacter plays. In such plays the character is compelled to achieve a goal—actors think of it as an *objective*, a key ingredient to finding the essence of the character—and faces a highly important choice that the situation demands he or she must make immediately. Reaching that goal isn't easy, because the character encounters contrary forces that appear to stop him or her from achieving that goal. The forces may be external, such as another (unseen) character's objections; or more often in a monodrama, the forces are internal, a personal decision that must be made, very much like Hamlet's "To be or not to be" uncertainty. Comic monodramas often exaggerate the desperation of the situation so the character must cleverly find solutions.

Other monodramas, however, may use less direct conflict and instead place the character in a situation that creates a tension, such as between dreams and reality, personal beliefs versus social mores, or the like. Often the character is struggling to cope with the death of a friend or relative or the loss of a personal dream or important goal.

In either case, tensions or conflicts make the character react. Those reactions are part of the *dimensionality* that playwrights, directors, and actors seek. To illustrate that point, imagine a play where the character wants something and easily gets it. Not much of a play, is it? The character's will to achieve isn't tested, and there's nothing to cause the character to react, to change, to develop. Conflict, however, prevents the character from getting what he or she wants. *Now what*? The answer creates suspense, so the audience will want to know, What will happen now? Encountering conflict makes the character more dimensional. Will he or she simply quit? Laugh at the challenge and move decisively to overcome the problem? Whimper? Cleverly sidestep the obstacle?

The Audition Piece

Because the monodrama sometimes is called a *monologue*, theatre workers may conclude it is merely a long speech (also often called a monologue) extracted from a longer play, useful as an actor's audition piece or exercise. An audition piece, however, is not intended for public performance but instead is an actor's tool to display abilities to a casting director. The audition piece cannot stand alone—it makes no sense by itself and needs to be perceived in the context of the rest of the play—and it is not structured with a beginning, middle, and end. The audition piece is usually short, perhaps a minute or two in length, because directors allow actors only a limited amount of time to show their talents.

In contrast to an audition piece, the monodrama is a complete work in itself, not an extract from a longer piece. Like a multicharacter play, it is a full theatrical communication that is expressly designed for presentation to an audience. Unlike a brief audition piece that may be two or three minutes long, the monodrama necessarily is longer in order to develop character, situation, and content.

Solo Moments in Other Art Forms

The monodrama's focus on one character's inner self is similar to other forms that focus on goals and emotions. We can learn more about the monodrama by comparing it with solo moments in musicals, novels, monologues within plays, or soliloquies.

Emotional Content. You will note that strong *emotions* almost always are involved in the following examples of solo musical numbers, soliloquies, and monologues. Monodramas also quite often deal with high emotional content.

Solo Musical Numbers. The monodrama's power is similar to certain solo numbers in musicals, such as Billy's "Soliloquy" ("My Boy Bill") from *Carousel*, "Far From the Home I Love" from *Fiddler on the Roof*, "Memories" from *Cats*, "Adelaide's Lament" from *Guys and Dolls*, or "But Not for Me" and "They Can't Take That Away from Me" from *Crazy for You*. When such musical numbers are effectively written and performed, the audience is not prompted to wonder why the character bursts into song to reveal inner thoughts, compelling emotions, and personal dreams or goals. So, too, the character in the monodrama faces a major emotional situation, so important that he or she simply has no choice but to encounter and reveal those significant intimate secrets and truths.

Novels and Short Stories. The theatrical monodrama also resembles insightful character monologues found in novels and short stories, illustrated by the opening section of William Faulkner's *The Sound and the Fury*, Molly Bloom's long stream-of-consciousness speech that concludes James Joyce's *Ulysses*, *I'm A Fool* by Sherwood Anderson, or *End of the Affair* by Graham Greene. These solo insights have markedly powerful language that carries the character though a mental and emotional self-examination process.

Monologues in Plays. The monodrama follows the same expression of internal personal truths that we find in solo speeches within multicharacter plays. One such example is Jerry's long tour de force monologue, "The Story of Jerry and the Dog," from Edward Albee's two-character one-act play, *The Zoo Story*. Vivid images dramatize that character's anguished attempts to confront and understand his world.

Soliloquies. The theatrical monodrama can be compared to a multicharacter play's soliloquy, a solo speech that shows the character's inner turmoil. To illustrate this point, consider a powerful and effective soliloquy from Shakespeare's *Macbeth*, Act One, Scene Five.

Lady Macbeth:
The raven himself is hoarse
That croaks the fatal entrance of Duncan
Under my battlements. Come, you spirits
That tend on mortal thoughts, unsex me here,
And fill me, from the crown to the toe, top-full
Of direst cruelty! Make thick my blood;
Stop up th' access and passage to remorse,
That no compunctious visitings of nature
Shake my fell purpose nor keep peace between
Th' effect and it! Come to my woman's breasts
And take my milk for gall, you murd'ring ministers,
Wherever in your sightless substances
You wait on nature's mischief!
Come, thick night,
And pall thee in the dunnest smoke of hell,
That my keen knife see not the wound it makes,
Nor heaven peep through the blanket of the dark
To cry 'Hold, hold!'

Soliloquies make forceful one-person theatrical statements, but unlike the monodrama they are not complete in themselves and cannot stand alone. To understand the preceding soliloquy, for example, the audience must know that Lady Macbeth is girding herself to assassinate King Duncan. A monodrama is equally compelling but does not require other information.

Soliloquies into Monodramas. Although by themselves soliloquies cannot stand alone, you can turn them into effective monodramas. Some actors construct monodramas with soliloquies, as singers do with arias, unifying units with introductory materials. Alternatively, Lady Macbeth's speech could become a monodrama if you were to create just enough exposition to let the audience know that the character believes she has reason to kill

King Duncan and then put her in conflict between those motivations versus equally strong reasons not to commit murder.

You may also borrow from such soliloquies to create monodramas that focus on contemporary issues, perhaps in this case using Lady Macbeth's concerns to illuminate modern feminist issues such as society's assignment of "appropriate" behavior for women or the struggle for personal empowerment to make decisions. These examples illustrate some ways soliloquies can stimulate your imagination to help you create your own monodrama.

THE MULTIPLE-CHARACTER EFFECT

A monodrama is similar to a multicharacter one-act or full-length play except for its most visible attribute of having only a single character. Or *perhaps we should say, more accurately, that we see only one actor.* Even though multicharacter plays may appear to have the advantage of revealing characterization through action and interaction with the interplay of multiple characters, the solo play also can bring in additional characters. Monodramas often make us sense the presence of other characters in the world offstage, adding size and scope to the monodrama with implied statements about social values or mores that directly affect the visible single character.

Evoking Additional Characters

The monodrama can create other people in the action, unseen to us but not to the solo character, who sees and hears them as if they were actually present. Through that character, we also see and hear the others. Actress-playwright Ruth Draper, a major influence on the modern monodrama, was especially noted for her ability to evoke other characters. For example, in her solo play A *Cocktail Party*, she performed one character who related to twenty-four other characters who surrounded her. Although the other characters were invisible, Draper's performance artistry made them so vivid they came alive in the audience's imagination.

The old woman at McDonald's is actively in contact with others she sees under the golden arches. Characters who enter her world are visible in our imagination, as shown in the following speech:

> I've seen a man healed by a Big Mac. I have. I was just sittin' there. Last summer it was. Oh, they don't never move you on. It's a sacred law in

McDonald's you can sit for a hundred years. Only place in this world. Anyway, a fella, maybe thirty-five, maybe forty, come on in there dressed real nice, real bright tie, bran' new baseball cap, nice white socks, and he had him that disease. You know the one I mean, Cerebral Walrus they call it. Anyway, he had him a cock leg. His poor old body had it two speeds at the same time. Now he got him some coffee, with a lid on, and sat him down and Jimmy the tow-head cook knew him see and he brought over a Big Mac.

She describes how the man was healed by eating the Big Mac sandwich. After eating it, she says, he "paraded out of there clean, straight like a pole-bean poplar, walked him a plumb line without no trace of the 'walrus.'" Her description enlarges the monodrama so it includes more than the solo character on stage.

One Actor but Multiple Characters

The monodrama has only one actor, but it isn't necessarily restricted to one character. In some solo plays the performer plays a number of characters on stage. Actors capable of playing multiple roles are called *protean performers*, a reference drawn from classical mythology's Proteus, the sea god capable of assuming a number of different forms. For example, through her acting skills, Ruth Draper could become a number of other characters in one monodrama, sometimes using a simple shawl to effect the change from, say, a young girl to an elderly woman or from a proud matron to a shy immigrant struggling with English. For instance, Draper portrayed six different characters in her In a Church in Italy.

Among the many other illustrations of solo plays with one actor but multiple characters is Kevin Kling's brisk comedy Twenty-One, a recent award-winner at the Actors Theatre of Louisville, in which Kling plays eight eccentric characters on a bus, simply staged with only chairs. Out of Spite: Tales of Survival in Sarajevo is another recent monodrama in which the performer plays multiple characters, in this case women who survive— endure with grace and dignity—unbearable conditions in that war-torn country. Canadians Damir Andrei and Cynthia Ashberger (who performed the one-woman show) adapted Out of Spite from works by Sarajevo resident Elma Softic, creating a haunting work that awakens our awareness of political inequities and of the strength of the survivors.

Modern performers enjoy the challenge of performing a variety of characters in a monodrama. Draper said she preferred monodramas to multicharacter plays because solo plays stretched her, encouraging her to grow as an actress. Lily Tomlin says that a highlight of her career was playing a number of different characters in *The Search for Intelligent Life in the Universe*. Anna Deavere Smith's *Fires in the Mirror* is based on the actress-playwright's belief that using another person's language will show what is normally not seen in that particular human, and through individualistic language she can capture a number of characters. Eric Bogosian's monodramas, such as *Drinking in America*, portray a number of characters that the playwright-actor brings to life through his vocal skills, use of various accents, and physicalization. For Hal Holbrook, who created *Mark Twain Tonight!* for himself to perform, the challenge was clear: young Holbrook became the elderly Twain, who became children such as Huck and Tom.

Popular with television audiences is another versatile protean performer: Tracey Ullman. Her *Tracey Takes On* series allows her to play a variety of characters, many memorably eccentric. Commissioned by HBO, the series has won numerous awards, including CableACE and Emmys. As do many solo performers, Ullman writes many of the scripts she performs. She also performed in the Broadway production of *The Big Love*, a one-woman show written by Jay Presson Allen.

Conversational Exchanges Between Characters

You'll find that it is often effective to bring in other characters' dialogue. Instead of having the character say something like, "My mother was always full of doom and gloom," you might elect to have a brief exchange of dialogue between child and mother, *showing* the parent's attitude rather than telling about it. Allison Boye uses that technique in *Harper Lee, I Suppose, Was a Child Once*. She could have had the character tell the audience that six-year-old Harper Lee grew up with equally young Truman Capote, but instead she shows Lee becoming a child playing with Capote, and they have a brief exchange of dialogue. The short moment not only *shows* the relationship, it is also savvy theatrical writing because it allows the actress to change voice and personality, reducing the potentially monotonous effect of a single voice and character.

EMPHASIS ON LANGUAGE

Monodramas often are considered *plays of language* because many carefully select images and metaphors such as the woman's description of a man afflicted with "cerebral walrus." Perhaps that emphasis is a residue of the modern monodramatist's poetic ancestors, such as the early Greek *rhapsodists* or the eighteenth-century solo platform performers, many of whom were poets. Certainly, too, language becomes more important in a play that is stripped of other theatrical qualities, such as numerous characters, stage scenery and machinery, and properties. We therefore often think of the solo play as theatre's equivalent to poetic forms.

French Fries illustrates the powerful diction you find in well-written solo plays. Martin uses diction to evoke the character while simultaneously enriching the dialogue with insightful images that awake the audience's visual imagination. We noted earlier the old woman's statement that plastic proves there is a God. Equally, her description of the man with "cerebral walrus" brings him to life: he "had him a cock leg" and "his poor old body had it two speeds at the same time." Although not all monodramas are as colorful, *French Fries* shows how language can be a major player in the scene: "Oh, they don't never move you on. It's a sacred law in McDonalds you can sit for a hundred years. Only place in this world."

Language, however, is tightly controlled. The monodrama, like poetry, demands clean precision. Thoreau's statement about clarity of writing could have been intended for the monodrama: "A sentence should read as if its author, had he held a plow instead of a pen, could have drawn a furrow deep and straight to the end." One common mistake in monodramas is loose overstatements, and what you decide not to write is as important as what you write, because effective solo plays demand careful editing and pruning to plow straight to the end.

LESS IS MORE PRODUCTION TECHNIQUES

Too much ornament is a fault in every kind of production. Uncommon expressions, strong flashes of wit, pointed similes, and epigrammatic turns, especially when they recur too frequently, are a disfigurement, rather than an embellishment. . . . Writers [may] seek for their favorite ornaments, even where the subject does not afford them; and by that means have twenty insipid conceits for one thought which is really beautiful. —David Hume

Theatre is a many-roomed mansion that consists of a wide variety of plays, performance styles, and production techniques. We are delighted to attend elaborate productions that stimulate our visual responses with spectacular scenery, lighting, and costumes, and we enjoy plays such as

Dracula, with its lush Gothic scenery and costumes, or K-2, which has a grand reproduction of a soaring ice-covered mountain. Visual spectacle excites us in musicals such as *Cats*, with imaginative and fanciful costumes, or *Starlight Express*, which uses roller skating platforms that circle the stage and jut into the audience.

Minimalist Theatre

Although we enjoy elaborate productions, we can be equally delighted by other rooms in theatre's expansive mansion. In contrast to productions with full-scale visual elements, productions of many monodramas are bare-bones minimalist theatre, using little or no scenery, lighting, properties, or costumes. Typical monodramas observe the *less is more* artistic concept, originated by Robert Browning in his poem, "Andrea Del Sarto," popularized by architect Ludwig Mies van der Rohe, and adopted by painters, sculptors, poets, and theatre artists. Less is more urges artists to pare away materials that are merely decorative, eliminating what architects call "gingerbread" (exterior moldings that adorn Victorian homes) and, equally for theatre, reducing or eliminating elaborate scenic, costume, and lighting design elements. The goal is restraint, removing excesses to leave an elemental beauty of form that matches purpose. In theatre less is more means tightly restrained productions, discarding nonessentials to focus attention on the character and story.

A Poor Theatre

The monodrama's basic production simplicity follows director Jerzy Grotowski's persuasive argument in *Towards a Poor Theatre* that "rich" theatrical productions are so ornate and complicated that they distract from the key elements of actor and audience, thereby inhibiting or even destroying theatre's ability to communicate effectively with audiences. Grotowski says that "poor" theatre productions, in contrast, avoid lavish staging techniques and thereby focus on the core of theatre: actor and audience. The typical monodrama eliminates production devices to make a more economical and direct theatrical statement, enhancing the performer's relationship with the audience and increasing the intimate contact between character and audience.

The great artist is the simplifier.   —Henri Frédéric Amiel
The art of art, the glory of expression and the sunshine of the light of letters, is simplicity.
—Walt Whitman

VARIETY OF MONODRAMAS

The monodrama can take a number of forms, differentiated by such factors as the reason the solo play was written, structural design, subject matter, and length measured by the performance playing time. All share common qualities such as artistic unification and focus on a single basic story; all have a beginning, middle, and end; and all depend on excellent, dimensional characterization. Those similarities aside, monodramas may vary in other aspects, reminding us that the monodrama delights in its freedom to be different.

Monodramas for Specific Performers

Some monodramatists write for specific actors, creating works that are specially suited to a given actor's talents. Samuel Beckett, for example, wrote two one-woman shows, *Rockaby* and *Footfalls*, for actress Billie Whitelaw. Jane Wagner wrote *The Search for Intelligent Life in the Universe* for comedienne Lily Tomlin, who won the Best Actress Antoinette Perry Award (popularly known as a Tony), Drama Desk, and Outer Critics' Circle awards for her performance. Tomlin repeated her successful solo stage role in a subsequent 1991 movie.

Commissioned Monodramas

Just as playwrights may create solo plays for specific actors, performers may commission a playwright to write a script for them. One example is the cleverly titled *Gertrude Stein Gertrude Stein Gertrude Stein*, which actress Pat Carroll asked playwright Marty Martin to write. Carroll won both the Drama Desk and Outer Critics' Circle Awards for her performance of the controversial American poet, novelist, and critic who was popularly known for her line, "A rose is a rose is a rose." Martin earned an Outer Critics' Circle Award for Best Play.

Biographical Monodramas

Ancient Greek *rhapsodists*, Roman *histriones*, and Middle Ages *scôps* and *gleemen* were solo performers who brought historical figures to life. So, too, many modern monodramatists are interested in showing the personal lives and professional accomplishments of contemporary men and women who have helped make us who we are today. The last quarter-century has seen the staging of a rather amazingly large number of one-person biographical monodramas, usually full-length scripts, proving popular with playwrights, actors, audiences, and critics. Typical subjects are public figures such as artists, actors, and politicians.

William Luce, for example, has written biographical full-length productions such as *The Belle of Amherst* about poet Emily Dickinson, which won Julie Harris a Best Actress Tony for her performance. Luce also dramatized the lives of other people in full-length monodramas such as *Brontë*, about author Charlotte Brontë, *Lillian*, the life of playwright Lillian Hellman, and *The Last Flapper* (originally produced as *Zelda*), about the wife of novelist F. Scott Fitzgerald. More recently he wrote about the life of John Barrymore, a member of a famous American acting dynasty. Christopher Plummer played the title role in *Barrymore*, winning a Tony in 1997.

Political Figures. Biographical monodramas may focus on politicians, such as Samuel Gallu's *Give 'Em Hell, Harry!* about President Harry S Truman, later made into a motion picture in 1975 and earning an Oscar nomination for actor James Whitmore. Playwright Donald Freed created Richard Nixon in *Secret Honor*, in which Philip Baker Hall played the beleaguered president.

Authors. Monodramatists may decide to focus on literary figures, such as Michaêl MacLiammoir's *Importance of Being Oscar* about playwright Oscar Wilde. Ray Stricklyn and Charlotte Chandler created *Confessions of a Nightingale*, "an intimate visit" with playwright Tennessee Williams; Stricklyn performed the solo role. Robert Morse played *Tru*, a one-person play about writer Truman Capote, in New York and on tour. While a college senior, Allison Boye transformed her decade-long fondness of *To Kill a Mockingbird* into a monodrama she wrote for herself to perform: *Harper Lee Was, I Suppose, A Child Once.* Boye's one-person show pays homage to Lee and relates the novel and the author to the playwright's own interests and experiences.

Motion Picture Actors. Michael Druxman used his experience as a screenwriter and movie historian-biographer to develop *The Hollywood Legends*, a collection of two-act monodramas about classical stars. Each play focuses on one star, including singers such as Al Jolson and Maurice Chavalier; actors such as Clara Bow, Carole Lombard, Clark Gable, Spencer Tracy, and Errol Flynn; and major contributors to film such as Orson Welles, the "boy genius" of theatre and motion pictures.

A *Variety of Biographical Monodramas*. Other biographical one-person shows include *Me and JFK*, *Eleanor* (about Eleanor Roosevelt), *Vincent* (about Theo Van Gogh's reactions to his famous brother), *Yr. Loving Mama*, *V. R.* (Queen Victoria), *Woodie Guthrie*, *Blasts and Bravos* (H. L. Mencken), *Papa* (Ernest Hemingway), *Paul Robeson*, *I Am His Wife* (Helene Schweitzer), and *His Satanic Majesty* (Lord Byron). More recent performances include the musical *Lady Day at Emerson Bar and Grill* (singer Billie Holiday) and *Full Gallop* (*Vogue* and *Harper's Bazaar* editor Diana Vreeland). Even Adolph Hitler has been the subject of a monodrama: *The Hitler Masque*.

Actors in Solo Plays. Actors are attracted to the challenges and opportunities of a solo turn. In recent years audience members dedicated to monodramas might have seen such well-known performers as Uta Hagen (*Charlotte*), Ben Kingsley (*Edmund Kean*), Henry Fonda (who won a Tony for creating the title role in *Clarence Darrow*), Zoe Caldwell (*Lillian*), Colleen Dewhurst (*My Gene*), Vincent Price (*Diversions and Delights*), James Earl Jones (*Paul Robeson*), Leonard Nimoy (*Vincent*), James Whitmore (*Will Rogers' U.S.A.* and *Bully!*), and Michael York (*Rogues and Vagabonds*).

Autobiographical Monodramas for Playwrights-Performers

Blending theatre and self, autobiographical monodramas tend to take on something of the atmosphere of folk stories for modern times, freshly created legends based on personal experiences that are expanded to comment indirectly on modern issues. For example, Spalding Gray, a popular and innovative modern solo performer, has written a number of autobiographical monodramas, performing them in New York and on tour. Among them are *Sex and Death to the Age of 14*, *Swimming to Cambodia*, *Terrors of Pleasure*, and *Monster in a Box*. Some have been presented on television and are available on video tape. Susan Miller took autobiographical writing into highly personal areas. Her *My Left Breast* is about her mastectomy—one highly memorable line is "One of these is not real. Can you tell which?"—and combines the frightening experience with lusty comedy.

Adaptations

Literary works are frequently adapted into monodramas, such as Everett Quinton's version of Charles Dickens's novel, *A Tale of Two Cities*. The Bible provides writer-performer Alec McGowen with a monodrama called *St. Mark's Gospel*. Shakespeare's works have long been popular with monodramatists. Lynn Redgrave, for example, toured the country and played on Broadway with her *Shakespeare for My Father: The Life and Times of an Actor's Daughter*, in which she combines some twenty Shakespearean characters with almost as many "characters from my life," such as Richard Burton, Dame Edith Evans, and, of course, her father, Sir Michael Redgrave. An abbreviated sample list of other excerpts from Shakespeare includes Fanny Kemble's *Readings from Shakespeare*, Benjamin Stewart's *Venus and Adonis*, John Gielgud's *The Ages of Man*, and Ian McKellen's *Acting Shakespeare*.

Playwright-Actor Monodramas

Actors can enhance their careers by writing solo plays designed for their particular interests and strengths. A case in point is Hal Holbrook. He was a college student intent on an acting career when he started in small clubs trying out what became one of the best known modern monodramas, *Mark Twain Tonight!* It sparked Holbrook's stage and television career through successful Broadway runs in 1959, 1966, and 1977, as well as many tours throughout the country, and Holbrook won a Tony for Mark Twain. Holbrook also used his Twain monodrama in a CBS television special in 1967 plus two record albums.

Professional actors often relish the challenges of the solo play. For example, stage, screen, and television actress Elizabeth Perry wrote *Sun Flower* for herself to perform, bringing to life Elizabeth Cady Stanton, the nineteenth century co-founder of the women's suffrage movement. When she performed *Sun Flower* at Arena Stage (Washington, D.C.) in 1997, Perry won praise for her bravura performance as she gave Stanton intelligence, wit, and vulnerability while also playing some two dozen additional characters. Director Anita Khanzadian shaped the performance to bring out Stanton's nobility. The script of *Sun Flower*, however, was criticized for an overall lack of conflict, essential to test a character's convictions.

Other actors also do well with pieces they write for themselves. Eric Bogosian, a popular modern monodramatist, has written several monodramas that he performs, including *Men Inside*, *FunHouse*, and *Drinking in America*. Whoopi Goldberg created her own *Whoopi Goldberg* for Broadway in 1984, igniting her acting career. Playwright Emlyn Williams created *Emlyn Williams as Charles Dickens*, which he performed; and Michaêl MacLiammoir wrote *I Must Be Talking to My Friends* for himself to play.

Rob Becker established a career with his *Defending the Caveman*, which he wrote for himself to perform. He spent three years writing the comedy about the classical battle between males and females, in the process studying history, psychology, sociology, anthropology, and mythology. *Caveman* became Broadway's longest running solo play, surpassing Lily Tomlin's *The Search for Intelligent Life in the Universe* and Jackie Mason's *The World According to Me*. To honor *Caveman's* record, New York Mayor Rudolph Guiliani proclaimed a "Caveman Day" and renamed West 44th Street Caveman Way. How's *that* for an illustration of the strength of a one-person play? You may have seen Becker's performance when he recently toured his solo play in a number of major American cities.

MUSICAL MONODRAMAS

Monodramas seem to have an almost humanlike impish delight in breaking boundaries. One-person musical solo plays may be increasing in popularity, as shown by works such as the one Beth Walters wrote for herself to perform: *Kooky Women Looking for Love*, which she presented in New York in 1993. Walters adapted a number of well-known fictional characters— Adelaide, Cinderella, Charity, and the like—in her humorous takeoff of musical theatre. Another example of the musical monodrama is *Herringbone*, with music by Walter Edgar Kennon and book and lyrics by Ellen Fitzhugh, which was developed in the BMI-Lehman Engel Musical Theatre Workshop and produced off-Broadway (starring David Rounds). In late 1991 actress Jean Stapleton performed two musical pieces scored by composer Lee Hoiby: *The Italian Lesson* (taken from a monodrama by Ruth Draper, one of the leading solo performers from 1920 until her death in 1956) and *Bon Appetit!* (interestingly, a Julia Child cooking recipe set to music).

EXPERIMENTAL AND CONTROVERSIAL MONODRAMAS

Monodramas can be controversial, illustrated by Annie Sprinkle's "performance art" one-person show: *Annie Sprinkle Post-Post Porn Modernist Still in Search of the Ultimate Sexual Experience*.* Her solo play prompted intense debates about using public funds to subsidize works that some politicians and clergy deem morally objectionable. Monodramas also can

---

* Performance art is a large category with many subdivisions, but generally we see that it often inserts personal life into fictional treatments, such as having the director or actor place his or her own concepts into an existing play. Performance art frequently performs in "untheatres" as part of the concept of eliminating audience-performer distinctions. Practitioners see links between modern performance art and ancient tribal rituals, such as

explore unexpected areas, such as Deb Margolin's *Gestation*, which deals with the character's decidedly mixed responses to pregnancy.

Karen Finley, perhaps best known as the performance artist who smeared her naked body with chocolate in one of her pieces, provoked additional arguments about the role of the artist in society and the role of governmental support for the arts. Finley and three other performance artists—Tim Miller, John Fleck, and Hollie Hughes—successfully filed suit against a statute, enacted by Congress, that required the National Endowment of the Arts to consider "general standards of decency" in awarding grants. In late 1996 the Ninth Circuit Court of Appeals ruled that statute was an unconstitutional barrier to artists' free speech.

More recently, Finley's *American Chestnut* deals with what she perceives as the superwoman complex. Her title resonates with the plight of the American Chestnut tree, the tall and stately tree that used to line suburban streets before it was afflicted with a terminal disease. Finley equates the tree's problems with social situations affecting women.

Also controversial is *Bitch! Dyke! Faghag! Whore!*, which toured cities such as Tampa, Boston, and Calgary and then had an unusually long run at New York's Village Gate in 1992–1993. Written, produced, and performed by Penny Arcade (whose real name is Susana Ventura), B!D!F!W! is a performance art show that mixes sexual motifs and avant-garde styles, including Arcade stripping naked before draping herself in an American flag. The author-actress plays a variety of characters, such as the hooker, the drag queen, and the junkie, who represent her various experiences and political views. It is called a one-person monodrama, although the production includes ten erotic male and female go-go dancers who add impact to the show's focus on sexuality.

Variations in Length

Monodramas can range in playing time from some ten minutes to more than two hours. The playing time of full-length monodramas is similar to that of full-length multicharacter plays, structured in two or three acts and providing an evening's entertainment of around two hours, ten minutes. One-act monodramas, like multicharacter one-act plays, tend to be

a shaman's. One outspoken proponent is Richard Schechner, whose *Performance Theory* is recommended for those wanting information about this alternative theatrical form. Doubters see performance art as merely a mod term to describe works that all too often are poorly conceived and sloppily presented, and they point out that *new* and *different* don't necessarily equate with *good*.

around thirty to forty-five minutes long. Short-short monodramas, a title I borrow from fiction's "short-short story" (limited to 2,000 words or less, in contrast to the short story, which is around 7,500 words) are around ten to twenty minutes long.

Most of the monodramas mentioned here are full evening entertainments, as long as full-length plays, but we must point out that shorter monodramas also are popular. Examples of excellent short solo plays include Samuel Beckett's *Krapp's Last Tape*, Lanford Wilson's *A Poster of the Cosmos*, Kenneth Jenkins' *Cemetery Man*, Jean-Claude van Itallie's *Struck Dumb* and *Rosary*, David Mamet's *Litko: A Dramatic Monologue*, Eugene O'Neill's *Beyond Breakfast*, August Strindberg's *The Stronger*, and the previously discussed Jane Martin *Talking With. . .* collection. Short monodramas are often experimental, illustrated by *Savage/Love* and *Tongues*, by Sam Shepard and Joseph Chaikin, which are jazz pieces that combine poetry and music, and Shel Silverstein's *The Devil and Billy Markham*, a rollicking poetic play.

VARIATIONS IN STRUCTURE

The one-person play varies in structure. It may be as carefully plotted as a multicharacter full-length play, with conflict and complications that create building action. Alternatively, it may be a brief character sketch or be a mood piece that seeks to evoke an emotion.

Plotted Monodramas

The structure of *plotted monodrama* resembles that of multicharacter plays. It usually contains essential elements of plot, such as inciting incident, foreshadowing, exposition, point of attack, complications and reversals creating rising action, and a climax. The character faces a major conflict between significant choices. For example, he or she might be considering marriage, divorce, suicide, abortion, an issue involving drugs, dropping out of school, quitting a job, dealing with a troublesome relative, or the like.

A significant aspect of the plot is a conflict that affects the character *now*, giving the play a sense of the present, not past, and giving the character a highly important vested emotional interest in the outcome. The conflict makes the action move to a future because there is a strong sense of urgency that the character must take some significant action. Conflict adds suspense by making the audience wonder what the character will do to solve his or her crisis.

Plot can be important regardless of the play's length, but longer pieces require careful plotting to give the character dynamic movement that will hold audience interest. For example, most full-length monodramas, such as *The Belle of Amherst*, *Clarence Darrow*, and *Give 'Em Hell, Harry*, have strong plots to sustain their length. Playwrights, actors, and directors find that well-designed plot creates stimuli and choices to which the character must respond, therefore becoming interesting, dynamic, and multidimensional with motivated emotional changes.

Not all full-length solo plays are as tightly plotted. *The Search for Intelligent Life in the Universe*, for example, is constructed with a number of short scenes or episodes similar to skits or blackouts. It is held tightly together by a common theme involving feminist issues and the central character's discoveries about her personal values. In contrast, critics praised Whoopi Goldberg's 1984 solo performance but criticized the script of *Whoopi Goldberg* because they believed it was too formless, without the adhesive power that plot contributes to a play.

Character Sketches

The term *character sketch* implies a relatively brief script that does not delve deeply into its subject's overall life but instead shows perhaps one or two highly interesting qualities of the character. A character sketch resembles a fiction writer's short or short-short story. For the playwright, as for the painter, a *sketch* suggests a relatively small work that shows selected, basic essentials of the subject but not all details.

The character sketch generally has little plot but instead relies heavily on a fascinating character whose unusual qualities and dimensions will attract audience attention. The character sketch often reflects the playwright's and actor's genuine fondness for the character. With little or no plot to sustain it, the character sketch tends to be relatively short, seldom more than ten or twenty minutes.

Enriched, Dimensional Characterization in Monodramas

Although some character sketches can be unfortunately thin, others gain strength when they make a subtle social commentary or observation, usually because the character's unique vision makes the audience see unusual aspects in a commonplace event or situation. Martin's *French Fries*, for example, starts with a common enough location—a McDonald's is about as commonplace as one can imagine—but the playwright gives the old woman an unusual concept of the place. Implied is a social comment about the needs of the elderly and homeless.

A fully dimensional study of a character shows details of the subject's life, conflicts, hopes, frustrations, successes, or failures. To continue the analogy with a painter, we can say that if a sketch is a small black-and-white pencil drawing, the dimensional character script is a canvas that is significantly larger, more colorful, more engaging, and more detailed. The playwright's canvas tends to be as long and complex as a major multi-character, one-act or full-length play.

Mood Pieces

A *mood piece* seeks to evoke an atmosphere through a character's emotional involvement with a particular event or issue. For example, a mood piece might focus on an old man or woman who lives in a retirement home and now is making detailed plans for a forthcoming visit from a son or daughter who, the character wants to believe, will arrive any moment. Such a monodrama would seek to make the audience empathize with the character's loneliness.

Evoking a mood requires delicacy. The playwright, actor, and director must be sensitive to the difference between *sentiment* and *sentimentality*. The former may be acceptable if handled with tasteful restraint, but the latter can become uncomfortably maudlin.

Some mood pieces take on an unfortunate single tone, holding too long to a given mood as if trying overly hard to evoke a mournful quality. For example, in a monodrama about an old person in a retirement home, some playwrights and performers might create a forlorn character with few dynamic changes. Others, with a more theatrical awareness of the difference between sentiment and sentimentality, will create a feisty, high-spirited character who can laugh or curse angrily in spite of loneliness. These effective monodramas have dynamic changeability that avoids overstating the single forlorn tone. Because the mood piece seldom has much plot, it is difficult to sustain for any substantial length of time, and most stay within the short-short time length.

Memory or Diary Monodramas

The Memory Monodrama. Scripts with dominant "I'll never forget the time when . . ." qualities most often are ill-suited for the theatre and may better be written as a novel or short story. Here's where we see the importance of keeping a play in the present tense, with action happening now. It is a matter of emphasis. If the past tense is important, those events must deeply and immediately affect the character now; merely relating events that once happened does not make effective theatre. Rather than writing a past-tense monodrama about already completed action, the playwright might consider revising the monodrama to put the action back in the time when the emotions and events took place, allowing the action to unfold rather than be told.

The Diary Monodrama. A play full of "my lover left me and I'm so lonely" or "I'm so mistreated because the world isn't fair" qualities may be appropriate for a personal diary but most often is a poor choice for public display in a theatrical production. Unfortunately, some writers seem to want to use the monodrama for introspective comments about intimate distress or whimpers about inequities the writer has experienced. Such pieces probably interest the author much more than an audience. Although playwrights certainly draw on their personal experiences, scripts that are only private tales of mournful misfortune just aren't likely to captivate an audience, and there's little even the most talented actor or director can do to enliven dreary pieces focused on "poor me."

The preceding list of basic categories of monodramas is not inclusive because monodramatists often search for new perspectives in theatrical writing, directing, and acting. Experimentations with music may indicate a direction future monodramas may take, and the popularity of Spalding Gray's autobiographical monodramas may herald a growing trend in this form. Still, most successful monodramas combine plot, characterization, thematic meaning, and mood, and they often include striking language and images.

THE MOST FREQUENTLY HEARD COMPLAINT

As you work on your solo play, remember that the number of possible forms of the solo play doesn't mean it has no limits. Audience suspension of disbelief is severely tested when the character is not deeply motivated to speak and when that motivation is not vital and clear. The most frequent negative comment in critics' reviews of monodramas can be summarized simply: "I couldn't understand what made the character want to talk." Some compare that lack of plausibility to the opening of the movie version of *The Sound of Music* when Julie Andrews, alone on a mountain, bursts into song accompanied by a lush orchestra as an ever-higher aerial view shows an increasingly distant Andrews within miles of empty mountains. Not often do we wonder about the source of the orchestra in musicals, but the highly visible empty space can make many of us have difficulty dealing with so much implausibility.

Playwrights, actors, and directors seek to eliminate that negative response by being sure the character's motivation to speak is both strong and clear. Plausibility and credibility are achieved by putting the character in a situation where he or she *must* encounter a conflict that centers on deeply held personal beliefs, giving the monodrama a sense of now. Significant is the honesty in writing and production.

THE MONODRAMA'S REWARDS

Drama is art, a poetic art in a special mode, with its own version of the poetic illusion to govern every detail of the performed piece. . . . Drama is neither ritual nor show business, though it may occur in the frame of either one; it is poetry, which is neither a kind of circus nor a kind of church. . . . Drama is poetry in the mode of action.   —Susanne Langer

Whether you are a playwright, actor, director, designer, producer, student of theatre, play reader, or audience member, you'll find the monodrama can be a rewarding experience. At its best, the solo play is a sharp laser beam that cuts through murky fog and confusing clouds that hide the human essence. Its intense single focus shows the internal heart and soul of a solitary character. Effective one-person plays awake the audience's imagination, mind, and soul. Like poetry, the solo play condenses the wide-ranging variety of life into a brilliant moment of illumination.

Artistic Advantages
Over centuries the one-person show has proved that it is a valid and important artistic form in its own right, no less significant than multi-character one-act or full-length plays. Your goal is to create a work of theatrical art, but you have few other limitations. The monodrama may be comic or dramatic, short or long, experimental or traditional. It may be primarily an entertainment piece or a strident protest. It may focus tightly on one character or evoke additional characters, on- or offstage.

Educational Advantages

An Entrance into Theatre. The monodrama serves as a significant entrance to theatre for students, play readers, playwrights, actors, directors, designers, and audience members. The short monodrama is a microcosm of the total theatre experience, allowing you to perceive what makes theatre. The monodrama's avoidance of nonessential theatrical trappings can help you see the essential elements of theatre, such as acting, directing, playwriting, and design, as well as play structure, characterization, conflict, emotional truths, thematic core, dialogue, the importance of showing instead of telling, entertainment, and communicating meaning. It lacks only the interactions between characters that one finds in more traditional one-act and full-length plays, but often even that interplay can be implied in monodramas that deal with one character in conflict with another (unseen) person or with the character's struggles with his or her own self.

Developing Playwriting Skills. The monodrama allows the playwright to concentrate on one character instead of being concerned about developing the many characters needed for a more standard one-act or full-length play. The more insightful, sensitive, and thorough the playwright's vision of the character, the greater impact the monodrama will have on audiences. Writing or performing a solo play is its own reward, but a very significant byproduct is that the one-person play also is an excellent method of improving theatrical skills for a one-act or full-length play. Learning how to achieve depth of characterization for a one-person play has obvious advantages if you turn to a multicharacter script.

Developing Directing and Acting Skills. Actors and directors find that the monodrama provides a unique opportunity to bring to life a richly dimensional character. It can be especially rewarding, as evidenced by the performers who have won important theatrical awards, performed on Broadway, or taken monodramas on tour. Furthermore, the lessons actors and directors learn in keeping a character truthful, vibrant, and alive during the course of a monodrama are directly applicable to other theatrical experiences.

Developing expertise through studies of a smaller unit, such as a short-short monodrama, allows playwright, actor, or director to feel confident about moving to larger projects, such as a full-length multicharacter play.

The short-short monodrama uses all the basics of theatrical storytelling, dialogue, characterization, emotional context, and structure; theatre workers who learn to present a quality monodrama gain valuable insights that are directly applicable for the more traditional and complicated forms of dramatic expression. Some theatre participants find that the microcosm of the monodrama is so rewarding that they decide not to move to multi-character plays and prefer instead to continue working with solo plays.

Audience Receptivity

Audiences tend to give the monodrama more space and freedom—they seem to suspend skepticism willingly—than they give full-length plays, apparently because the solo play appears to have an experimental quality and because its intimacy draws audiences directly into the situation. Because the solo play is more flexible than its multicharacter relatives, you can take advantage of Samuel Taylor Coleridge's often-quoted concept of the ideal audience response to theatre: "That act of poetic faith, the willing suspension of disbelief." The one-person show allows you an excellent opportunity to experiment with enhanced or elevated diction, fantasy and other departures from realism, jumps in time and place, and comparable appeals to the audience's imagination.

Opening Employment Possibilities

In contrast to multicharacter plays, the monodrama can be produced relatively quickly and inexpensively, and it tours easily. Therefore, whether you are playwright, actor, or director, you'll find that the solo play can give you production opportunities. Consider, for example, Roy Dotrice, who is the record-holder for number of performances by an actor in a monodrama. He performed his *Brief Lives* 1,700 times, including a 400-performance-run at the Mayfair Theatre in London. That's almost five years of work as an actor. To put Dotrice's record in perspective, compare his 1,700 performances with popular, long-running Broadway shows such as *South Pacific* (1949–1954), which had 1,925 performances, or *Cage aux Folles* (1983–1987), with 1,761 performances. No one should promise you'll equal or beat Dotrice's record, but no one can ignore the solo play's possibilities.

Increased Possibilities for Production Experience

The monodrama not only offers theatre workers exciting artistic challenges and lessons, it also gives them a significant practical bonus: stage experience. Many monodramas are produced in the today's theatre, providing valuable creative opportunities for playwrights, directors, actors, and designers. Compared with plays or musicals, monodramas can be produced easily, so theatrical organizations can schedule solo plays for production while major shows are in rehearsal. As a result, the theatre is more active, attracting audience interest and support. Expenses for cast salary are less than for multicharacter plays, and one actor (instead of many) means less expenditure for costumes, props, and the like. In most cases the focus on the performer and story means carefully designed minimal settings, decreasing construction expense and time.

Some theatres select a number of short monodramas for an evening's entertainment, sometimes using different playwrights and actors but usually involving the same designer and one or more directors. Busy theatres may plan an evening of monodramas while a major production is in progress, perhaps presenting the monodramas on Sunday afternoons and Monday nights when the main stage is not in use. Theatres also combine monodramas with one-act plays.

Local or Touring Theatre. The lack of complex and expensive production devices make monodramas a good choice for your local community or educational amateur theatres as well as for professional regional theatres. The production simplicity also makes monodramas popular as touring shows, illustrated by writer-performers such as Spalding Gray, who tours his *Monster in a Box* about his novel *Impossible Vacation.* Regional and educational theatres often sponsor touring monodramas.

New York Productions. Monodramas also have had successful New York productions that have won critical awards. Although cynics may conclude that New York producers are willing to gamble on presenting monodramas only because they are less costly than traditional plays, that view is too simplistic and overlooks the artistic qualities of effective monodramas. Nonetheless, the low overhead certainly is a factor, and although no one promises that you'll get to Broadway with your monodrama, history indicates that possibility exists.

A COMPELLING THEATRICAL EXPERIENCE

As you've seen in the extracts from the monodrama about the old woman in McDonald's, the solo play is a curiously insightful experience. This unique form of theatre allows us to see past one individual's exterior public mask into her most private interior thoughts and emotions. The absence of other characters makes the solo player more important and creates a rapport between character and audience.

Although *French Fries* is short, in that brief 15 minutes' playing time we can intuit much about the old woman's entire life. We feel the character's values, attitudes, dreams, and emotions, empathizing and becoming one with her as we see a world through her eyes. When it is over, we feel we've made a discovery no less significant than the boldest explorer's, but our journey is into a human heart—and into ourselves. The result is a compelling theatrical encounter.

For playwrights, actors, directors, and designers, the monodrama is no less a significant artistic form than the one-act or full-length play. At its best, the monodrama is theatre in its basic fundamentals. Eliminating excess baggage makes it a brilliant single ray of light instead of a diffused shadowy event. It is a private sharing, a direct theatrical one-to-one communication with the audience, a close-up lens that demands naked truth from all participants.

Challenging? Yes, very.

Rewarding? Most certainly.

EXERCISES

Write your responses to the following exercises. Keep your materials in your Monodrama Notebook where you can use them for creating your own monodrama.

1. If you've read or seen one or more monodramas, what was your reaction? What made the monodrama effective? What made it ineffective? What were your responses to the techniques used by the playwright, director, and actor? What changes would you have preferred?

2. One key to writing a successful monodrama lies in developing a character who is compelled to speak. That compulsion often is a response to a major dilemma the character faces and a major goal the character deeply wants to achieve. Write brief outlines, perhaps a page or two long, of short monodramas based on the following characters, keeping action in the present tense and moving to the future. Decide if you want to create a comedy or a drama. Think of a dimen-

sional human with dynamic emotional qualities.

a. A proud elderly man or woman is homeless and impoverished. The character has an opportunity to go to a shelter but does not like to accept charity. Add complications to the situation. For example, suppose winter is coming or the character is hungry or ill. What if the character knows a friend who went to that shelter and seemed to lose her individuality? Think of dynamic emotional variations the character experiences.

b. A young man just found out that he impregnated the woman he dates. What will he do? What if the character is selfish and does not want to accept responsibility but has an active conscience? Alternatively, think of the woman's view. What will she do? Consider adding complications such as pressures from family or friends, the character's religious beliefs, or the character's life-long goals that the pregnancy influences.

c. A romantic young woman is deeply in love with a young man but everything went wrong on their date last night and they separated angrily. What if she now wants to telephone him but cannot because she is afraid he'll reject her?

3. Select any soliloquy you wish, such as Hamlet's "To be or not to be" or Macbeth's "Tomorrow and tomorrow," and imagine turning it into a monodrama. Feel free to adapt it. Ignore any background details you wish so it needs little or no exposition and instead focus on the character's emotions and thoughts. How would you write it so it has a beginning, middle, and end? What would you do to keep it in the present tense, with action happening now, and moving to a future? Can you change the Shakespearean character into a modern-day equivalent? Write an outline or sketch of the monodrama you'd create.

4. Think of an issue that deeply concerns you. Perhaps you'll select a major social problem such as AIDS, abortion, or drugs, or you may wish to consider certain human traits such as honesty, charity, or ambition. Feel free to choose any topic that is important to you. Now create a dimensional character who is presently encountering a situation involving that topic. Be sure he or she is deeply involved in the action and has a compelling goal. Write a brief outline of a monodrama based on that character.

A play's an interpretation. It is not a report. And that is the beginning of its poetry because, in order to interpret, you have to convince, you have to distort toward a symbolic construction of what happened, and as that distortion takes place, you begin to leave out and over-emphasize and consequently deliver up life as a unity rather than as a chaos, and any such attempt, the more intense it is, the more poetic it becomes. —Arthur Miller

3
CHAPTER

French Fries *and* Twirler
Two Monodramas by Jane Martin

THROUGHOUT THIS BOOK YOU'LL FIND EXAMPLES OF MONO-
dramas to help you better understand the form so you can develop your
own solo play. To start us off, in this chapter we look at two complete
scripts. Following each monodrama you'll find exercises that call your
attention to specific aspects of the monodrama.

As you read these plays, note their ability to explore ideas and form as
well as develop rich characterization. Use your imagination to stage plays
in your mind. Read them aloud, using the character's voice, projecting her
emotions, goals, and motivational drives, showing her dreams and
hungers, and using gestures and physical movements to help you bring
her to life.

JANE MARTIN

The monodrama can bring you theatrical productions, publications, hon-
ors, and prizes, as illustrated by the works of one of modern theatre's fascinating mysteries, Jane Martin. Paradoxically, she is a well-known, yet

unknown, playwright. Martin catapulted into world-wide attention in 1981 when the Actors Theatre of Louisville (Kentucky) first presented her collected monodramas, a series of eleven short-short monodramas called *Talking With . . .*, which received critical and popular acclaim. Later the Actors Theatre presented the collection in New York's Manhattan Theatre Club. Since then her monodramas have been published by Samuel French, Inc., and performed throughout America and the world (winning "Best Foreign Play of the Year" in Germany). She also has written a number of multicharacter plays.

Well-known? Her work, yes. But Jane Martin is a nom de plume, and only a very few people know the playwright's identity. An executor handles all business and legal matters involved with productions and publications of her plays. Ms. Martin deliberately remains anonymous, despite her fame—or perhaps because of it. Jon Jory, Artistic Director of Actors Theatre, says that apparently Ms. Martin does not want her personal life affected by being viewed as "the person who writes about those fascinating people."

With the mystery about her identity come rumors. Some people claim that the plays were actually written by Jon Jory, although he denies that, whereas others say that a number of playwrights secretly collaborated to write the plays attributed to Ms. Martin.

Ms. Martin has been steadfast in maintaining her anonymity.

A theatre person who won't step forward and bow to acknowledge the well-deserved applause?

That's the stuff on which theatrical legends are built.

In the previous chapter we quoted from *French Fries*. Because it may be difficult to obtain copies of monodramas to show the form's power and versatility, we include here the entire scripts of *Fries* and *Twirler*, another Martin play. These help you better understand some of the solo play's characteristics, form, techniques, stylistic approach, construction, and flexibility. *Fries* and *Twirler* are part of Martin's eleven-play collection, *Talking With . . .*, and should you wish to read the others you can order acting editions from Samuel French, Inc.

As you'll discover by timing *French Fries* and *Twirler* while you read them aloud, they are examples of the brief monodrama. You'll note that they are shorter than the typical one-act play, so short, in fact, that we adapt fiction's short-short story description to refer to these works as *short-short monodramas*.

French Fries and Twirler illustrate the monodrama's ability to bring intriguing characters to life and the power of language to expand the universe of the play. They were first performed at the Actors Theatre of Louisville in 1981. The first New York production of the full set of monodramas, an Actors Theater of Louisville production, opened at the Manhattan Theater Club in October, 1982. The director was Jon Jory. The solo actress in French Fries was Theresa Merritt. Lisa Goodman performed the solo role in Twirler.

FRENCH FRIES
by Jane Martin

An old woman in a straight-back chair holding a McDonald's cup. She is surrounded by several bundles of newspapers. She wears thick glasses that distort her eyes to the viewer.

ANNA MAE: If I had one wish in my life, why I'd like to live in McDonald's. Right there in the restaurant. 'Stead of in this old place. I'll come up to the brow of the hill, bowed down with my troubles, hurtin' under my load and I'll see that yellow horseshoe, sort of like part of a rainbow, and it gives my old spirit a lift. Lord, I can sit in a McDonald's all day. I've done it too. Walked the seven miles with the sun just on its way, and then sat on the curb till five minutes of seven. First one there and the last to leave. Just like some ol' french fry they forgot.

I like the young people workin' there. Like a team of fine young horses when I was growin' up. All smilin'. Tell you what I really like though is the plastic. God gave us plastic so there wouldn't be no stains on his world. See, in the human world of the earth it all gets scratched, stained, tore up, faded down. Loses its shine. All of it does. In time. Well, God he gave us the idea of plastic so we'd know what the everlasting really was. See if there's plastic then there's surely eternity. It's God's hint.

You ever watch folks when they come on in the McDonald's? They always speed up, almost run the last few steps. You see if they don't.

Old Dobbin with the barn in sight. They know it's safe in there and it ain't safe outside. Now it ain't safe outside and you know it.

I've seen a man healed by a Big Mac. I have. I was just sittin' there. Last summer it was. Oh, they don't never move you on. It's a sacred law in McDonald's, you can sit for a hundred years. Only place in this world. Anyway, a fella, maybe thirty-five, maybe forty, come on in there dressed real nice, real bright tie, bran' new baseball cap, nice white socks and he had him that disease. You know the one I mean, Cerebral Walrus they call it. Anyway, he had him a cock leg. His poor old body had it two speeds at the same time. Now he got him some coffee, with a lid on, and sat him down and Jimmy the tow-head cook knew him, see, and he brought over a Big Mac. Well, the sick fella ate maybe half of it and then he was just sittin', you know, suffering those tremors, when a couple of *ants* come right out of the burger. Now there ain't no ants in McDonald's no way. Lord sent those ants, and the sick fella he looked real sharp at the burger and a bunch *more* ants marched on out as nice as you please and his head lolled right over and he pitched himself out of that chair and banged his head on the floor, loud. Thwack! Like a bowling ball dropping. Made you half sick to hear it. We jump up and run over, but he was cold out. Well those servin' kids, so cute, they watered him, stuck a touch pepper up his nostril, slapped him right smart, and bang, up he got. Standin' and blinkin'. 'Well, how are you?' we say. An he looks us over, looks right in our eyes, and he say, 'I'm fine.' And he was. He was fine! Tipped his Cincinnati Reds baseball cap, big 'jus-swallowed-the-canary' grin, paraded out of there clean, straight like a pole-bean poplar, walked him a plumb line without no trace of the 'walrus.' Got outside, jumped up, whooped, hollered, sang him the National Anthem, flagged down a Circle Line bus, an' rode off up Muhammad Ali Boulevard wavin' an' smilin' like the King of the Pharaohs. Healed by a Big Mac. I saw it.

McDonald's. You ever see anybody die in a McDonald's? No sir. No way. Nobody ever has died in one. Shoot, they die in Burger King all the time. Kentucky Fried Chicken's got their own damn ambulances. Nooooooooooo, you can't die in a McDonald's no matter how hard you try. It's the spices. Seals you safe in this life like it seals in the flavor. Yesssssss, yes!

I asked Jarrell could I live there. See they close up around ten, and there ain't a thing goin' on in 'em till seven A.M. I'd just sit in those nice swingy chairs and lean forward. Rest my head on those cool, cool, smooth tables, sing me a hymn and sleep like a baby. Jarrell, he said he'd write him a letter up the chain of command and see would they let me. Oh, I got my bid in. Peaceful and clean.

Sometimes I see it like the last of a movie. You know how they start the picture up real close and then back it off steady and far? Well, that's how I dream it. I'm living in McDonald's and it's real late at night and you see me up close, smiling, and then you see the whole McDonald's from the outside, lit up and friendly. And I get smaller and smaller, like they do, and then it's just a light in the darkness, like a star, and I'm in it. I'm part of that light, part of the whole sky, and it's all McDonald's, but part of something even bigger, something fixed and shiny . . . like plastic.

I know. I know. It's just a dream. Just a beacon in the storm. But you got to have a dream. It's our dreams make us what we are.

BLACKOUT

EXERCISES

The following exercises are designed to help you find methods to create richly drawn characters. Use the following questions as guides, answering those you can and freely adding other insights and comments that indicate how you *see* and *hear* the play. Make your answers as specific as possible. Approach the exercises with good-faith determination to learn and explore the world of the theatre and you'll find that they stimulate your imagination and help you to create your personal theatrical vision.

Some questions, for example, ask you to sketch various aspects of the plays to show what you envision. Ability to draw is not important; instead, express your imaginative response to the play. Use photographs from magazines or books (of course, don't destroy library copies!), swatches of material to indicate clothing or other aspects of the play's environment, and the like.

Write your responses in your Monodrama Notebook, in which you keep notes and ideas about the monodrama you will create.

1. Imagine the play's environment. Forget that *French Fries* is a theatre piece—these questions aren't for scenic design but instead are part of the creative search for characterization that is crucial for playwrights, actors, and directors. Think of the location as if you are Anna Mae. See her surroundings and atmosphere in your imagination. Describe them in Anna Mae's terms, perhaps using phrases such as "I *see a picture of my daddy on the wall*" or "*This place makes me feel like an ol' red coon dog all tied up and no place to run.*" Note the use of the present tense verbs: plays take place in a perpetual present, never in the past.

   Is she in her own home? In a home that belongs to someone else, such as a relative? An apartment? An institution?

   What's the size of the room? Large? Small? Is it brightly lit and cheerful? Dark? What's the source of illumination? A lamp? The sun? A street light shining through the window?

   What's inside the room? What furniture? What does she see on tops of tables or bureaus? Are the walls painted or covered with wallpaper? What color? Is the floor bare wood, linoleum, or carpet? Is the place neat or messy?

   Find swatches of fabric that represent aspects of the room such as the rug, wallpaper, bed linen, and so forth.

   Are there pictures and paintings on the walls and tops of tables? Old pictures or new? Of whom? Draw pictures or find photographs that look like the paintings or photographs you see in her room.

   Are there things in this room that Anna Mae crafted herself?

   Does Anna Mae live in one room? If not, sketch a plan of her place and describe the other rooms.

   Is there a special item she picks up or touches for comfort?

   What about this place does she like? Dislike? What are her emotional attitudes toward the room?

2. To better envision the character, actors, directors, and playwrights, think of numerous specific details, even if—often especially if—such information doesn't appear within the script itself. This approach is often compared with *the tip of the iceberg*, which asks creative artists to understand that one-tenth of the play (like an iceberg) is visible above the surface, supported by the nine-tenths that is hidden. The result can be enhanced and dimensional characterization. Therefore, you want to expand the universe of the play by looking at the world

outside Anna Mae's place. Does she live in a small town?
Metropolitan area? What does her name suggest to you about the
geographic region? Does she live in the north? South? What clues
are you given? (Muhammad Ali Boulevard is a major street in
Louisville, where Martin's plays are frequently presented, and we
might assume she lives there. Still, let the tenor of the play itself
help you identify the region.)

Who lives next door? Does she know them? Like them or fight with
them? What are their names? What are their emotional responses
to Anna Mae?

What does she see when she looks out of her window? What can she
smell and hear? What are her emotional reactions to those senso-
ry stimuli?

When she leaves this place does she walk down stairs? Go through a
hallway? Exit directly to the outdoors? What stores or shops does
she notice when she leaves this place? Does she know people
who work in those stores? What do they think of her?

What is the time of day? The season? What's the weather like? How
does she feel about the time?

What are her emotional attitudes toward Jarrell?

How does she feel about Jimmy, the tow-head cook?

3. Look carefully at Anna Mae. Respond to the following questions with
words as well as sketches that you draw. Look in magazines for photographs that remind you of her and put the pictures in your
Notebook.

Is her general appearance neat or unkempt? Are her clothes ironed
or wrinkled?

Is she wearing perfume? If so, what kind?

How old is she? Is her face wrinkled or smooth?

What color is her hair? Is it long or short? Does she wear it in a bun
or loose?

What does she wear? Blouse? Sweater? Skirt? If a skirt, is it long or
short, plain or flowered, new or old? Or does she wear jeans?
What color are her clothes? What fabrics? What is most striking
about her hat?

What accessories does she wear? A locket? Earrings? Does she wear
a wedding ring?

Does she wear glasses? If so, are they metal-rimmed or plastic?

What sort of shoes does she wear? Heels or flats? Heavy boots? Tennis shoes?

How does she move? Gracefully? Does she have pains in certain joints?

What is her characteristic gesture (also called *psychologic gesture*) that she does habitually? Does she frequently push her glasses back in place on her nose? Reach out as if to stroke an imaginary cat?

She starts the play seated in the chair. Does she get up during the play? On what lines? Where does she go? Why? Does she return to her chair? On what lines?

4. Listen to Anna Mae. Hear her voice, her individualistic way of expressing her thoughts, her rhythm when she speaks, and her choice of words.

   Is she a soprano or alto?

   Is her voice strong or faltering? Assured or doubtful?

   What do you learn about her from words such as *'stead* rather than instead, *ol'* instead of old, *sittin'* for sitting, or *nooooooooooo* and *yessssss* for no and yes?

   What does she mean by "Old Dobbin"? By "cerebral walrus"? By "cock leg"?

   Which sentences and phrases would she say quickly? Which would she say slowly? Where would she pause?

   Does she sound self-pitying? Bold? Does she whimper? Cry? Does she laugh? Is she exuberant?

5. Actors and directors learn that the key to performing a character is to look for her *objective*, or *goal*, which refers to something the character most wants or has to achieve at all costs. What is Anna Mae's objective? Why does she want that goal? How strongly does she want it? What is Anna Mae's emotional stake in that objective? What does she lose if she doesn't achieve it? What is Anna Mae's primary emotion throughout the script?

6. A well-written monodrama or play has three parts: beginning, middle, and end. Identify this play's beginning and ending. Are they roughly the same length? Where does the middle begin and end? Of the three parts, which is the longest?

7. In the previous chapter we noted that monodramas often are called *dramas of language* because words are so important. Note the playwright's choices: "tipped his Cincinnati Reds baseball cap" instead of "tipped his cap," "flagged down a Circle Line bus" instead of "got on a bus," and "Jimmy the tow-head cook" instead of "one of the workers." What's the effect of such specific references? Review the script to note phrases or lines you think are especially strong. What gives them that extra strength?

8. What do you believe motivated the author to write this play? What do you think she wanted to say? What does she want the audience to feel and think? Where do you think she got the idea for Anna Mae's character? Do you think the playwright likes Anna Mae? What do you learn about Anna Mae? What do you learn about society, especially the world in which Anna Mae lives? What do you learn about yourself? How do you respond to her final lines, starting with "*I know. I know. It's just a dream*"?

We turn from *French Fries* to another one-person play. *Twirler* starts with an apparently mundane subject but it evolves into a much larger and quite disturbing journey.

TWIRLER
by Jane Martin

A young woman stands center stage. She is dressed in a spangled, single-piece swimsuit, the kind that is specially made for baton twirlers. She holds a shining, silver baton in her hand.

APRIL: I started when I was six. Momma sawed off a broom handle, and Uncle Carbo slapped some sort of silver paint, well, grey really, on it, and I went down in the basement and twirled. Later on, Momma hit the daily double on horses named Spin Dry and Silver Revolver and she said that was a sign so she gave me lessons at the Dainty Deb Dance Studio where the lady, Miss Aurelia, taught some twirling on the side.

I won the Ohio Juniors title when I was six and the Midwest Young Adult Division three years later and then in high school I finished fourth in the nationals. Momma and I wore look-alike Statue of Liberty costumes that she had to send clear to Nebraska to get and Daddy was there in a T-shirt with my name, April. My first name is April and my last name is March. There were four thousand people there, and when they yelled my name golden balloons fell out of the ceiling. Nobody, not even Charlene Ann Morrison, ever finished fourth at my age.

Oh, I've flown high and known tragedy both. My daddy says it's put spirit in my soul and steel in my heart. My left hand was crushed in a riding accident by a horse named Big Blood Red, and though I came back to twirl I couldn't do it at the highest level. That was denied me by Big Blood Red who clipped my wings. You mustn't pity me though. Oh, by no means! Being denied showed me the way, showed me the glory that sits inside life where you can't see it.

People think you're a twit if you twirl. It's a prejudice of the unknowing. Twirlers are the niggers of a white University. Yes, they are. One time I was doing fire batons at a night game, and all of a sudden I see this guy walk right out of the stands. I was doing triples and he walks right out past the half-time marshals, comes up to me, he had this blue-bead headband, I can still see it. Walks right up, and when I come front after a back reverse he spits in my face. That's the only, single time I ever dropped a baton, dropped 'em both in front of sixty thousand people and he smiles, see, and he says this thing I won't repeat. He called me a bodily part in front of half of Ohio. It was like being raped. It shows that beauty inspires hate and that hating beauty is Satan. (Breaks focus, identifies a person in audience; focus, pause, line.)

You haven't twirled, have you? I can see that by your hands. Would you like to hold my silver baton? Here, hold it.

You can't imagine what it feels like to have that baton up in the air. I used to twirl with this girl who called it blue-collar Zen. The 'tons' catch the sun when they're up, and when they go up, you go up too. You can't twirl if you're not inside the 'ton.' When you've got 'em up over twenty feet it's like flying or gliding. Your hands are still down, but your insides spin and rise and leave the ground. Only a twirler knows that—so we're not niggers.

The secret for a twirler is the light. You live or die with the light. It's your fate. The best is a February sky clouded right over in the late afternoon. It's all background then, and what happens is that the 'tons' leave tracks, traces, they etch the air, and if you're hot, if your hands have it, you can draw on the sky. Charlene Ann Morrison, God, Charlene Ann! She was inspired by something beyond man. She won the nationals nine years in a row. Unparalleled and unrepeatable. Last two years she had leukemia, and at the end you could see through her hands when she twirled. Charlene Ann died with a 'ton' thirty feet up, her momma swears on that. I did speed with Charlene at a regional in Fargo and she may be fibbin' but she says there was a day when her 'tons' erased while they turned. Like the sky was a sheet of rain and the 'tons' were car wipers and when she had erased this certain part of the sky you could see the face of the Lord God Jesus, and his hair was all rhinestones and he was doing this incredible singing like the sound of a piccolo. The people who said Charlene was crazy probably never twirled a day in their life.

Twirling is the physical parallel of revelation. You can't know that. Twirling is the throwing of yourself up to God. It's a pure gift, hidden from Satan because it is wrapped and disguised in the midst of football. It is God throwing, spirit fire, and very few come to it. You have to grow eyes in your heart to understand its message, and when it opens to you it becomes your path to suffer ridicule, to be crucified by misunderstanding, and to be spit upon. I need my baton now.

There is one twirling no one sees. At the winter solstice we go to a meadow God showed us just outside Green Bay. The God-throwers come there on December twenty-first. There's snow, sometimes deep snow, and our clothes fall away and we stand unprotected while acolytes bring the 'tons.' They are ebony 'tons' with razors set all along the shaft. They are three feet long. One by one the twirlers throw, two 'tons' each, thirty feet up, and as they fall back they cut your hands. The razors arch into the sky and find God and then fly down to take your blood in a crucifixion, and the red drops draw God on the ground and if you are up with the batons you can look down and see him revealed. Red on white. Red on white. You can't imagine. You can't imagine how wonderful that is.

I started twirling when I was six but I never really twirled until my hand was crushed by the horse named Big Blood Red. I have seen God's face from thirty feet up in the air and I know him.

Listen. I will leave my silver baton here for you. Lying here as if I forgot it, and when the people file out you can wait back and pick it up, it can be yours, it can be your burden. It is the eye of the needle. I leave it for you.

BLACKOUT

EXERCISES

The previous exercises for *French Fries* also apply to *Twirler*, so return to those and adapt them to this play. Here we focus on other aspects of the monodrama.

1. Consider the playwright's choice in writing about a baton twirler. Some of us might think that twirlers simply do not deserve such attention, and April herself says that twirlers aren't respected: "People think you're a twit if you twirl," she says. "Twirlers are the niggers of a white University." She illustrates her point vividly. Once when she was twirling a man spat on her face and "called me a bodily part in front of half of Ohio." Given a potential negative attitude about twirlers, how does the playwright awaken audience interest in this character? If the audience might initially lack respect for a twirler, does this monodrama change their minds? If so, how?

2. Names are significant indicators of character. The playwright could have avoided naming her characters and simply labeled them, generically, "a typical young baton twirler" or "an ordinary old lady in a rocking chair." But Martin wisely gives each character a colorful name that makes her a distinct individual. What images do the characters' names evoke in your mind? Note, by the way, that the playwright uses dialog to identify April's name, a clever writing device that contributes to making the play complete and self-contained without the need for outside information such as a program.

3. Like *French Fries*, *Twirler* certainly illustrates the power of language. The play starts with a rather mundane tone, but the playwright shifts gears radically with the poetic first sentence of the third paragraph, "Oh, I've flown high and known tragedy both," amplified by the next sentence, "My daddy says it's put spirit in my soul and steel in my heart." How do those two sentences change the play's focus? What was the play's tone before those sentences? What is the new tone?

4. Language also becomes more powerful with specific references. Instead of a general statement such as "Momma won some money," the playwright writes, "Momma hit the daily double on horses named Spin Dry and Silver Revolver." Instead of "so I took twirling lessons," April says "so she gave me lessons at the Dainty Deb Dance studio where the lady, Miss Aurelia, taught some twirling on the side." April didn't just "win titles," she won "the Ohio Juniors title" and the "Midwest Young Adult Division." She didn't simply wear a "fancy costume," but instead "Momma and I wore look-alike Statue of Liberty Costumes that she had to send clear to Nebraska to get." There weren't just cheers for her performance but "when they yelled my name golden balloons fell out of the ceiling." She didn't simply have an accident: "My left hand was crushed in a riding accident by a horse named Big Blood Red." She doesn't say "you gotta have faith" but instead says "You have to grow eyes in your heart to understand its message." Identify other specific references in *Twirler* and *French Fries*. Why does the playwright use definitive names and terms instead of more generic allusions? What do these specifics contribute to the play? Which creates "universality" in a play and which appears more effective—abstract generalizations or concrete specific references?

5. We expect plays to follow a "law of conflict" that places the characters in forceful opposition, conscious will versus conscious will, a struggle to overcome odds. Conflict may appear easier to achieve in a multicharacter play when one character is opposed by another, protagonist against antagonist, such as a Hamlet versus a Claudius, but can the writer achieve conflict in a one-person play? Is there conflict in *Twirler*? In *French Fries*? If so, identify it. How does the playwright achieve conflict?

4

Bridges Across a Chasm

Three Plays by Eric Bogosian, Anna Deavere Smith, and Lanford Wilson

The late Lorraine Hansberry in To Be Young, Gifted, and Black *creates an image of a bridge across a chasm. It is a bridge filled with all of her favorite artists, many of them are indeed the greatest American artists of the twentieth century. . . . I have for many years been living with her image of the bridge across the chasm. A dream of hers which so intoxicated me, inspired me as a young artist, that it became a memory. Even though it never was.*

Art is our connection to the universe, it is our connection to what came before, and to what will be, and to what will never be. —Anna Deavere Smith

A BOOK DEALING WITH THE MONODRAMA FACES PROBLEMS WITH selectivity—so many excellent contemporary solo performers, but, unfortunately, limited space to devote to them. Just as art is a matter of making choices, so choices must be made here, although sometimes the exclusion process is painful when—by necessity—we omit favorite artists.

In this chapter we select three notable contributors to the contemporary solo play—Eric Bogosian, Anna Deavere Smith, and Lanford Wilson—who illustrate the solo performance as a "bridge across a chasm," as Smith quotes playwright Lorraine Hansberry, connecting artist and audience with past and future. We include samples of their writing, discussions of their techniques, and their statements about their work. Their artistry provides models you may wish to consider, hence their selection here. Subsequent chapters introduce you to additional notable monodramatists.

Bogosian, Smith, and Wilson share certain commonalities. All are remarkably talented, have achieved critical and popular acclaim, and have won significant awards. They grasp their audiences' attention and hold it with superior storytelling techniques. All three have excellent theatre sense—an awareness of what theatre is and what it can become—although each has a different approach to the theatrical experience. They also differ in one aspect of their use of the solo play: Bogosian and Smith write scripts for themselves to perform; Wilson is a playwright but not a performer.

These three make observations about their society based on clear visions of their corners of the universe. Their scripts have a sharp point of view. For those reasons I venture to assume that they also have distinct personal credos, a firm knowledge of "this I believe." Whether or not they have formally written credos is less important than that presence in their works. As you read their plays you may find that for each that sense of credo—a personal commitment—gives their work additional dimensionality.

"A theatre in your head." Whether you are a playwright, director, or actor, as you read these (and other) plays you will want to work to see and hear them in the imaginary theatre in your mind. Playwrights will want to note how each playwright develops character, uses language, and structures the script with action. Actors may wish to find a private place to read them aloud. Directors may want to sketch a floor plan to plan movements of each solo character, make notes about line readings and interpretation, consider the tempo in performance, and think of how they would work with the actor to achieve characterization.

Looking at the stuff my artist friends produced, I saw the answer [to what I wanted to achieve]: make a gallery of people, each going "all the way" into his world. Individually the characters might be repulsive, unnerving, pathetic or melodramatic, but taken together a large picture could be seen. Like a collage. But not a dreamy one; rather, a "switching-stations" one. I had enjoyed watching performers like Andy Kaufman and John Wood make lightning changes during a performance, but disliked the presence of the performer "himself." So I just cut out all the in-between stuff. Like you were turning channels: first this guy, then that guy. Fragments. Chunks of personality. . . . I borrowed types from television and, from the streets, I grabbed the derelicts, homeboys and punks I had been watching since I had arrived in New York. All I had to add was the energy.

The greatest performers I had seen live were rock stars. Jimi, Mick, Janis—they played

*to the audience, they used their presence, they went all the way and that's the way I want-
ed to perform.*

*Of course theater isn't rock-and-roll. But I'd seen rock-and-roll energy in a theatrical
production enough times to know it could be done: John Wood in* Travesties *(and later
John Malkovich and Gary Sinise in* True West*). There were other models: great underground performers like Brother Theodore, Jeff Weiss, James Chance (of the Contortions)
and Tomatoe (of the Screamers). And I couldn't ignore Richard Pryor in his first live concert film. Nor De Niro in* Mean Streets*. And let's not forget Jimmy Swaggart!*

—Eric Bogosian

Multitalented Eric Bogosian is a stage and film actor plus playwright and
screen writer. Quite possibly the high energy—as he says here, for his performances he seeks the dynamics of a rock concert—that is so clearly
shown in his performances also contributes to his multiple creative talents. As a film actor he has appeared in *The Substance of Fire, Beavis and
Butthead Do America,* and *Under Seige* opposite Steven Segal. He also was
Barry Champion in Oliver Stone's film of his own *Talk Radio.* He was cocre-
ator of the television series *High Incident.*

Bogosian writes monodramas for himself to perform. Comic, dynamic,
sardonic, boiling with frenzied energy, his one-man shows are portraits of
an American society hooked on finding pleasure through any available
means. He writes short vignettes, and in a given evening's performance he
rapidly changes among widely different characters. They resonate with
life, sometimes violent, often profane. They may mock establishment
practices, be involved with drugs or alcohol, or threaten others' security.

Bogosian also seems especially fond of creating television or radio
commercials to make satirical statements about American values. Those
of us in his audience feel he takes us on a roller coaster, not in a sanitized
theme park but in an inner city reality that is colored by his intense
amazement at life's diversities and peculiarities.

In the 1980s, following experimentation with what he describes as pretentious New York avant-garde art, Bogosian shifted focus:

My love affair with the avant-garde had ended. It was time to get practical. I was out of money, so I had to make work cheap. Solos were the
answer. No rehearsal space had to be rented, no actors paid, no costly
sets, costumes, or lights.[1]

Certainly minimalism is a crucial element in his monodramas. They can be performed in virtually any locale. Once he has rehearsed and prepared them, he is ready to perform them almost immediately. More importantly, the minimalist approach stimulates the audience's imagination to see the environment and other characters.

Before turning to the solo play, Bogosian had developed a comic persona to perform in nightclubs. He found that unsatisfying: "I wanted the pieces to exist in the theater and, when I went home, I wanted to go home as me." As he started his monodramas he had several basic premises:

> I had nothing to say to anybody. Only questions. I wanted to rock and I wanted to act. I loved making believe I was somebody else. And I wanted to be an artist.[2]

Ritual. In the previous chapter we discussed the significance of ritual to theatre. In his preface to *Pounding Nails in the Floor with My Forehead*, a collection of 16 short solo plays, Bogosian discusses theatre as a holy ritual:

> Theater is ritual. It is something we make together every time it happens. Theater is holy. Instead of being bombarded by a cathode ray tube, we are speaking to ourselves. Human language, not electronic noise. Theater is laughter, which is always a valuable commodity.
>
> Above all, theater is empathy as opposed to voyeurism. All good theater is about imagining a walk in someone else's shoes. And all theater asks the same question: What would I do if that were me up there?[3]

In the 1980s Bogosian began creating one-person pieces—collections of short scripts that combine to make a total evening's performance—such as *Men Inside, Voices of America, FunHouse, Drinking in America,* and *Sex, Drugs, Rock & Roll.* They opened off-Broadway in such houses as the Public Theater or the American Place Theatre. *Drinking in America,* which premiered at the American Place Theatre in 1986, won a Drama Desk Award for Outstanding Solo Performance plus a Village Voice Off-Broadway Award—better known as an Obie—for best new play. Several have been shown on television, such as *Drinking in America* on Cinemax and *Sex, Drugs, Rock & Roll* on HBO.

Example From Men Inside

Bogosian's characters often are street people, such as the character in *Nice Shoes*, one vignette from his collection called *Men Inside*. We include the full script here. Punctuation and capitalization are Bogosian's.

NICE SHOES

(Very friendly, but with growing menace)

Hey . . . hey . . . you . . . you with the glasses. Come here. Come here for a second, I wanna ask you a question. . . . No, come here. I never seen you around the neighborhood before and I just want ta meet ya. . . . What's ya name? . . . Mike? Michael . . . Michael . . . Mike. How ya doin' there, Mike? I'm Sonny, this here's Joey and this is Richie. He's a big guy, huh?

And the shoes! Nice shoes! I like those shoes, huh? Richie, check out Mike's shoes. . . . I like those shoes, Mike. . . . Hey! You know what we call shoes like dose? "C-Shoes," "C-Shoes." . . . You wanna know why? 'Cause dey cost a C-note . . . hundred bucks, get it?

(laughing, he turns to Joey) Pretty funny . . . C-shoes, huh? . . . *(whips around, noticing Mike getting away)*

Hey-hey-hey-hey-hey. . . . Mike, don't walk away from me when I'm talkin' to you here now! That's very impolite, you know? You're being impolite to me . . . and you're embarrassing me in front of my friends. . . . You're insulting me in front of my friends . . . and when somebody insults me I get angry. . . . I get angry and I hurt people . . . heh, heh.

RICHIE, SHUT UP! SHUT YA FUCKING MOUTH!

Don't listen to him, he's full a shit. I won't let him lay a hand on you. . . . This fight is between you and me. . . .

Look, it's OK . . . it's OK . . . all youse gotta do is apologize to me and everything'll be cool, all right? Just get down on your knees and apologize and—

RICHIE! STAY OUT OF IT! . . . PUT IT BACK. . . . Put the blade back in ya pocket.

Now, Mike, look what you started, everybody's gettin' excited around here. Richie's gettin' angry, next thing Joey's gonna get angry. . . . Just get down on ya knees and apologize and then Richie won't think I'm an asshole. . . .

(*condescendingly*) That's great. . . . Just for a second . . . just stay down there for a second. . . . YA NOT A HOMO, ARE YA MIKE? Hey, Joey, this guy down on his knees ya think maybe he's a homo? Haha. . . . And do me a favor while you're down there. Just slip your shoes off for a minute, will ya? Joey! Get the shoes!. . . . You comfortable there, Mike? You're sure ya not a faggot, are you? You better not be, walking around this neighborhood. We'll castrate ya!

Here, Mike, get up. You don't want to stay down there all day. Let me brush you off. Hey, Mike, we're just fucking with ya head. You can take a joke, can't you? Sure you can! I wanna tell you something, Mike: you're good shit. Anytime you need anything in this neighborhood, you just come see me, Sonny, and I'll take care of you, OK? You need fireworks, anything like that, you come see me, OK? OK! (*shaking hands with him*) Well, it was nice talking to you, but we gotta get going, I'll see you later. . . .

Hmmmm? What? What shoes? (*turning back to Joey*) These shoes? These are my shoes, Mike. These are my C-shoes. I just bought these shoes up in Bloomingdale's. Joey? Richie?

(*looks down at Mike's feet*) Oh, you don't got no shoes! Hey, Joey, look-it dis guy's got no shoes! Richie, look! . . . Hey, how come you got no shoes? . . . All those nice clothes and no shoes! How'd dat happen? You're gonna get cold with no shoes? Ain't he gonna get cold?

(*laughing right into Mike's face*) Oh! I think we got a crybaby here! I think he's gonna start crying. (*Suddenly Sonny stops laughing, gets a very cold look in his eyes.*) Hey Richie, did you hear that? What was that word he just said?

(*lunging for Mike, grabbing him and talking slowly*) Hey Mike, we don't like swearing around here. Huh? Fuckface? Scumbag? (*fast, dangerous, pulling him up off the ground, so that we can see Sonny's eyes just over his fists*) Hey, hey. You come walking around this neighborhood, embarrassing me around my friends, swearing at me in front of my friends, hey let me tell you something, Mr. Nice Shoes, Mr. Faggot: You worried about not having no shoes? You're lucky you still got feet! (*pause; he throws Mike to the ground.*) Get the fuck out of here! (*pause*) Asshole!. . . . Come on. (*laughing as he walks away with Richie and Joey*) . . . Joey, lemme see my shoes. . . .[4]

Bogosian's Playwriting Craft

Alan Schneider (1917–1984), one of America's outstanding theatrical directors, once spoke of his admiration of short plays. "I like one-acts," he said. "My grandmother taught me that diamonds aren't as large as bricks." He could have been describing the short or short-short monodrama. Certainly *Nice Shoes* is a sparkling gem that exemplifies the best of the short-short solo play. If you seek an expertly crafted model, Bogosian's technique is especially worth noting:

☐ The script is carefully constructed with a strong specific conflict.

☐ The protagonist's objective is quite clear—to dominate, to be king of his turf—and it motivates him throughout the play.

☐ The protagonist's objective provides the play's plot, the structure of action.

☐ The character is dimensional and dynamic. He goes through quick changes.

☐ The play has a clear subject and theme. The playwright shows, without comment, a significant social problem: street violence. More frighteningly, perhaps, it appears to be senseless violence, violence for its own sake, even violence for merely recreational purposes.

☐ Bogosian uses foreshadowing to create suspense. At the very beginning we are aware that Sonny has a dark ulterior motive behind his apparent friendliness. Sonny's early admiration for Mike's clothes, especially his shoes, is clear foreshadowing of events to come.

☐ The playwright manages to avoid exposition, yet gives us enough clues so we easily imagine Sonny's history. The locale is implied so strongly it needs no mention in the play.

☐ His script plunges immediately into action by omitting unimportant introductory materials. (This effective quick beginning is known as *in medias res*, starting "in the middle of a narrative or plot." It is especially recommended not only for short-short solo plays but also for longer works.)

☐ The play's point of attack, which begins the action, is sharp. Bogosian makes it perfectly clear with repetition: "Come here," "Come here for a second," "Don't walk away from me when I'm talking to you."

☐ Bogosian involves the audience by stimulating imagination. We can *see* and *hear* the unseen other characters.

☐ The monodrama is built with a clear beginning, middle, and end.

☐ Bogosian deftly evokes three other characters. We know all necessary information about the unseen participants.

☐ Throughout the script you are aware the author has a sharp sense of theatre, perhaps best exemplified by the way he implies the major properties, the shoes and the knife.

☐ Language is crisp, vital, and directly part of the character. There are no excess words.

☐ The play rings with truth.

☐ Finally, the playwright twice inserts the name of the solo character into the dialogue to help the audience identify Sonny.

All that in a matter of a few minutes, with no props or scenery, with no other characters visible on stage? Surely *Nice Shoes* illustrates the power of the solo play.

Bogosian's Performance Techniques

The best thing about being an actor is that you can be somebody you never were and never would be. Like a soldier. Or a cowboy. Even more interesting is how you figure out how to act like a cowboy. I've never met one in my life. I must have learned how to act like a cowboy from John Wayne, an actor. . . . My problem was that I would go to a movie, come out of the theater and try to make my life work the way the movie worked, with me in the lead role. And then I'd run into a wino acting like Red Skelton, and I'd think this guy was having fun. . . . So I made Men Inside *in an attempt to sort out all these people inside me.* —Eric Bogosian

Bogosian's solo performances, like those of many other monodramatists, are minimalist productions. There is no special scenic environment, and the only items on stage are a microphone and a few pieces of furniture such as a chair and table. His costume also is simple: white shirt, black pants, and black shoes. His performance is highly energetic, full of large physical actions and vocal variations. He has a wide vocal range and enjoys using accents to depict characters.

ANNA DEAVERE SMITH: INTERVIEWER AND CHRONICLER OF INDIVIDUALS ENCOUNTERING SOCIAL PROBLEMS

My goal has been to find American character in the ways that people speak. . . . Words have always held a particular power for me. I remember leafing through a book of Native American poems one morning while I was waiting for my Shakespeare class to begin and being struck by a phrase from the preface, "The word, the word above all, is truly magical, not only by its meaning, but by its artful manipulation." This quote, which I added to my journal, reminded me of something my grandfather had told me when I was a girl: "If you say a word often enough it becomes your own." [Later my father] told me that my grandfather had actually said, "If you say a word often enough, it becomes you." I was still a student at the time, but I knew even then, even before I had made a conscious decision to teach as well as act, that my grandfather's words would be important.

—Anna Deavere Smith

Anna Deavere Smith, a playwright, actress, and Stanford University drama professor, has developed an exciting new monodramatic form that encompasses social commentary about contemporary issues that burn in our nation's consciousness, fidelity to actual people involved in major events, and a style of acting that runs counter to the more standard Stanislavsky approach. Smith writes full-length monodramas for herself to perform, playing several dozen actual people in short vignettes. Her full-length, one-person shows such as *Fires in the Mirror* and *Twilight: Los Angeles*, 1992 have been praised for their artistic achievements and insight into racial and class conflicts.

Theatrical Journalism: Research for Authenticity

Smith's solo plays defy easy labeling but perhaps we can introduce her work by calling it *theatrical journalism* because she is rather like an investigative television news reporter who seeks to show how major abstract social issues concretely affect specific individuals. In this sense Smith is a chronicler of her times, similar to earlier solo performers such as the Greek *rhapsodist*, Roman *histrione*, or medieval *scôp*, who shaped stories of significant contemporary events and people to enlighten audiences.

Smith's drive for authenticity separates her from other monodramatists. She combines detailed research and creativity. She interviews witnesses and participants who were involved in critical events; then she edits the interviews and selects materials for her solo performances. She performs each different character in her full-length monodramas.

Twilight: Los Angeles, 1992

Smith's *Twilight: Los Angeles, 1992* opened at the Mark Taper Forum in Los Angeles. Her full-length monodrama is based on the Los Angeles riot of 1992, which followed the acquittal of police accused of beating Rodney King, an event captured on amateur videotape and frequently shown on network television to shocked Americans. In the riot 58 people were killed, 2,382 were injured, more than 12,000 were arrested, and some 20,000 lost their jobs primarily because their places of employment were reduced to ashes because more than 10,000 buildings were burned to the ground.

Smith spent nine months interviewing people affected by the riot. She then transcribed the interview tapes and edited them into her own form of theatrical verse. In performance she becomes almost two dozen people who were affected by the riot, bringing to life such real-life characters as an aunt of Rodney King, Los Angles police chief Daryl Gates, and a juror at the trial.

Fires in the Mirror

Fires in the Mirror *is a part of a series of theater (or performance) pieces called* On the Road: A Search for American Character, *which I create by interviewing people and later performing them using their own words. My goal has been to find American character in the ways that people speak. When I started this project, in the early 1980s, my simple introduction to anyone I interviewed was, "If you give me an hour of your time, I'll invite you to see yourself performed." At that time I was not as interested in performing or in social commentary as I was in experimenting with language and its relationship to character.* —Anna Deavere Smith

Fires in the Mirror deals with riots in Crown Heights, Brooklyn, in August 1991. More significantly, Smith's monodrama reflects America's troubled path of discrimination, polarization, misunderstanding, religious and racial tensions, and police and governmental policies. Although one specific event sparked the Crown Heights riots, the area was a tinderbox of tensions that had grown over a period of years. Smith's *Fires in the Mirror* focuses on the people involved, directly or indirectly, with the event and the underlying bitterness.

The facts of the event that started the riots can be stated simply. On the evening of August 19, 1991, one car of a three-car motorcade carrying Rebbe Menachem Schneerson, a member of the orthodox Hasidic sect known as the Lubavitchers, struck two Guyanese American children playing on the sidewalk. One, a seven-year-old boy, was killed; his young cousin was injured. Testimony indicated that the car ran a red light. A private Jewish ambulance arrived on the scene and removed not the injured children but the Lubavitchers. In apparent retaliation, three hours later Yankel Rosenbaum, a Hasidic history professor, was stabbed to death a few blocks from the accident. The next day riots began between Lubavitchers and Blacks.

In *Fires in the Mirror* Smith performs twenty-six different men and women. Among them are Angela Davis (activist and author), Rabbi Joseph Spielman (Lubavitch spokesperson), Reverend Al Sharpton (activist and minister), Monique "Big Mo" Matthews (Los Angles rapper), Carmel Cato (father of Gavin, the young boy killed in the accident), and Norman Rosenbaum (brother of the history professor who was stabbed to death a few hours after the accident).

Fires in the Mirror premiered at the New York Shakespeare Festival in 1992, where it ran four months. Smith was both author and solo performer; the production was directed by Christopher Ashley. *Fires* also has been presented by such notable theatres as the American Repertory Theatre (Cambridge, Mass.), McCarter Theatre (Princeton, N.J.), Brown University (Providence, R.I.), Brooklyn Academy of Music (N.Y.), and the Royal Court Theatre (London). A version of the play was filmed by *American Playhouse*.

Example from Fires in the Mirror
Smith's *Fires in the Mirror* consists of a number of vignettes tied together by two themes: the specific incidents in Crown Heights and more general tensions between peoples. Each vignette is titled and is prefaced by a short description of the person Smith interviewed. An example of one—Robert Sherman, Director, Mayor of the City of New York's Increase the Peace Corps—is quoted here in its entirety.

ROBERT SHERMAN
Lousy Language

(11:00 A.M. *Wednesday, November 13, 1991. A very sunny and large, elegant living room in a large apartment near the Brooklyn Museum. Mr. Sherman is sitting in an armchair near an enormous bouquet of flowers for the birth of his first child. He wears sweats and a bright orange long-sleeved tee shirt. Smiles frequently, upbeat, impassioned. Fingers his wedding ring. Each phrase builds on the next, pauses are all sustained intensity, never lets up. Full. Lots of volume, clear enunciation, teeth, and tongue very involved in his speech. Good-humored, seems to like the act of speech.)*

Do you have demographic information on Crown Heights?
The important thing to remember is that—
and I will check these numbers when I get back to the office—
I think the
Hasidim
comprise only ten percent
of the population
of the neighborhood.
The Crown Heights conflict has been brewing on and off for twenty
    years
since the Hasidic community
developed some serious numbers
and some strength in Crown Heights and as African Americans and
Caribbean Americans came to make up the dominant culture in
Crown Heights.
Very important to remember that
those things that are expressed really as
bias, those things that we at the Human Rights Commission
would consider to be bias,
have the same trappings of bias,
which is complaints based on a characteristic, not on a knowledge
    of a
specific person.
There sort of is a soup
of bias—
prejudice, racism, and discrimination.
I think bias really does relate to
feelings with a valence,
feelings with a, uhm,
(*Breathing in*)
feelings that can go in a direction positive or negative

although we usually use bias to mean a negative.
What it means usually
is negative attitudes
that can lead to negative behaviors:
biased
acts, biased incidents,
or biased crimes.
Racism is hatred based on race.
Discrimination refers to
acts against somebody . . .
so that the words actually tangle up.
I think in part
because vocabulary follows general awareness. . . .
I think you know
the Eskimos have seventy words for snow?
We probably have seventy different kinds of bias, prejudice, racism,
    and
discrimination,
but it's not in our mind-set to be clear about it,
so I think that we have
sort of lousy language
on the subject
and that
is a reflection
of our unwillingness
to deal with it honestly
and to sort it out.
I think we have very, very bad language.[5]

Smith's Playwriting Craft

Smith's goal is to capture each individual's particular way of speaking. She starts with interviewing the subject, then she artistically shapes the results to express personal characteristics. She focuses on oral communication devices such as word choice, pauses, verbal advances and retreats, and emphasis through restatement and repetition. No doubt her interview with Robert Sherman was much longer than that shown above, but she expresses the essence of what he was saying: Our "lousy language" reflects our unwillingness to address concerns about racial prejudice directly. Especially pertinent are metaphorical images such as seventy words for snow or racial bias as a sort of soup.

Form and Content. The content of *Lousy Language*—of the entire *Fires in the Mirror*—dictates the script's form. Smith does not create a traditional structure of protagonist's goal, clear point of attack, complications or obstacles, climax. There's no special emphasis on beginning, middle, and end. Why? Because the historical situation she dramatizes lacks such structural clarity. Content and form are closely married.

Performance Techniques

To Smith, words are the origin of characterization, of acting. She describes an acting assignment she once received: a short Shakespearean passage that, when she read it the first few times, made no sense to her. Dutifully rereading it over and over, she found that she became transformed, almost magically, into the character. As the passage entered her being, she understood its meaning and the character. For her (as we quote before), "The word, the word above all, is truly magical, not only by its meaning, but by its artful manipulation." When young she had learned from her grandfather that "If you say a word often enough, it becomes you." In acting classes, she found that through the word the actor becomes the character. In this sense her approach is an interesting refinement of the Stanislavsky method that is popular today.

Smith's performance gives each character an individualistic rhythm and style. One may be hesitant, another brassy, and a third nervous. She shifts comfortably between male and female, young and old, using minimal costume effects. Her technique of moving quickly and easily from one character to another gives the overall performance a dynamic life. By the end of the evening the audience feels it has met two dozen different humans. The applause shows admiration for her insight and talent.

Influences on Smith's Monodramas

Smith's solo plays are highly original, but—perhaps expectably with artistic works by a theatrical scholar—they resonate with other theatrical forms. Such similarities do not diminish Smith's creativity but instead enrich the impact of her work. Two forms—the Living Newspaper and documentary dramas—appear especially relevant to Smith's theatrical work.

The Living Newspaper. The social thrust of Smith's monodramas echo the Living Newspaper multicharacter productions under the wing of the Federal Theatre Project (1935–1939), part of the government's Works Progress Administration, which sought to employ millions of Americans during the Great Depression of the 1930s. Conceived by Elmer Rice and mostly written by Arthur Arents, Living Newspaper plays dramatized the headlines of the day, just as Smith focuses on major contemporary events that are important to our society.

Smith's plays also echo the Living Newspaper plays' call for immediate political action for social reform. For example, *Triple-A Plowed Under* (1936) deals with the contemporary plight of the nation's farmers, *Power* (1937) looks at electrical utility companies, and *One-Third of a Nation* (1938) is taken from President Franklin D. Roosevelt's second inaugural speech, which said one-third of the depression-struck United States was "ill-housed, ill-clad, and ill-nourished." Smith achieves her effect by showing the events but avoiding direct didactic statements, encouraging her audiences to see the need for reform.

However, where Smith's monodramas use minimalist production techniques, Living Newspaper productions were elaborate multicharacter events, similar to those popularized by earlier directors Vsyevolod Meyerhold and Erwin Piscator, whose vision of theatre included elaborate visual spectacles and multimedia presentations. The Living Newspaper used dramatic scenes to show the plight of individuals, projections of films and images, and large casts to represent the citizens who were victimized by social injustice. Smith shows not groups but individuals affected by prejudices.

Documentary Dramas. Smith's focus on factual events also may remind us of a relatively new theatrical form called documentary dramas, or docudramas, which are multicharacter plays that examine recent historical events, often using actual testimony drawn from court records. Proponents say docudramas are superior to journalistic reporting because they eliminate self-serving official sources of information.

Typical docudramas, like Smith's monodramas, have political and social ramifications. For example, Rolf Hochhuth's *The Deputy* (1963) accuses Pope Pius XII of refusing to take action to prevent the Holocaust, Eric Bentley's *Are You Now or Have You Ever Been* (1972) focuses on Senator Joseph R. McCarthy's witch hunts in the House Un-American Activities Committee,

Peter Weiss's *The Investigation* (1965) uses transcripts from the war crime trials involving the Nazi extermination camp at Auschwitz, and Daniel Berrigan's *The Trial of the Catonsville Nine* (1971) shows the trial of nine protesters (including nuns and priests) of American policy in the Vietnam war.

LANFORD WILSON: CHARACTERS RICH WITH MAGIC

It is difficult to imagine a theatrical honor Lanford Wilson has not received. Among the list of his plays that have won awards are *The Rimers of Eldrich*, which received the Drama Desk-Vernon Rice Award; *The Hot L Baltimore*, which won the Obie Award, New York Drama Critics' Circle Award, and Outer Critics' Circle Award; and *Talley's Folly*, winner of the Pulitzer Prize for Drama, the New York Drama Critics' Circle Award, and Theatre Club Inc. Award for best play. His *5th of July*, *Angel's Fall*, and *Talley's Folly* were nominated for Tony Awards. The American Academy of Arts and Letters honored Wilson for his contributions as a playwright, and he has received a number of significant fellowships, such as the Guggenheim, Yale, and Rockefeller.

It is equally difficult to imagine theatrical form and content he has not written. Wilson is the author of a number of monodramas, one-act plays, full-length plays, the libretto for an operatic version of Tennessee Williams's poetic drama *Summer and Smoke*, and a translation of Anton Chekhov's drama, *The Three Sisters*.

Wilson says he started writing plays almost by accident. Then he learned the importance of conflict to create dramatic events.

> When I moved to Chicago from San Diego, I was working for an advertising agency, but thinking of being an artist, an editorial illustrator. I was writing stories, and began one that didn't really sound like a story; it sounded like a play. I was not two pages into it when I said, "I'm a playwright." If anyone had asked me that night what I did, I would have said, "I write plays." It didn't matter that I didn't know a damned thing about plays.
>
> The University of Chicago had an adult education playwriting class. I took twelve sessions. The professor would say, "A play must have conflict. Here in an example of conflict. Now that everyone understands what conflict is, go home and write a scene with conflict and bring it in typed next week." The next week, four actors from the Goodman Theatre would come and read the scripts, sight unseen. There we were, sitting and hearing real, professional actors reading our work. It was absolutely thrilling, just thrilling.[6]

Wilson is especially noted for his ability to write vivid, interesting, unique characters. His one-act and full-length plays resonate with dimensional humans. Often the Wilson characters may appear to be social outsiders, perhaps even "losers," but they are able to endure and continue. If they do not struggle heroically, neither do they whimper and quit. His Hot L Baltimore, for example, takes place in a run-down hotel—in such poor condition that the e has disappeared from hotel—and its residents appear to be social misfits. Faced with losing their home because the hotel faces demolition, they are able to find ways to continue to survive.

A primary strength of Wilson's plays is rich and interesting characterization, although he feels that characterization was pale in his early plays. He says he learned to write colorful characters from reading novelist Charles Dickens:

> Just before I started working on Hot L Baltimore, I read Dickens' Our Mutual Friend. I had just done Lemon Sky and Serenading Louie, and they seemed pale and quaint compared to Dickens. I knew I had to goose my work. I knew I had to have characters that were more far-out. Your characters have to have some magic.[7]

A Poster of the Cosmos

A Poster of the Cosmos was first presented in New York City in June 1988 by the Ensemble Studio Theatre, Curt Dempster, Artistic Director. Jonathan Hogan directed. Tom Noonan performed the solo character. We include the full script in its entirety.

A Poster of the Cosmos illustrates the monodrama's power to dramatize a social problem through the life of a specific individual. Read this solo play aloud to yourself, becoming the character, seeing his environment, and feeling the depth of his emotions.

A POSTER OF THE COSMOS
by Lanford Wilson
For Tom Noonan

Character: Tom—a large, brooding, and most of this time quite angry man of thirty-six.
Scene: A police station in Manhattan, 1987.

Tom, most of the time, sits at an institutional table in an institutional chair.

There is a tape recorder on the table. He is in a white pool of light in a black void. He wears a white T-shirt, white work pants, and sneakers.

He is addressing a cop who would be at the other end of the table, and another off left or right who would be slouching against a door. When he gets up, something in the cops' posture tells him he'd better sit back down.

When he smokes the smoke rises up in the white downspot like a nebula.

TOM (*He is standing and quite pissed off*): All right, I'm sitting down and I'm staying down. Okay?

He sits.

Now, are you happy?

He glares at the cops in disgust.

Jesus, you guys slay me with that crap. "You don't look like the kinna guy'd do somethin' like dat." You're a joke. Cops. Jesus. I mean you're some total cliché. I don't have to be here lookin' at you guys, I could turn on the TV. "What's that white stuff on your shirt?" Jesus. I'm a baker, it's flour. You want a sample, take to your lab? (*Shaking his head in wonder*) "You don't look like the kinna guy'd do somethin' like dat." What does dat kinna guy who'd do somethin' like dat look like to a cop, huh? And what kinna *thing*? You don't know nothin': you know what you think you know. You seen every kinna dirty business there is every night, lookin' under the covers, spend your workin' day in the fuckin' armpits of the city and still ain't learned shit about people. You're totally fuckin' blind and deaf like fish I heard about, spend their life back in some fuckin' cave.

He looks around, taps the tape recorder, looks at it.

Is this on? You got your video cameras goin'? 'Cause I told you I'd tell you but this is the only time I'm tellin' this. So, you know, get out your proper equipment, I'm not doin' this twice.

He looks around, still disgusted.

"You don't look like the kinna guy'd do somethin' like dat." Johnny said I didn't look like no kinna guy at all. Just a big ugly guy. Said I was like Kurt Vonnegut or somebody. Somebody had the good sense not to look like nobody else. He said that. I read every word Vonnegut wrote. He's good. He's got a perverted point of view, I like that. There was a time I wouldn't of understood that, but we change, which is what I'm sayin' here.

Beat.

"You don't look like the kinna guy'd do dat." What kinna guy is *that*? *What* kinna guy? Oh, well, you're talkin' *dat* kinna guy. The kinna guy'd *do* that. *Dat* kinna guy. . . . Well, I *ain't* dat kinna guy. I'm a kinna guy like *you* kinna guys. That's why you make me want to puke sittin' here lookin' at you. "Hey, guys, dis guy is our kinna guy. I can't believe he's dat kinna guy." Well, I *ain't* that kinna guy.

He is almost saddened by the cops.

You guys move in the dark, inna doorways, if you didn't look right through people 'steada at 'em, you'd maybe know there ain't no *"kinna* guys." You'd maybe know you can't sort guys out like vegetables. This is a potato, it goes wid the potatoes; this is a carrot, this here's celery—we got us an eggplant, goes wid the eggplant. That's vegetables, that ain't people. There ain't no kinna guys, 'cause *guys*, if you used your *eyes*, you'd know, are V-8 juice, man. You don't know *what* kinna thing's in there.

Tom pauses, takes cigarettes from his pants pocket, puts them on the table with a Zippo lighter, takes one from the pack and lights it. He has a new thought that annoys him lightly.

For all you know Johnny was a junkie. Didn't see you lookin' for the tracks, and you'da found 'em by the way, so what kinna guys are we talkin' about here? It depresses people to sit here and talk to this kinna massive stupidity.

Beat.

Johnny'd love it. He'd laugh his ass, man. No shit, he'd wet himself over you guys. And I don't wanna make him sound simple. He was like this anything-but-easy sort of person. He used to, you know, when he was a kid, had this prescription for hypertension medication, but he said he didn't take it 'cause it messed up his bowels so bad. *Thinking* was Johnny's problem. Like 'cause his mind was goin' like on all these tracks, like it had all these connections and he was always repluggin' everything and crossin' over these wires, till you could almost like *see* this complicated mess of lines in his head. Like he'd wait till he was like fuckin' droppin', like his eyes had been closed for an hour before he'd even get in bed at night. And then he'd lay there and in a minute he'd be up again. And like you know, you'd think, aw, shit, 'cause he's smokin' all these cigarettes and this shit and half the time he don't know if he's sittin' up or layin' down. The whole apartment could go up and he'd never know it. He'd just have to go on repluggin' those wires till finally, sorta totally uncon-nected, somthin' would short-out in his head. You could almost hear like his whole system shut down, and he'd be out cold some-where. Maybe ona floor, ina chair.

Maybe a beat, but he continues the same.

Then, you know, he was a twitcher. Like a dog. Even in his sleep, which was something I never saw on a human being while they was sleepin'. Like a dog is chasing maybe a rabbit, or gettin' run after by a wolf, but you'd watch Johnny and say, Johnny what the hell are you dreamin' you're chasin'? Then he'd wake up and keep right on twitchin'. You know, the foot is goin' or the fingers are goin'. He'd be biting at his lip or digging at his cheek like a fuckin' junkie, which I don't think he ever was, 'cause he worked for a hospital, procuring, and coulda brought anythin' home but never did, except stories about the fuckin' nurses and orderlies tryin' to steal him blind, fal-sifying records on him, but he never said he was, and he'd lie, but his lies was always telling things on himself like he was worse than he was. Like he said he'd left his wife and kid back in Arkansas when he was seventeen, and really missed the little daughter, but like he fuckin' never had no kids. The wife, yeah, but—and a lot of shit like he'd been in jail, which he hadn't and all. But he, you know, used to shoot up but he never worked up a habit, 'cause probably he never, at that time, had the bread for it and you can't imagine a worse thief than Johnny, so he'd never make it as a junkie. But he never said he was even an out-and-out user, so you can be pretty sure he wasn't.

Which also he wasn't the type 'cause junkies are zombies even before they get hooked. They're basically lazy people don't want the responsibility of livin'. Anything, you're not gonna catch no twitcher on the shit, 'cause it'd be like, you know, a waste of good shit. And Johnny was this, you know, he'd get his fingers goin' in his hair, I'd look over and say, "Aww, Jesus, Johnny," 'cause there'd be this like patch of red hair in the middle of his like dirty blond and he'd say, "What, have I got myself bleedin' again?" And you couldn't figger what a basically nice-lookin' guy was always fuckin' himself over like that, but that was just all those wires he was repluggin' all the time. Like the only reason he had a good body was he had these weights, but he'd use 'em like to work off energy not to build himself up. That's what I say, his mom said he was born with it. But he like burned calories like nothin' I ever saw. Ate more than me and he's what? Five-eight, which he thought was short but it isn't like freakish or nothin' to worry about and weighed maybe a buck forty but he used to say like basically his body was a very inefficient machine. He was like a real gas burner.

Beat. He thinks a minute.

He was gonna open a delivery service. This from a guy who had a money job—and he'd be the only deliverer. On his bike. He used to sit and map out routes one place to another. He called himself the Manhattan Transit. Used to make practice runs; you know, during rush hour. But this was just a way to blow off that nervous stuff he had but it didn't work out 'cause he had no business sense. He went so far he made up this ad and put it in the *Village Voice* two weeks running with our phone number on it. This was during a two-week vacation he had. We was goin' to go down to St. Pete, then he got this idea. Only the damnedest thing, the phone never rung once. No, that's not true. Once about six months later I picked up the phone, said, hello, this guy says, "Is this the Manhattan Transit?" I said it used to be but they sold their bicycle.

Beat.

He would of been good at it. I said he should work at some place where they use messengers but he wasn't interested in workin' for somebody else. He was already doin' that, he had a regular job you'd think kept him so crazy he wouldn't have time to dream up some schemes, but you got to remember all those wires in his head—and he wasn't meant to work in a office. Twitchers are hell in an office. He was at St. Vincent's first, then up to Doctors Hospital and back to St. Vincent's, runnin' procurements for like the whole hospital. Ordering truckloads of rubbing alcohol and all the prescription stuff, the bedpans and walkers, so you know it wasn't no snap, but one wire in his head was always out in the rain on his bike using this like photographic map of the city: the one-way streets, and places blocked off for school kids at recess time. You probably seen him. He's the guy goin' about five times faster than the traffic. And fightin' everythin'. Nothin' was easy. Went at everythin' crazy. He'd get off work, his face all red, you'd know he'd been diggin' at himself again. That he'd be up all night workin' on the bike. So I don't want to make him sound easy. He was anything butta easy sort of person. I was the easy one.

Pause. He stretches, or even gets up, then sits back down. He looks off, thinking.

I was the easy one. He was always wantin' to change things, I didn't care how things was. Then he was always changin' jobs, or tryin' to. He'd blow up at somebody and walk out, they'd always ask him to come back and I been workin' at the same bakery twenty years. Since I was sixteen. And I like it 'cause they're old fashioned and do it the same way they always did. You'd think bakin' bread is nothin' with the machines they use. Doin' all the measuring and mixin' and kneadin', what's to do but carry the trays to the ovens and back, but yeast is a livin' thing; it can't be taken for granted. One batch ain't like the next, and the humidity and temperature in the room makes a difference. Johnny liked it. I couldn't smell it on me but he liked the smell. He said people take on the character of their work and I figured I was gradually becoming this nice crusty loaf of Italian bread. But the way I think of it it's good, 'cause, like I said, it's nourishing and it's a live thing. Bread. But I wasn't foolin' myself that it was a job that calls for a lot of thinkin'. Like Johnny's. Instinct, maybe. Also the money ain't bad and you always got fresh bread. Only thing I didn't like was I worked nights and he worked days.

Pause. He looks at the cops.

Hell, that got a reaction, didn't it? Now you're thinkin', "He ain't our kinna guy after all. Good, we ain't gotta worry about it." But I was, I used to be, I know all that. But circumstances are crazy things; the things that can happen all of a sudden change everything. Like I'd never thought much of myself as part of anything. I was, you know, I thought I was above everything. I just watched it. But really, I didn't know how to get involved in it.

Beat.

So, I get off work at seven, I'm eatin' at this place I always did, Johnny's havin' breakfast. He's depressed because the Cosmos folded. Soccer team. I think they'd folded about five years back but he'd got to thinkin' about it again. And we're talkin' about atmospheric pressure, which is something it happens I've read a lot about, and we're both readers that only read factual stuff. Only I read slow and forget it and he reads like tearin' through things and remembers. And we'd both been married when we was kids, and had a kid of our own, only, you know, it turned out he didn't. And he said he was gay now and he'd been like fuckin' everythin' in sight for five years only he'd got frustrated with it and hadn't been laid in a month, and we're bitchin' our jobs and he got up and goes off for a minute and comes back and says why don't we go around the corner to his apartment 'cause we're takin' up two seats at the counter and this is a business based on volume and I said, no, you got to go to work and he said . . . "I just called in sick."

He smiles, then thinks about it. A frown, a troubled pause.

That's funny. He really did, first time I met him, called in sick. I never thought about that till right now.

Beat.

Jesus, all that talkin' about food makes me realize I ain't eaten in two days.

A beat. He looks at the cops expectantly. Apparently there is no reaction.

Fuck it, skip it. So anyway, if you'da said I'd be livin' wid a guy I'da said, you know, go fuck yourself. And it stayed like that. It was somethin' that always surprised me, you know? Well, of course you don't. Assholes. But I'd wake up, go in the livin' room, he'd be in a chair or somethin', you know, twitchin' like he was deliverin' somethin' somewhere. Or actually sometimes he'd be in bed there. And it always like surprised me. I'd think, what the hell do you know about this? If he'd been a big old hairy guy or something probably nothing would have happened, but Johnny didn't have hair on his body, he had like this peach fuzz all over him that make him feel like . . . skip it. I'm your kinna guy, right? I don't think. I don't analyze. So you know . . . we had like . . . three years. We did go down to St. Pete. He'd heard about it, he'd always wanted to go. We didn't like it. We went on down to Key West, he'd heard about that, too. That was worse. We come back, rented a car, went up to Vermont. And that was good. Except for Johnny drivin', I couldn't let him drive 'cause he'd go crazy. We'd get behind a tractor or somethin', he'd go ape. Also I'd get dizzy on the roads all up and down and curvin' and Johnny being this like aerobic driver.

Pause.

So after three years, when he started gettin' sick—they was very good about it at the hospital. They let him come to work for a while. Then, you know, like I said, he'd dig at himself and bleed, so that wasn't possible. That'd be real bad. So then I started being the one that was crazy all the time and I'd get off and come home in the morning, he'd be starin' out the window or somethin'. He'd say, "I slept fourteen hours." It was like this blessing for him; like this miracle, he couldn't believe it. I guess everything that was goin' on in him, I guess was interesting to him. He was like studying it. I'd say, "What?" And he'd hold up his hand for me to be quiet for a long time and then he'd say, "I'd never have believed pain could be that bad. This is amazing." You know, he had like his intestines all eaten out and that and he had insurance and the hospital was good to him. They all visited him, but he'd didn't take the painkillers. He was curious about it.

He looks around, then goes on rather flatly.

Then he got worse and started takin' 'em.

Beat.

You could see by his expression that he hadn't thought he was gonna do that. The staff, the nurses and you know the volunteers, the ghouls that get off on that, they were okay. They didn't get in our way much. (*Searching, becoming frustrated*) What I couldn't believe was that I didn't have it. I got the fuckin' test, it was negative. I couldn't believe that. Twice. I couldn't figger that, 'cause like the first time I was with him, I just fucked him and he like laid up against me and jerked off. And that was sorta what we did for a while. That was our pattern; you know, you fall into routines. But after a while, you get familiar with someone, I was all over him. No way I wasn't exposed to that like three times a week for three years. What the hell was goin' on? I got to thinkin' maybe he didn't have it, maybe it was somethin' else, but . . .

He settles down, pauses, thinks of something else.

He had these friends at the hospital, offered him somethin', I don't know what, take him out of his misery, he didn't take it, he wanted to see it through to the end like. (A *little frustration creeps back*) See, my problem was I didn't really know what he was goin' through. You help and you watch and it tears you up, sure, but you don't know *what*, you know, whatta you know.

Beat.

He wanted to come home, but . . . uh. . . .

Pause. He regards the cops.

This is the only part you fucks care about, so listen up. We wanted him to be home for the end, but it slipped up on us. We thought he'd come home another time but he went into this like semicoma and just went right outta sight, he just sank. I didn't know if he recognized me or not. I got this old poster of the Cosmos and put it up on the wall across from the bed. They had him propped up in bed, but he just looked scared. He saw it and he said, "What's that?" You know, you know you know everythin' in the room and it's all familiar, and he hadn't seen that before. Probably it was just this big dark thing in front of him that he couldn't tell what it was and it scared him. He didn't understand it. (*Looking around*) This gets bloody, so if you're faint of heart or anything . . . (*Looking up*) all you fuckers out in TV land, recordin' this shit for fuckin' prosperity; check your focus, this is hot shit, they're gonna wanna know this.

Pause.

So the nurse comes by, I said he's restin'. She was glad to skip him. And I took off my clothes and held him. He was sayin', it sounded like, "This is curious." And there was just like nothin' to him.

Pause.

See the problem is, like I said, I was the one who was crazy now. And, uh, well, to hell with it. I'm your kinna guy, fellas, I won't think about it. We do what we do, we do what's gotta be done. (*And rather coldly, or that is what he tries for*) So he died in my arms and I held him a long time and then I cut a place on his cheek where he used to dig and on his chest where he used to gouge out those red marks and in his hair. And when the blood came I licked it off him. Cleaned him up. So then the nurse come, you know, and shit a brick and called you guys. But they let me hold him till you come. I guess they was afraid of me. Or maybe of all the blood. Then they knew I had to be crazy, 'cause like we agreed, I'm not the kinna guy'd do somethin' like that. What they thought, I think, was that I'd killed him, but that wasn't what he wanted and what I had to consider now was myself. And what I wanted.

Pause.

So if it don't take again, then I'm like fucked, which wouldn't be the first time. I guess there's gonna be maybe some compensation in knowin' I did what I could.

A long wandering pause, then he looks at the cops.

So. Are you happy now?

A *pause. Eight counts. Blackout.*

THE END[8]

Wilson's Playwriting Craft

Wilson constructs his play like a tapestry, with subtle motifs carefully woven throughout. We may be only vaguely aware of them initially, but as the play progresses the pattern becomes more clear. One motif that becomes quite clear through repetition is Tom's statement, "I'm your kinna guy," although at first we may wonder just what he means precisely by this "everyman" statement. "I'm not a criminal"? "I'm an ordinary working guy"? "I'm straight"? The repetition is a form of foreshadowing that creates suspense.

A second motif is built with references to blood, intertwined with Johnny's twitchings and diggings at his body. "He'd get his fingers goin' in his hair, I'd look over and say, 'Aww, Jesus, Johnny,' 'cause there'd be this like patch of red hair in the middle of his like dirty blond and he'd say, 'What, have I got myself bleedin' again?'" We are left wondering if this is a form of self-destruction, and we then ask ourselves if that intertwines with Johnny's disease. The motif develops into a climax at the end of the play when Tom describes licking the blood off Johnny's body.

Wilson's subtlety also deserves attention. He never specifies Johnny's medical problem precisely, never mentions AIDS. But we in the audience know through implication. We anticipate the problem and are not surprised when Tom says, "So after three years, when he started gettin' sick—they was very good about it at the hospital." We know what was making Johnny start "gettin' sick." Furthermore, the play's title has a subtle double meaning: It resonates with an implication larger than the specific name of a soccer team.

A *Poster of the Cosmos* evokes other characters. We do not need to actually see the cops because they are clear in our imagination. More significantly, we also learn a great deal about Johnny. The result is a solo play that is similar to the complexity of a multicharacter play.

Wilson's craft also is shown in the way he handles the "conversation" between cops and Tom. A lesser playwright might have had Tom say something specific that echoes a cop's statement, such as "Oh, you want me to just stay seated, huh?" or "So you want me to talk into your tape recorder, right?" Wilson deftly avoids the trap of having Tom repeat something a cop says. (This sort of problem also often occurs when a character is involved with a telephone conversation. A playwright's goal is to avoid obviously repeating the statements and instead to imply what the other person says.)

As we noted at the beginning of this chapter, these three monodramatists, along with Jane Martin, whose monodramas you read in an earlier chapter, can provide writing and performance models you may wish to consider. You no doubt noticed differences in approach and concept between the scripts. Among those differences is the playing time. Bogosian's *Nice Shoes* is so brief we'd call it a short-short monodrama. Wilson's *Poster* is longer, with playing time closer to that of a typical one-act play. Smith's *Fires in the Mirror* is a full-length play, constructed with short episodes such as *Lousy Language*.

EXERCISES

These exercises encourage you to consider solo plays similar to those we've discussed in this chapter. Here you are to create outlines for a number of short plays. For these exercises to be effective, write the outlines (in contrast to merely thinking about them). An outline should describe the character, what he or she wants, why that goal is important, the character's manner of speech and physical movement, and the environment in which the action takes place. Your outline then should list in order what happens. Each outline may be between two and six pages long, depending on how much detail you create. Expect to write several drafts of each outline to shape it into a form that satisfies your needs. Keep the outlines in your notebook.

1. Write an outline for a short monodrama that will be charged with electricity, rapid moving, raging with the fire of truth. Capture the energy of rock and roll.

2. Think about particular social issues that are important to you. Construct an outline for a short monodrama about a character actually living through such an issue.

3. Imagine you are performing Bogosian's *Nice Shoes* and Smith's *Lousy Language*. Read them aloud repeatedly so the words become you,

seeking the character's attitude and emotions as shown through vocal and physical qualities. Notice how each monodrama's unique language dictates a pace and rhythm and also pulls you into the character.

4. Imagine you are directing *Nice Shoes* and *Lousy Language*. Show what is on stage by sketching a floor plan. Envision the characters' movements and note them on the script. Decide the basic tempo and rhythmic variations. Imagine your conversations with the actors, outlining what you'll suggest to them to help them establish characterization.

5. In the introduction to A *Poster of the Cosmos*, Lanford Wilson says that a playwriting class assigned him to "go home and write a scene with conflict." Conflict is one of the most important parts of drama— most theatre practitioners argue it is the single most important aspect—and playwrights are urged to follow the assignment given Wilson. His emphasis on the point is worth remembering. The following questions refer to conflict in the three monodramas.

   a. What is the conflict in A *Poster of the Cosmos*? What abstract forces are in opposition? What concrete, specific forces? What is the outcome of the conflict?

   b. What is the conflict in *Twirler*? What in the **play** leads you to your conclusion about the nature of the conflict?

   c. What is the conflict in *French Fries*? Who specifically has a goal that is opposed by whom? What does that conflict lead you to conclude about the play's subject and theme?

6. Some believe that plays should contain *surprise*, a bold, even audacious new event or discovery, yet a logical part of the whole. Did *Poster* give you that surprise at the ending when Tom described his actions after Johnny died? What was its effect?

7. In an earlier chapter we discussed the significance of primitive rituals, and we indicated that rituals can make important contributions to theatre. What ritual or rituals are evoked by Tom's actions at the ending of *Poster*?

Hamlet speaks of the theatre holding a mirror up to nature. I think in fact it is society to which theatre holds up a mirror. The theatre and all drama can be seen as a mirror in which society looks at itself. . . . *The manners and lifestyle shown in the theatre inevitably become a potent influence on the manners and lifestyles of the times. Unconsciously we tend to reflect in our own life the attitudes, the accepted modes of behavior, we have seen in the theatre, or for that matter in the cinema or on television. How do courting couples know what to say to each other when for the first time they have to find the right words to break the ice or declare their feelings? I am certain that unconsciously they will use dialogue of a style of approach they have seen on the stage or screen. And similarly with people who are faced with death, bereavement, victory or defeat in sport, etc. Of course, the playwrights who wrote the dialogues concerned have imitated dialogues they have observed in real life. Yet they have selected the manner of speech and the words which they felt most appropriate, so they have reinforced a certain way of behavior as against another.*

—Martin Esslin

NOTES

1. Eric Bogosian, *Drinking in America* (New York: Random House, 1987), 16.

2. Ibid., 16–17.

3. Eric Bogosian, *Pounding Nails in the Floor with My Forehead* (New York: Theatre Communications Group, 1994), xii.

4. Bogosian, *Drinking*, 115–118.

5. Anna Deavere Smith, *Fires in the Mirror* (New York: Anchor Books, 1993), 63–66.

6. Lee Alan Morrow and Frank Pike, *Creating Theater: The Professionals' Approach to New Plays* (New York: Vintage Books, 1986), 10–11.

7. Ibid., 17–18.

8. Lanford Wilson, *A Poster of the Cosmos*, in *The Way We Live Now: American Plays & the AIDS Crisis*, ed. by Elizabeth Osborn (New York: Theatre Communications Group, 1990), 63–75.

5

The Playwright, Actor, and Director as Visionary, Lawmaker, and Storyteller

You see things;
and you say "Why?"
But I dream things that never were;
and I say "Why not?"

—George Bernard Shaw

MONODRAMATISTS YOU MET IN PREVIOUS CHAPTERS REVEAL significant insights not only into the solo play but also the nature of theatre. Here we draw together some of those insights to suggest concepts that can help you enlarge your vision and transform your ideas into staged experiences. We look at selected aspects of the nature of theatre overall as well as the solo play specifically.

THEATRICAL LAWMAKERS AND VISIONARIES

We live in a changing world: man is whispering through space, soaring to the stars in ships, flinging miles of steel and glass into the air. Shall the theatre continue to huddle in the confines of a painted box set? The movies, in their kaleidoscopic speed and juxtaposition of external objects and internal emotions, are seeking to find visible and audible expression for the tempo and the psychology of our time. The stage too must experiment—with ideas, with psychological relationship of men and women, with speech and rhythm forms, with dance and movement, with color and light—or it must and should become a museum product.

—Hallie Flanagan

"Why not?" As a theatrical artist you are, like the Serpent in George Bernard Shaw's *Back to Methuselah* (quoted at the beginning of this chapter), a visionary who chooses to dream things that never were, seeking to create what has never before existed. Whether you are an actor, director, playwright, designer, or technician, you start with a vision of a new theatrical experience and ask, Why not? The question ignites your imagination and creativity and propels your drive for excellence.

Think of the various monodramatists from previous chapters: Do you think they are visionaries who are challenged by the Why not? question? Surely the answer to that must be a resounding yes. Each clearly has a vision—the art of seeing the invisible—that stimulates the creative spirit and leads to a theatrical voice. As those monodramatists indicate, asking Why not? leads you to express your personal beliefs in language for the theatre.

Those soloists help us become more aware of the monodrama's special challenges for playwrights, directors, designers, and actors to create a theatre that shall not, to quote visionary Hallie Flanagan, leader of the Federal Theatre Project, "continue to huddle in the confines of a painted box set." Instead of such limited confines, as a monodramatist you seek to create a theatrical experience that will meet the need for what she calls the "visible and audible expression for the tempo and the psychology of our time."

The solo play is well suited to meet that need. The monodramatist thinks of the audience's hunger to discover the inner secrets of the soul. With that in mind, the solo performer crafts a theatrical experience that will stimulate the audience's imaginations to leap in time and space, to see and hear characters who are not on stage, and to experience the wonders of a human's determination to achieve an objective. As you have seen in earlier examples and discussions, the solo play can show a human's private dreams, secret thoughts, and compelling hungers. With fewer production effects than the multicharacter play, the monodrama is free of the cumbersome confines of the box set and is like a single brilliant ray of focused light that cuts through to the theatrical nucleus—the inner spirit of a character in action.

Theatrical Artists as Lawmakers

Existentialist philosophy teaches, in part, that each of us is a lawmaker. In that regard, our actions are our direct statements, "This is how I believe things should be," a code of beliefs that apply not only to ourselves but to the rest of humanity. Some existentialists believe that what one individual chooses to do or not to do implies a law for others.

The concept is especially applicable to artists, who necessarily bring firm personal convictions and standards to their art. Each time we create theatre—whether we write, direct, act, design, manage, or work on crews—we are making a bold pronouncement: *this is what I believe theatre should be.* In that existentialist sense each production defines, at least partially and for now, our conscious and unconscious concepts of a model theatre.

Happily, given the often frustrating complexities of achieving goals in theatre, we don't require ourselves to define our ideal in a single production. Although as theatre creators we must continually pursue an elusive standard called perfection—any lesser goal is simply unacceptable—we also recognize that as artists we will change, grow, and improve. We expect that each production will venture closer to that elusive standard. Over a broad period of creative life in the theatre, our concept of "what theatre should be" evolves as it is honed, refined, and clarified. The monodrama encourages us to experiment with theatrical techniques and to explore new insights as we work through personal expression of our goals.

Negative and Positive Lawmakers

Aware that productions may define an ideal theatre, it is no wonder that theatre artists are disgusted by those who insult and diminish the art by making it a vanity vehicle for narrow, self-serving personal interests and agendas, failing to uphold high artistic standards, treating audiences with an elitist condescension as if that proves a personal excellence, and responding to all criticism with a fireball "kill the messenger" rationalization. Is *that* what a model theatre should be? Hardly. Will those attitudes encourage a growing, vital theatre that attracts dedicated participants and earns the respect of audiences? Not likely. If theatre does become the museum oddity that Flanagan fears, surely such self-serving attitudes will be at least partially responsible.

Fortunately, the self-servers are a minority. Many will self-destruct and disappear under the weight of their own preoccupation with serving only themselves. Monodramatists such as those you've met in previous chapters have earned admiration for their focus on giving of themselves to further theatre. Theatre artists deeply respect the majority who give freely of themselves to honor the art, subordinating personal interests, determined to help participants improve, dedicated to the highest possible standards, and committed to create a rich theatrical experience that communicates with audiences through emotional and intellectual appeals. From such "lawmakers" comes the model theatre of the future: vital, dynamic, communicative, honest.

Theatre Artists as Visionaries

Theatre is an art of dreams and ideals, and artists are more than lawmakers. All who work effectively in theatre share another significant attribute: *the artist as visionary*. The examples of monodramatists we've discussed show that theatre artists are dreamers following a vision, which is the art of seeing the invisible, to dream "Why not?" Where there is no vision, theatre art fades. With vision, theatre art is enriched and enhanced. Because vision may be lofty, romantic, even idealized, it can elevate theatre art into unexplored heights, just as our society is lifted into new consciousness by political, philosophical, and religious visionaries who dream things that never were.

The theatre visionary seeks to *share* with coworkers and colleagues and with audiences, to communicate, to make vision accessible. Aware that only a small percentage of the population attends theatre, the visionary has a missionary's zeal to bring audiences back to the theatre with exciting, insightful works that show the essence of a human.

Necessary for effective vision is a *sense of the theatre*, an awareness of what works on stage, or a dream of what can work, to transform your vision into lively theatre. Such vision leads to theatrical characters in action, richly drawn with emotions and thoughts, gestures and metaphors, actions and inactions, objectives and conflicts, speeches and silences. Like monodramatists we've discussed, think of transforming your vision into concrete reality in the theatre so your monodrama will come to life on stage.

THE SEARCH FOR THE HUMAN ESSENCE

If vision is the art of seeing the invisible, theatrical vision is the art of showing the invisible, communicating from stage to audience. —Eric Bentley

As a theatrical artist developing your sense of what works on stage, you necessarily are deeply involved in what critic-playwright-scholar Eric Bentley calls "the search for human essence" that lies under outer appearances. Because the monodrama is a study of humanity, it particularly excels in daring to examine fundamental questions about what it means to be a thinking, feeling, conscious human facing questions about morality, ethical conduct, relationships with others, personal responsibilities and goals, social obligations, mortality.

Each such question is a troublesome grit of sand that invades your personal shell of consciousness to create a pearl—your theatrical statement. As you have seen in monodramas, the solo play shows personal insights into the human essence in their works. Some solo play authors, for example, may elect to show a human within an enigmatic, even hostile world that is constructed of dire consequences made more troublesome because they appear senselessly random. Others with a different outlook might show the human within a universe that is full of delights, wonders, and charms that are a result of a deity's carefully structured master plan. Which outlook is "right" isn't as relevant as that there is a personal statement, a point of view, a concept about the human spirit. That leads to a powerful theatrical statement. After all, theatre echoes our personal concerns about the nature of existence because the business of theatre is to show images of our lives reflected in the actions of humans who are vitally in contact with issues that affect humanity.

Thanks to art, instead of seeing one world, our own, we see it multiplied and as many original artists as there are, so many worlds are at our disposal. —Marcel Proust

Showing the Private Human Beneath the Public Mask

The monodrama is particularly adept at showing the essence of humanity, the inner secrets of a private human that normally are hidden beneath his or her public mask. The solo character is free to express private truths that could not be disclosed if others were in his or her world. It becomes an intimate one-to-one expression from and to the inner self, the soul-mind and the heart-mind. You've seen the power of such revealed secrets in monodramas that go beyond surface appearances, such as Jane Martin's *Twirler*, Eric Bogosian's *Nice Shoes*, Lanford Wilson's A *Poster of the Cosmos*, and Anna Deavere Smith's *Fires in the Mirror*. Because theatre is an art focused on human struggle to prevail, you can shape your monodrama into a powerful theatrical experience about the human essence in whatever world you see.

Searching for the Human Essence

Bentley says the dramatist has a responsibility to search for the human essence. True enough, but *all* theatre participants—directors, actors, designers, managers, producers, and technicians, as well as playwrights—are involved in that active exploration to discover and dramatize the basic nature of humanity. The writer creates a personal interpretation of the significant core of a distinctly individualized human; actors and directors rely on analysis, interpretation, creative imagination, and technique to bring to life that essence; producers and managers support and encourage the process; designers and technicians provide the environment and atmosphere that will best show the human in the universe of the play. All share similar interests in searching for ways to dramatize the human essence.

PERSONAL GOALS

Life is very nice, but it lacks form. It's the aim of art to give it some.   —Jean Anouilh

Exploring Your Creative Vision

As a theatre artist, you develop a vision, a purpose, an underlying motif for your creation. Often your goal is only vaguely perceived during your initial stages of invention. Contrary to popular myths, creative ideas seldom magically explode full-blown into life in a lightning flash burst of inspiration. Instead, the artist actively *searches* for a vision that will lead to a unified work of art.

You recall, for instance, that Eric Bogosian first tried the New York avant-garde scene before he found he was really looking for the truth the monodrama can show. Like Bogosian, encourage yourself to explore, instead of demanding an immediate, full-fledged, richly developed idea. Don't be dismayed if your initial exploration appears disorganized or random, because the artist's search necessarily must involve experiments, false starts, trying one idea only to throw it out, searchings, and consciously or unconsciously asking questions such as, What am I trying to create? and What do I want this to be?

The "Eureka" Experience

The Greek inventor Archimedes supposedly called out "Eureka!"—I've found it!—when after long research he discovered how to determine the amount of gold in a king's crown. Artists experience similar exaltation when they finally see their objective after long search. If the creative spirit were a daffodil, it would spend as much energy burrowing straight down into the dark underground as it would reaching up to claim the sun, but when it finds its direction it becomes a brilliant explosion of life. Regardless of how long it takes to perceive the ultimate goal, sooner or later the playwright, actor, or director experiences a Eureka! moment—Ah! Now I know that *this* is what I'm trying to do!—and discovers a goal that harmonizes all of the individual parts into a cohesive whole.

ONE ARTIST'S SEARCH FOR A GOAL

Often we must intuit what artists wanted to achieve because writers, directors, and actors usually prefer to let their work speak for them instead of explaining their goals. Occasionally, however, an artist's statement gives us insight into the creative process. For example, in the introduction to his full-length monodrama, *Mister Lincoln*, playwright Herbert Mitgang explains the thoughts that guided him. He started by identifying basic theatrical concepts he'd use, such as using powerful theatrical language, including unities of time, place, and action. He also knew he would avoid the lecture technique. Mitgang searched for the essence of Lincoln's life, as he describes here:

> In writing *Mister Lincoln* for the theatre, I decided from the start that a one-man play would be ideal for my subject and concept. I was aware that this form had been evolving in recent years; that what had to be avoided was a feeling by the audience that it was watching a play with a lectern at dead center for high-minded speeches. I had seen most of the current one-man shows and found that those I admired were most dramatized, most theatrical.
>
> Why, I wondered, did some personages—political or literary—work better than others in a monodrama? I felt that it had to do with language rather than actions; that the theatre is still a self-contained area of eloquence where words count. The words have to come first;* without them the finest actor must falter. . . . It struck me that the one-man form could serve as a concentrate for Lincoln's language without distillation or distraction. . . . I still wanted to achieve the Aristotelian unities of action, time and place; I aimed to do so by making thematic connections between life-incidents. As in a novel, one can plant certain ideas in early chapters—the first act—that can be called to mind and pay off at the end—in the second act.

* Mitgang's belief that in theatre "words count" and "the words must come first" has an interesting similarity with Anna Deavere Smith's emphasis on "the word, always the word."

And so, as the play took shape in my mind, I was forced to think harder on Lincoln and the centrality of his life than I had ever done before as a Lincoln biographer or film documentarian. The central theme that emerged was his own evolving stand on slavery that led to the Emancipation Proclamation. "If I ever get a chance to hit the Institution [of slavery]," he says in Act I, "I'm going to hit it hard." With his Proclamation in Act II as a high moment, he does.[1]

Goals Taking Shape and Evolving

Although Mitgang had a basic vision of the play he wanted to write—he knew it would be a solo play about Lincoln and it would emphasize language—it is important for us to note that he didn't begin his writing process with full awareness of his goal. On the contrary, he says he researched the life of Lincoln and the play slowly took shape in his mind and then a theme emerged. Finally he had a grasp of his specific goal: to show what he identified as the centrality of Lincoln's life, his stand on slavery.

The decision that the slavery issue would be the central theme gave Mitgang ideas for a number of scenes as well as a driving compulsion for the character to achieve an objective. Those ideas led to a unified play structure, as you see in the following extract from his play. Early in the first act the playwright creates a scene for Lincoln to speak about his first exposure to a slave auction when he was in New Orleans:

FROM MISTER LINCOLN
by Herbert Mitgang
Act One

On the block was a beautiful girl called Eliza. A Frenchman from New Orleans bid $1,200 for her but his bid was topped by a young Methodist minister. The auctioneer pulled the dress from Eliza's shoulders, exposing her breasts, and said: "Who's gonna lose a chance like this?" The sweating Frenchman bid $1,465, once again the young minister outbid him. The auctioneer lifted Eliza's dress, baring her body from her feet to her waist, slapped her on the thigh, and said: "Who's gonna win this prize?" The Frenchman bid $1,580, the auctioneer raised his gavel, the girl looked at the minister in terror and pleading. He bid $1,585.

He strikes handle of umbrella against bench like auctioneer

The gavel came down, and the girl fell in a faint. The auctioneer said: "Well sir, you got her damn cheap. What are you gonna do with her?" The young minister, whose name was Fairbanks, and who was one of the leaders of the anti-slavery movement in Ohio, said: "Free her!"

I have since learned that Fairbanks has spent seventeen years in the state penitentiary for his antislavery activities. Mind you, he was one of the lucky ones. In the Southern states, leaders of slavery revolts could and had been hanged.[2]

Mitgang's decision to concentrate on the slavery issue gives him a reoccurring leitmotiv for the action: Lincoln repeatedly wrestles with the question of enslaving others until the thematic climax with the Emancipation Proclamation in the latter part of the play. For the playwright, identification of the character's major objective became the key for the play's organization.

Thinking of a character's objective is important for all members of the production team, not just the playwright. Finding the character's goal is equally important for the actor and director. To create a dimensional human for the theatre they search through the script to discover the character's driving compulsion. Awareness of the objective leads director and actor to understand how to perform the character and what aspects of the play deserve most emphasis in production.

THE CREDO: IDENTIFYING YOUR PERSONAL POINT OF VIEW TO CREATE THEATRE

Playwright Tina Howe speaks about the writer's need to show a personal vision:

I tell my students not to be afraid of their vision. I think it's funny that young playwrights tend to be rather tentative and fearful and to second-guess themselves. So my advice is to go for broke. If there is some impulse that makes you want to write a play, you've just got to put everything you have into it and let out all the stops. I think that the only way theater is going to be exciting again is if the next generation will be braver and more audacious.

Theatrical director Lloyd Richards says he believes in the necessity of a personal investment:

In the early days of my career, I sometimes chose to work on plays that I didn't feel strongly about. But never again. . . . I don't believe in doing a play in which I can't invest myself totally. It takes blood to do a play. You can't make that kind of investment without caring about the work.

Actor William Redfield discusses the actor's use of self:

Should the actor work out the details of his part in personal terms, should he succeed in engaging his own secret anxieties and enjoyments—his private beliefs, his dreamlike characteristics, should he then insinuate those secrets into the ebbing and flowing of the play, he will be inevitably swept into the main lines of action—he will be forced unconsciously from point to point in his performance.

Actor Tom Hulce says he enjoys working with colleagues who have a strong vision that results from personal beliefs:

I've worked with a lot of nice people, and boy, am I not interested in nice. I want to work with people who are opinionated, who have a real vision. You might have big or little disagreements, but you know there is a vision at work. I will take that any day, no matter how difficult or neurotic or complicated the people I'm working with. I would prefer to be bad, more than I would prefer to be safe. If you're working with people who have a clear vision, then you feel free to take the biggest risks. You know that if you fall, they'll catch you; if you go off track, they'll put you back on.

As we discuss the artist's personal credo, we return to the idea of actress Uta Hagen's statement that personal conviction is essential to work in theatre, with which the introduction to this book began. In *Respect for Acting* Hagen says, "It is necessary to have a point of view about the world which surrounds you, the society in which you live; a point of view as to how your art can reflect your judgment." She adds, "You must ask yourself, 'How can I bring all this to the statement I wish to make in the theater?'"

Her concept deserves emphasis. Note how other theatre artists echo Hagen's belief. Playwright Robert Anderson, for example, says the playwright's responsibility is "to look in his heart and write, to write whatever concerns him at the moment; to write with passion and conviction," and playwright Mary Gallagher says, "Good theatre incorporates the personal, the social, the political, seamlessly." Director Tyrone Guthrie has a sweeping concept of universals when he says, "The purpose of theatre is to show mankind to himself, and thereby to show to man God's image." As you work in theatre, you're guided by your personal conviction about what makes the essence of effective theatre.

Developing and Using a Personal Credo

Whether you are playwright, actor, or director, you benefit from discovering your personal point of view by writing a *credo*, a statement of *what you believe*. Your credo defines who you are by your values, philosophy, and concept of the essence of humanity. The key is to *write* your credo, not merely say you'll think about it, because the writing process forces you to think more deeply about your personal standards, organize beliefs into priorities, and define the parameters of what drives you. Don't be surprised if you uncover opposing beliefs or concepts you didn't know you held: many who write credos report such unexpected personal discoveries. Possibly you may encounter the same sort of self-revelations as you construct your credo.

The length and detail of your credo depends on your investment in it. Theatre artists tell me that their credos range in length from a dozen pages to several hundred pages. One writer says she starts a new credo every year, keeping each annual credo in a separate notebook. Your credo may include perhaps half a dozen basic subjects or twice as many. No one can tell you what topics your credo will include, but perhaps some of the following subjects may suggest ideas:

☐ belief in a deity, faith, sharing, giving;

☐ love, relationships, marriage, family;

☐ goals, ambitions, dreams, future;

☐ prejudice, hate groups, lies, violation of human rights, persecution;

☐ divorce, unwanted pregnancy, abortion, child or spousal abuse.

Personalize your list of subjects. Your goal is to learn, by writing, your most important beliefs.

Your strongest beliefs should become the raw materials for your monodrama. Playwrights create plays from their credo; directors and actors search for plays that bring to life beliefs that most awaken their interest. Throughout, ask yourself how you will make your beliefs a statement in the theatre.[3]

Personal Conviction

Your credo focuses your creative process toward matters that involve you emotionally and intellectually. Your next step is to create a character who *lives* that subject, who is compelled to face the questions and take the actions that involve that idea. Theatrical writing requires *concrete action*, not abstract theories or didactic sermons. Whether you elect to create a comedy or a tragedy, your monodrama will take on dramatic tension and vitality when both you and the character have a gut-level involvement with the topic.

If you decide your monodrama will focus on love, marriage, death of a loved one, family values and relationships, religious concepts, acquaintance rape, abortion, AIDS, or the like, it's safe to assume you already have formulated strong feelings and opinions to lead you to that particular subject. You're creating from your credo. Your attitude and opinions will lead you to write because, as Scott Fitzgerald says, you have something you feel you *must* say. You've seen that passion in such monodramas as Anna Deavere Smith's *Fires in the Mirror* and Lanford Wilson's *A Poster of the Cosmos*, among others.

In contrast, if the playwright selects a subject because it is a "hot topic" that's in the news, quite likely the play will be thin and dull, lacking the central driving force that comes with personal commitment and conviction. Imagine that a theatre worker—playwright, actor, or director—decides to base a play on, say, the issue of the homeless or the plight of women simply because he or she thinks that the homeless or feminists are currently in vogue and dramatizing the issue will somehow prove that the theatre worker has an alert social consciousness. Or imagine a theatre artist decides to adopt a particular approach—say, performance art, or shock, or social drama—simply to prove that he or she is on the cutting edge of new movements. Imagine a director forcing changes on an existing play to achieve such a goal, taking an otherwise strong play and adding numerous effects to turn it from the playwright's original intention into a play about homelessness or the like.

What will such theatre workers prove? Not much worthwhile. What's the difference between a theatre person selecting the *issue du jour* and others with such variable standards, such as a slick politician desperately seeking votes by claiming to embrace a mod issue or a supermarket tabloid's mentality? Pity the poor audience.

We may be amused by a chameleon's ability to change colors according to the current situation, but we expect more integrity from a serious artist.

At best, such a selection process suggests that the individual has shallow thinking but no personal beliefs about life or society. It's one thing to create theatre to focus on the homeless or to adapt performance art techniques because one's gut cries for that expression. It's quite different to use such an approach for self-aggrandizement. Worse, using the theatre simply to be in vogue is an unfortunate exploitation of the art solely to satisfy vanity. Surely it is better to want to create from personal conviction and to maintain a respectful dedication to theatre.

Originality

Creating monodramas with situations and characters that interest you will make your monodrama original. That's quite different from deliberately *seeking* originality, which too easily can lead to being different merely for the sake of difference. In this context we need to remember that new and different or experimental does not necessarily equal good and worthwhile or artistic.

Instead of the results of *trying* to be original, you achieve an artistic work as unique as your fingerprint when your work represents your personal insight into human weaknesses or strengths, particular subjects or social concerns, and human behavior, values, and attitudes. Experienced theatre artists know that originality resulting from personal belief is more desirable than originality for its own sake or to prove one's cleverness.

Appeal to Others

Plays based on personal conviction have an intensity that will awaken the audience's emotions and thoughts, as we've seen in monodramas such as Jane Martin's *French Fries*, with the playwright's ironic statement about plastic equaling eternity and the importance of dreams. Lanford Wilson's *A Poster of the Cosmos* shows the writer's emotional involvement with devastating effects of AIDS, and Jane Wagner's *The Search for Intelligent Life in the Universe* illustrates the playwright's personal insight into the women's movement and self-proclaimed political activists. Your preoccupation with the subject and characters you select will reflect in the character's attitudes, giving him or her a personal stake in the outcome.

A PERSONAL VISION OF TRUTH

Whether you write, act, or direct, expect your monodrama to show your vision of truth and your insight into the human essence in a story you carefully craft to capture the audience's imagination with emotional, sensual, and intellectual stimuli. Your vision then leads the audience to a perception you want to share about a selected aspect of life, society, or particular people. As playwright Arthur Miller says, plays illuminate a certain mystery, and just as primitive rituals dramatized the mysteries of the universe, so theatre brings to life significant experiences that speak to our fears, hopes, and dreams.

As lawmaker and visionary, you create a monodrama that reflects your beliefs about society and theatre. Your vision begins to take shape as you decide what you want to say through the theatre. You ask yourself questions such as these: What personal statements are important to me? What social problems or aspects of human relationships awaken my emotions and mind? What do I believe theatre must be? How will I use the monodrama to bring my concepts to life?

For example, perhaps you are trying to come to grips with the results of failed dreams and unfilled ambition, as Samuel Beckett does in his one-man play, *Krapp's Last Tape*. Or perhaps you are fascinated by mysticism and decide your monodrama will express your vision of such experience, as Jane Martin does in *Twirler*. If you are concerned about racial prejudice and violence, you may want to put together interviews such as those that resulted in playwright-actress Anna Deavere Smith's monodrama, *Twilight: Los Angeles, 1992*, which dramatizes aspects of the 1992 Los Angeles riots. Alternatively, you might be interested in acting challenges that use the solo play's ability to stimulate the audience's imagination, and so you decide to follow examples of monodramatists such as Ruth Draper, Cornelia Otis Skinner, Lily Tomlin, or Patrick Stewart, who each performed a number of characters in their monodramas.

STORYTELLING

Personal storytelling is very important to me because we've become so media-ized that we begin to think that the stories the stars tell on Johnny Carson are more important than ours. If I am a preacher or a proselytizer at all, it's to say, "Get together with friends, tell stories, listen. Turn off the TV, put down the book, listen to a story." Because the more we are fragmented and the more people are moved around and are in motion and are the bigger this country gets and the more media-ized it gets, tied together only through television, the more healing it is to tell personal stories about your day. It gives you a personal history and it gives you a sense of existence and place. —Spalding Gray

Think of your monodrama as a form of storytelling, lively and engaging, an art as ancient as primitive rituals and as modern as today's plays. "The dramatist must be by instinct a storyteller," says playwright-novelist Thornton Wilder, because storytelling brings your creative vision to life in theatre, using characterization, rituals, suspense, emotions, and language to show the human essence and express the artist's personal point of view. Actor and playwright Spalding Gray, whose works such as *Swimming to Cambodia* and *Monster in a Box* make him one of today's leading monodramatists, says that storytelling is the important aspect of his art. Showing his intention to create monodramas that reflect his concept of theatre's role in society, Gray says he believes storytelling is a form of *healing*, a way of making connection between individuals who are otherwise separated.

Story Enactment

In theatre we think of storytelling as *story enactment*, shaping a story to be shown on stage by the character, who lives the action and involves the audience. You create a monodrama that will use the stage's power to show actors enacting action—what the character feels and thinks, wants but cannot achieve, does and does not do, and says and does not say—that is in process *now*, moving inexorably to a future. Theatrical storytelling differs from, say, a novelist's storytelling technique, which describes past events that are completed by the time we pick up the book, or an essayist's or preacher's direct, even didactic, statements. Theatre is not literature but dramatized events, using illusion to create an enhanced poetic reality.

Playwrights, Actors, Directors, and Designers as Storytellers

The dramatist must be by instinct a storyteller. There is something mysterious about the endowment of the storyteller. . . . It springs not, as some have said, from an aversion to general ideas, but from an instinctive coupling of idea and illustration; the idea, for a born storyteller, can only be expressed imbedded in its circumstantial illustration. The myth, the parable, the fable are the foundation of all fiction and in them is seen most clearly the didactic, moralizing employment of a story. —Thornton Wilder

Although Wilder calls the dramatist a storyteller, the writer is not the only theatre worker actively involved in telling a story. Actors, directors, and designers also are authors of human action. Just as playwrights use metaphors and images to create action that illuminates the play's meaning and uncovers the character's internal self, so directors and actors apply their artistic variations of those devices—voice, movement, gesture, and use of time and space—to communicate to the audience. Scenery, lighting, and costume designers also create images and metaphors involving mass, shape, line, color, light, and shadows to show the environment of the action. All theatrical artists seek to hold the audience's attention by weaving a hypnotic tale that shows the human spirit in action.

The theatrical monodramatist—playwright, actor, director—seeks a personal relationship to the audience, like an expert storyteller bringing to life a ghost story to youngsters gathered around a campfire, involving them in the events, seeking to tell the story *with* the audience rather than *at* them. You use the monodrama's intimate one-to-one relationship with the audience, its sense of close *sharing* of the human experience, unhampered by the ornate production machinery that often distances multi-character plays from the audience. The close relationship necessarily demands a basic honesty from playwright and performer, ruling out bombastic dialogue, artificial situations, or stage trickery; and the intimacy gives you an opportunity to make a direct impact on your audience through character revelation.

Show, Don't Tell

Expert storytelling, says Wilder, illustrates the underlying idea. From Wilder's comments we draw one of the inescapable rules of theatre: *show, don't tell*. Your idea is brought to life in an "illustration," to use Wilder's term, which means showing the idea in human terms. Rather than expressing your idea bluntly as an essayist would do, in theatre you imply your idea through action.

What Wilder calls a myth, parable, or fable is a story that shows your personal point of view or concept. For example, many essays are written about AIDS, but Wilson's A *Poster of the Cosmos* personalizes the disease, making it vivid by bringing it to life in the theatre. Although some people may view AIDS as a distant abstraction that is discussed in statistical reports, Wilson's theatrical sense gives the disease a more meaningful concrete immediacy by showing the tragic results for the two specific humans. So, too, your monodrama transforms an abstract concept into concrete form by showing an individualized character living through aspects of the problem, which leads the audience to sense your vision and idea.

AN OBSESSIVE NEED TO TELL A STORY

You don't write because you want to say something;
you write because you've got something to say. —F. Scott Fitzgerald

Playwrights, actors, and directors bring to their solo plays what monodramatist Spalding Gray calls "an obsessive need to tell a story," a strong desire to communicate with others through the theatre. Needing to write is important, as playwright Marsha Norman emphasizes: "Most of us who continue to write need it in some central, absolutely critical way. If it were against the law to write plays, if people were put in prison for writing plays, I would still do it." Your desire to tell a story and your dedication to theatre become excellent motivational drives that will help you create a monodrama you will respect.

Think of playwriting less as writing and more as a passion to share with others a story that shows your ideas about people, issues, and situations that arouse your emotions and challenge your intellect. As writer Sholem Asch points out, "Writing comes more easily if you have something to say," and your monodrama will be easier to create and become a more powerful theatrical piece if you want others to see your comic or dramatic view of an aspect of society or life that preoccupies your attention. As a playwright, you are a master storyteller using entertainment, actions, emotions, and metaphors to show audiences your view of your corner of the universe. Select human qualities that you believe are most important, such as a character's struggles to endure and prevail, his or her achievements or failures, the tragic heart or the impish comic spirit, the warm soul full of love or the bitter hate-filled spirit, the enduring strength of purpose or the weakness of indifference, the proud or the meek.

Stubbornness is extremely important to writing success and almost as important as talent. The world is not waiting for anyone to write a new play and the world will not stop if you don't write that play. The play has got to be very, very important to you if you expect it to be important to anyone else. —Ted Tally

Writing to Discover What You Want to Say

Nonwriters often are surprised to discover that playwrights often must go through a number of versions of their plays to discover what they want to say, instead of knowing in advance their precise goals. They ask, "Don't you start by knowing what you want to say?" Well, no, not always. For example, Tina Howe says her search to find what she wanted to say took years of active writing: "For three years, *Painting Churches* was about a girl coming home and having her mother make a dress for her debut as a pianist," and Howe wrote eight drafts for that concept until "finally I got the idea that the girl would be a portrait painter and was coming home to paint her parents' portrait. It was a moment of blinding awareness, an epiphany. And everything fell together." Concludes Howe, "That's how we playwrights work."[4]

RITUAL

The influence of the shaman's ceremonial ritual is seen in modern monodramas. Jeffrey Goldman makes the point while interviewing monodramatist Spalding Gray:

> **GOLDMAN:** I've often thought that your role as a monologist in today's society is similar in many ways to the figure of the Shaman. Because in a world dependent so much on surfaces, where appearance counts for so much, you are appearing naked on stage, revealing universal, but often unmentionable, fantasies. Likewise, the Shaman tells stories that relate to and help people deal with their own lives and problems. Unfortunately, he often tells them things they don't want to hear, and so they sacrifice him.
>
> **SPALDING GRAY:** I think that's a good analogy. . . . I'm highly ritualized . . . and I find that I'm very interested in ritual and structure. . . . I think people who are into any kind of acting or performance are that way. And they're also into what Freud would call "the repetition complex," where a certain security is found in repeating gestures.

Whether you write, direct, or act, as a storyteller you are like the prehistoric shaman as you create rituals, actions, images, metaphors, or analogies that illustrate and show the human essence in motion. The shaman told stories that appealed to the audience's interests and needs. Even if his audience had not been aware the subject interested them, the shaman's storytelling expertise turned them from disinterested observers to active participants. The shaman used impersonation, gesture, movement and dance, costume, forms of magic, and other theatrical forms of entertainment to communicate with his audience.

Rituals in Modern Society

Rituals enrich our lives, make special events more meaningful, and give us comfort. Rites of passage are marked by rituals, such as a bar mitzvah to celebrate a boy's change into adulthood, bridal showers, marriage celebrations, birthday parties, and funeral ceremonies. Initiation into clubs is based on rituals. Rituals are major forces in various religions: communion, confession, benediction, liturgy, mantra, meditation, Kaddish, and celebrations of events such as Easter, Christmas, or Hanukkah. Sports are full of rituals, such as the traditional flipping of a coin to decide which team will be defender or attacker, the ring announcer's stylized incantation to announce the fighters, or sailboats' maneuvering dances to get in position for the racing start.

Rituals in Theatre

Rituals enrich theatre, too, as previous chapters have indicated. Theatre itself is a ritual: conventions such as a stage space, audience facilities, ways of beginning a production, the display of human actions, enactment and impersonation, and creation of a certain magic are ritualistic. Plays, too, are rituals in action. Think, for example, of Sonny's ritualistic defense of his territory or April March's ritualized ceremony with other baton twirlers who gather to wipe the sky away to expose God.

As a theatre worker you share the prehistoric shaman's desire to make rituals meaningful experiences for the audience. Select rituals that are important to you, and then adapt them into theatrical metaphors. Available to you are techniques similar to those the shaman used, such as impersonation, gesture, movement and dance, costume, and forms of magic. You'll use actions, images, or metaphors that illustrate and show the human essence in motion as you bring to life rituals that you make important to the audience. Your own commitment to the ritual helps draw and sustain the audience's interest.

ENTERTAINMENT

I've heard it argued . . . that one has a duty and an obligation in a classical theater to re-educate the audience, to make them listen, to bring back to them, by force as it were, the appreciation of the spoken word, of lyric writing, and redevelop their powers of concentration even at the expense of entertainment (which has a kind of shabby connotation associ-

ated with Broadway). I disagree with this. I think "entertainment" is a perfectly sound word and a desirable reason for going to the theater. —Hume Cronyn

Theatrical storytelling must be entertaining, it must be *fun*. Despite some who seem to distrust the idea of theatre as entertainment or fun, as if that somehow weakened the art's intellectual thrust, *entertainment* does not implies a lightweight, sugary confection. On the contrary, according to no less a theorist than Bertolt Brecht, often hailed as one of theatre's intellectual and nonconformist playwrights, entertainment is one of theatre's highest goals. Says Brecht, "From the first it has been theatre's business to entertain people as it also has been of all the other arts. It is this business which gives it its particular dignity; it needs no other passport but fun."

Entertainment, as actor, director, and playwright Hume Cronyn says, is a perfectly acceptable theatrical quality. A desire for entertainment makes people want to attend the theatre. They stay in the theatre because entertainment draws them into the story's environment, holding their attention, awakening mind and heart. Entertainment diverts audience members from their daily concerns and takes them into new worlds, and entertainment helps the audience concentrate on daily life more intensely by showing them inner truths of their own experience. Entertainment makes theatre meaningful.

Cronyn repeats a popular theory when he says he's heard some people talk about *making* audiences attend the theatre, even "by force as it were," while expressing an elitist scorn for "entertainment." That's hardly a model theatre. After all, entertainment encompasses comedy, drama, or tragedy, and theatrical works from *King Lear* to *The Sound of Music*, *Krapp's Last Tape*, or *The Break-Up Diet*. Your monodrama can show psychological sensitivity, tragic loss, anger about social problems, philosophical awareness, or pure enjoyment of life. Whatever the form you choose, you seek to create a compelling story that entertains, and thus grasps, the audience, to sustain its interest throughout your monodrama.

SURPRISE

"Etonne-moi!"—"Astonish me!"—says Sergei Pavlovich Diaghilev, the Russian ballet producer and art critic. Closely related to entertainment is the element of *surprise*, a twist, event, or discovery that gives new insight into the problem.

A play's action is driven forward by the difference between the anticipated versus the event that actually takes place. For example, if you imagine being in the audience watching Jane Martin's *French Fries*, you can sense the feeling of surprise when the character says she wants to live in McDonald's, shows her reasons for believing McDonald's provides eternal life, and concludes that we must all have our dreams, for dreams make us what we are. Equally, imagine watching Martin's *Twirler* and experiencing the astonishment when the character equates baton twirling with a religious experience, the baton wiping away the sky to expose the face of God, and the special sacrificial ritual that involves catching the falling baton that has razor blades in the handle. So, too, there is surprise in Lanford Wilson's A *Poster of the Cosmos* when Tom discloses his actions when his friend died.

But an effective surprise cannot be a trick or gimmick. We've all heard playwrights read first drafts of scripts that put a character in remarkable dilemmas and tortured situations, ending with "and then I woke up." We feel let down because it all was merely a trick: the playwright did not let the audience know the character was dreaming or even asleep. Equally, the surprise "O. Henry ending" is only a gimmick twist at the end of the story, pulling in information the author knew but hadn't disclosed. Yes, such tricks may surprise, but they also cheat. They're like *deus ex machina* endings that are contrivances, far less satisfactory than ingenuity and insight.

Although multicharacter plays often achieve surprise with news brought in by an offstage character, in the monodrama you use depth of characterization to achieve Diaghilev's demand, "Astonish me!" As you have seen in *French Fries*, *Twirler*, and A *Poster of the Cosmos*, surprise is a logical part of the character's emotions, goals, motivations, insights, discoveries, and conclusions.

EXERCISES

1. Recall a favorite storytelling experience from your childhood. Perhaps it was a parent making up stories at night, a school teacher's weekly story session, a special story reading presentation at your local library, or a campfire story late in the evening. What do you recall about that experience? Did it stimulate your imagination and emotions? What captured your attention? Did the storyteller act

out the story? What did you enjoy most about the experience? How can you adapt that to a monodrama?

2. Spalding Gray speaks of the *healing* power of storytelling. What does healing mean to you? How would you use that idea in a monodrama you'd create?

3. What about theatre makes you dream and ask Why not? What do you believe makes the most powerful theatrical experience? What is your vision of the ideal theatre? How can you use the monodrama to achieve that goal?

4. Theatre involves, among other things, an expression of *the human essence*. What are the most important essences that you wish to bring to life in your monodrama?

5. Write your personal credo and keep it in your monodrama notebook. Perhaps the approach following will help you organize your thoughts.
   a. Using free association, list all the subjects that deeply interest you, preoccupy your attention, or make you angry or delighted. List, too, rituals that make your life more meaningful. This initial phase may take several days or weeks until you are certain you have exhausted possibilities. Avoid censoring your ideas and instead accept all subjects that come to mind.
   b. Examine your list for groupings. Quite likely you'll find that some listings actually are repetitions. Put similar subjects together.
   c. Organize your subjects into priorities, starting with those most important to you.
   d. When you are satisfied you have completed the first three steps, start with the first subject on your list and write your personal beliefs about that topic. Continue the process with other subjects.

6. Using the first two or three first subjects of your credo, construct outlines for monodramas. For each monodrama, construct an outline that addresses the following questions.
   a Imagine a character who faces a major crisis that relates to a specific issue from your credo. In as few words as possible, state the *specific* conflict the character faces, a goal in which the character has a compelling interest. What emotions force the character to speak?

b. Identify basic aspects of the character. In a page or two describe the character.

    i. What is the character's name?

    ii. How old is the character?

    iii. What are the important physical aspects of the character?

    iv. What are the important emotional aspects?

    v. What does he or she wear?

    vi. What physical items must be present? (For example, the character may need certain things such as a scrapbook, picture, telephone, or the like.)

    vii. Where does the monodrama take place?

    viii. What is the season of the year? What month? What time of day?

    ix. Describe the outside world that surrounds the character. What is the environment? What does he or she see, hear, and smell through the window? Who lives nearby? How does the character feel about those people?

7. Describe the ideal audience for your monodrama. Young people? College age? Elderly? A secular audience? A religious group? Sophisticated?

8. What is the ideal audience response? What effect do you want your monodrama to have on the audience? What do you want them to feel? Think? What emotions do you want the audience to experience for the character? What tone do you want your monodrama to convey? Do you want this to be a comic play? Dramatic? Ironic? A sense of personal fulfillment?

NOTES

1. Herbert Mitgang, Mister Lincoln (Woodstock, IL: Dramatic Publishing Co.), 5–6.

2. Ibid., 16–17.

3. For further information about the credo, I invite you to read Chapter 4 of my book Playwriting: Writing, Producing, and Selling Your Play, published by Waveland Press, P.O. Box 400, Prospect Heights, IL 60070.

4. Lee Alan Morrow and Frank Pike, Creating Theater: The Professionals' Approach to New Plays (New York: Vintage Original, 1986), 32.

Skill without imagination is craftsmanship and gives us many useful objects such as wickerwork picnic baskets. Imagination without skill gives us modern art. —Tom Stoppard

Form, to me, is the shape any creative work must take in order to exist with its ultimate force, beauty, and meaning. —William Inge

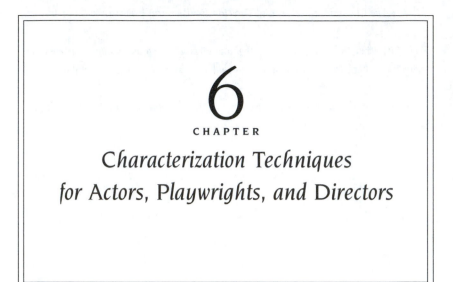

6

CHAPTER

Characterization Techniques
for Actors, Playwrights, and Directors

I'm convinced that there are absolutely unbreakable rules in the theatre, and that it doesn't matter how good you are, you can't break them. . . . You must state the issue at the beginning of the play. The audience must know what is at stake; they must know when they will be able to go home: "This is a story of a little boy who lost his marbles." They must know, when the little boy either gets his marbles back or finds something better than his marbles, or kills himself because he can't live without his marbles, that the play will end and they can applaud and go home. He can't not care about the marbles. He has to want them with such a passion that you are interested, that you connect to that passion. The theatre is all about wanting things that you can or can't have or you do or do not get. Now, the boy himself has to be likable. It has to matter to you whether he gets his marbles or not.

—Marsha Norman

The playwright. 6 A.M. The writer rose early to have quiet time for solitary work and now stares glumly at the computer screen. This morning's goal: revise to make a passive character more lively and dynamic. *What if I make the character react differently to the stimuli of the situation? Maybe I ought to invent a new obstacle that will force the character to react more strongly?* Although aware the revision will be difficult, the playwright takes a deep breath and begins yet another rewrite: "Act One, page 1. At rise. . . ."

The actor. A break in rehearsals. Gulping a cup of coffee, the actor worries about the scene they've just run for the third time this evening. *Damn! My character just isn't coming to life but instead is static, unresponsive, small, even—* the dreaded word—*dull. What if I increase what the character has at stake? Am I really showing what the character wants? What if the character reacts differently to obstacles?* The actor forces a cheerful smile to hide inner worries and goes back on stage.

The director. A scene in progress. The frustrated director paces restively in the back of the dim auditorium. *The scene just doesn't work. It seems—phony. Characterization isn't on target. Why is the character so limp? Is the problem limited only to this one scene, or is there something inherently flawed in our basic foundation? What if we go back to the early scene when the character first initiates a goal?* The director calls, "Okay, let's do it again. We'll try some different things this time. From the top, please."

In the these scenarios the consistent element is artistic concern for *characterization*, the people of the play—in the monodrama, the solo character. We mustn't forget the other unseen characters who may be evoked, however. Often the invisible characters are also crisply drawn active contributors to the play, as you noticed with Mike and Joey in Eric Bogosian's *Nice Shoes*, or the cops and especially Johnny in Lanford Wilson's *A Poster of the Cosmos*.

"This is a story of a little boy who lost his marbles." In the quotation that begins this chapter, playwright Marsha Norman makes clear the importance of a key aspect of characterization: a drive to achieve a goal. As Norman says, "The theatre is all about wanting things that you can or can't have or you do or do not get." Playwright, actor, and director create a character who passionately *wants* something—Norman's little boy absolutely *must* get his marbles—and both the play's structure and its characterization are constructed with that struggle to achieve a specific objective despite obstacles. The passion and the struggle create a character in action.

For all plays, rich characterization is an important goal for the playwright, actor, and director. For the monodrama with its single character, dimensional, interesting, and vital characterization is crucial.

CALL IT SPINACH? TERMINOLOGY AND DEFINITIONS

[Playing an objective] has been called many things in many books and some people don't call it anything; but it is a process that is going on, if they are really acting. I myself don't care if you call it spinach, if you know what it is, and do it, because it is one of the most important elements in acting. —Robert Lewis

Theatrical vocabulary becomes remarkably confusing because many of our terms have different meanings. Adding to the confusion, various practitioners develop their own terminology. In *Method—or Madness?* Robert Lewis spoofs the frustrating problem the jargon creators make with confusing terminology to define the character's motivating drive to an objective. In the preceding quotation he says he doesn't care if the actor calls the process spinach as long as the actor does it. To reduce this unfortunate confusion, we need to define terms more clearly. Here we look at selected basic terminology for characterization.

☐ *Action*. You'll encounter at least three meanings of *action*. First, action is a structural reference, pertaining to the play's dramatic movement, shown to the audience by the character's determined efforts to achieve an objective, the progression of the plot, and the conflicts that characters face. Secondly, dialogue also can be action, sharp and forward moving. Finally, action is a a component of characterization, the basic inner motivation (see also *intention*) that compels the character to move to achieve an objective or goal.

☐ *Intention*. A character has a basic overall objective. Intentions are the character's set of actions toward that objective, tactics the character uses to achieve that goal.

☐ *Given circumstances*. A Stanislavsky concept, given circumstances refer to dramatic events, actions, and environment that influence the character. Given circumstances may occur before the play begins (if major, called the *inciting incident*), such as Mike's appearance on Sonny's turf, the effect of Johnny's death on Tom, or the death of Hamlet's father. They also may be part of the play's ongoing physical and social environment, such as when and where the action takes place, the identity of the major participants, and the action that is happening. For example, the given circumstances in *Nice Shoes* must include a contemporary urban street corner, a small gang of toughs, and a stranger.

☐ *Obstacles*. The traditional example of the dramatic structural model is "boy wants girl, girl's parents say no, boy loses girl, boy overcomes parental objections and gets girl." The first action phrase—boy wants girl—is the *objective* (he wants the girl) and *intention* (how he will go about making her respond positively to him). The second—her parents say no—is the obstacle phase of the dramatic action. Playwrights and directors call those phases *complications*, counter-forces that change the direction of the plot by impeding the character's progress toward the objective. Without such barriers, there'd be no conflict or drama. Obstacles can be physical (often added by the actor or director), psychological (part of the playwright's creation of character), or structural (the playwright's plot construction).

☐ *Subtext.* The actual dialogue is the text; the underlying unspoken meaning is the subtext. Sonny says he won't hurt Mike, but the subtext clearly is full of latent violence; his visible smiles and laughter appear to indicate congenial friendliness but under them is a bitter hatred of outsiders. Anna Mae sees a man cured of a physical disease and her subtext is a wistful hope that she also can be cured. She says she wants to live in McDonald's, and under that expressed wish is a subtext concerning what she feels about where she now lives.

☐ *Spine.* The same as *superobjective*, spine is a different way of describing the artistic unification of a play on the premise that all individual pieces of the play are connected to a master plan, like vertebrae to a body's spine. Playwrights ensure unification of their scripts by knitting closely all units with the spine; directors approaching a play must first find its basic core; and actors examine their characters' connection to the play against the broad framework of the play's action. The spine includes the play's primary action, the characters' objectives, and the major conflict.

☐ *Superobjective.* Although some acting texts or teachers use superobjective to refer to an individual character's major goal, more precisely this term describes the play's structural design that dramatizes a single subject, which unifies the play. Stanislavsky discusses the actor's relationship to the play's superobjective, saying that all the actor's thoughts, feelings, and actions should carry out the plot's superobjective. Any detail, no matter how small, is incorrect if not directly connected to the superobjective. Directors and playwrights in particular must understand the play as a whole, its very reason for being, and they cannot be certain that have accurately positioned characters into the action until they have a full grasp of the play's basic thrust.

COMMON TECHNIQUES FOR CREATING
DIMENSIONAL CHARACTERS

The creative talents of playwright, actor, and director harmonize most closely with the creation of a theatrical character. Too often, however, that harmony is overlooked. Theatre texts and teachers seem to discuss characterization only from the narrow point of view of each individual set of artists. For example, most books on acting treat characterization with little or no consideration of the artistic contributions of the playwright or director, and you find similar parochial attitudes in texts for playwrights or directors. Such books can lead you to conclude that playwrights, actors, and directors do not share common techniques, as if each creator were somehow compartmentalized away from the others. That's unfortunate. As we discuss here, playwrights, actors, and directors have more significant similarities than differences, and you can use your knowledge and experience in one of these aspects of theatrical art to nurture and strengthen your insights and abilities in the other two.

As you learn more about the working techniques of each individual theatrical artist, you conclude that apparent differences are more semantic and less substantial. Granted, the director and playwright tend to have more objectivity about the play's overall effect than the actor, who is apt to look at the character in terms of subjective moments. Granted, too, we seem to have developed separate vocabularies for each, implying substantial differences.

Such differences, however, are less important than our mutual similarities. After all, playwrights, actors, and directors are creative artists whose personal standards drive them to create rich, dynamic, vital characterization. An ideal education for anyone most interested in any given creative theatrical art—whether playwriting, acting, or directing—includes hands-on work in the other arts. That's especially true with the techniques of developing dimensional and interesting characters, the core of the theatrical experience. The solo play offers playwrights, directors, and actors rich opportunities to create richly drawn characters. Challenging? Yes, certainly. But also potentially remarkably rewarding.

Similarities of Playwriting, Acting, and Directing

☐ *Playwrights*, *actors*, and *directors* are all storytellers who seek to develop theatrical techniques to communicate ideas and emotions from stage to audience.

☐ *Playwrights* and *directors* use the "What if?" questions that Stanislavsky recommends to actors to stimulate imagination.

☐ *Playwrights* can use actors' techniques, such as improvisations, exercises, preparation of character biographies, and focus on characters' objectives. Writers also think of themselves as directors by visualizing the stage action and environment, hearing and seeing the action.

☐ *Directors* work more effectively with actors if they borrow performers' characterization techniques, and they improve their use of the stage by thinking of themselves as playwrights of action and visual storytellers. Additionally, learning playwrights' techniques helps directors ensure accurate play analysis, a crucial first step that leads to interpretation.

☐ *Actors* and *directors* better understand why characters have certain speeches or actions if they are aware of the playwright's storytelling techniques. For instance, the playwright may have decided the script needed exposition or foreshadowing and therefore wrote lines to communicate information to the audience without thinking whether the character actually *wanted* to say them. The director and actor sensitive to the playwright's techniques will recognize why such possibly out-of-character lines were necessary and will find ways to make them appear motivated.

Dialogue Versus Character

. . . . the character must be construed from his own words. Not the information contained in them, but their taste, their flavour, because, when it comes down to it, the essential question is: what kind of man talks like that? —Simon Callow

"What kinna guy would say that?" says Tom in A *Poster of the Cosmos*. That question is always in the minds of playwrights, directors, and actors. Dialogue is characterization; characterization is dialogue. What the character says—and the way he or she says it—reflects the essence of the person. For example, think of what you learn about Anna Mae when she says, "He had him . . . Cerebral Walrus," or about Robert Sherman when he concludes we have "lousy language" when addressing issues of prejudice.

The playwright's challenge is to find the precise dialogue the character says—and that *only* this particular character can and *must* say. Therefore, the playwright crafts distinctive dialogue for the particular character—a tapestry of images, incomplete or complete sentences, elevated or more common expressions, and rambling or precise and long or short sentences. The challenge in multicharacter plays is to have each character speak in his or her his distinctive verbal patterns; in monodramas, that challenge is equaled by the need to create a character whose speech is not only distinctive but also active, lively, and colorful so that the dialogue moves the play forward and holds audience interest.

For directors and actors, dialogue is a vitally important key to understanding the character. A novelist can describe what a character is thinking and feeling, but in theatre those interior qualities are inherent in dialogue. Significant, too, is what is *not* said, the emotions and meanings that lie unspoken beneath the dialogue—the *subtext*. The director helps the actor first to discover the subtext and then to develop ways to express it by using such techniques as vocal inflection, attitude, pauses, and body language.

Using Photographs to Help Envision Characters

Students in makeup classes learn to accumulate a large file of photographs of interesting characters, especially faces and expressions, to help them learn makeup techniques. Costume designers collect pictures of clothing styles that show period, class, and personality. Playwrights, actors, and directors can adapt that exercise to create characterization.

Imagine you are writing a play about, say, an elderly woman like Anna Mae in Jane Martin's French Fries or are going to direct or act a street character such as Sonny in Eric Bogosian's Nice Shoes. You can stimulate your imagination to discover more aspects of the character with pictures. Start the process by examining books and magazines for photographs or paintings that seem similar to the character. Perhaps you will strike gold and find a picture that you feel is exactly like the character. More often, however, you find *aspects* of the character—this picture shows the character's hair, another looks like the character's face, here's a good image of the clothing, this picture shows the character's hair, and so forth. You meld the various pictures together to give a total view of the character. Think of expanding your search to other elements of the play: as pictures can help you envision the person, so they also can give you images of furniture, wall decorations, favored photographs, and other aspects of the character's environment. For actors and directors that search-and-collect process can be equally significant.

File such pictures in your Monodrama Notebook, where you can refer to them during the process of creating the character. You may also want to collect pictures of interesting faces, situations, or environments that may lead to a different play in the future.

Casting Your Monodrama

Playwrights create characters by drawing from real humans, personal experience, and imagination, but they can kindle new fire in their characters by thinking of actors who would be ideal for the role. For some playwrights the actor may be a friend or perhaps a member of a company where the playwright works. Lanford Wilson, for example, started writing A *Poster of the Cosmos* because he wanted to create a role for actor Tom Noonan, and Jane Wagner wrote *The Search for Intelligent Life in the Universe* specifically for actress Lily Tomlin. However, you aren't limited to available actors or even living ones. To sharpen your vision and awaken your imagination, you may want to think of movie or stage actors, past or present, with particular vocal qualities, physical attributes, or mannerisms that can flesh out the character as you write. Put the actor in the theatre in your head and watch and listen to him or her become the character.

Directors, too, can use that same imaginary mental theatre as they study a play for production. Often you find thinking of a particular actor may help you envision the play more clearly so you can better plan to transform the play from page to stage. Some directors may blend aspects of several actors for just one character, selecting one given actor's vocal qualities and another actor's physical techniques. Your goal is to free and stimulate your imagination to think of flesh and blood, not words in a script. However, although those images help during initial planning, you'll want to be free of them when you hold auditions and during subsequent rehearsals.

For actors, this imaginary casting technique is less helpful. You want to search out original qualities. Acting imitates life, not imitations. Thinking of how a given actor would do your role is a bad idea because you would be imitating someone who might have been imitating yet another actor who was imitating an actor who also had been. . . . Better is to observe real-life humans and to find the character in yourself and yourself in the character.

We've been discussing *imagination*, a way of seeing something new where nothing had existed. Freeing your imagination often can mean deliberately returning to the freshness you had as a child. Recapturing that childlike imagination may require deliberate efforts.

CHILDLIKE IMAGINATION

Every child is an artist. The problem is how to remain an artist once he grows up.

—Pablo Picasso

Konstantin Stanislavsky (1863–1938), the Russian director and actor who formulated our modern approach to acting, urged actors to learn to develop a childlike freshness. *Dream*, he encouraged actors. *Bring forth the child within you so you can use that youthful imagination to invent mental images and experiences*. The same imaginative process is equally important for writers and directors who use fantasies and daydreams in creating a character who is dynamic, alive, and vital.

For playwright, actor, and director, the creative process is like a free-wheeling child's game, playing make-believe, pretending to be a different person, making up a different world, day dreaming adventures, delighting in unrestricted opportunities to play. The uninhibited child's creative spirit ignores the conformist's barriers and relishes freedom to go where it wishes. It cherishes whimsy and craves flights of fancy. The creative process is an expedition into dreams of things that never were.

Creative theatre artists try to recapture the child's freshness of spirit to act out dreams, freely using body, heart, mind, and soul to create a new experience. We take special effort to revive that youthful freedom because too often as we grow up we are taught that we must put childish things behind us so we can "be mature," which leads us to fear that make-believe games somehow are wrong and that daydreaming is a nonprofitable waste of time for people who should be focusing their lives on "adult" business in the real world.

Perhaps the best analogy of the restrictions we develop as we age is the coloring book. As children we used crayons boldly to express our personal feelings, making trees a fiery red, turning houses into fantastic rainbows, splashing colors freely across the page. As we mature, however, we're taught to color tightly. Quite possibly you had a teacher tell you,

"No, no. You must be careful to stay *inside* the lines." Bad advice, inhibiting and rigid. Conforming to such "adult" values of a teacher or parent can be restrictive lessons that inhibit the child's freewheeling creative spirit and, later, the adult's creative instincts. We want to return to that fresh-eyed freedom so we can invent and daydream, in effect coloring trees as we see them or wish they appeared. We encourage ourselves not to submit to other people's rigidity.

Developing Dynamic Characterization

Characters are born of the artist's imagination, sired by the artist's personal experiences, nurtured by a love of adventure. They inherit the artist's sensitive insight into other humans; their genes carry the artist's knowledge of basic motivational drives. From the artist's heart and soul the characters receive genuine emotions and deep involvement in issues.

The creative process avoids stereotypes and instead looks for the unique, the specific qualities that make a character as distinct as a fingerprint. To give the character a dynamic life, look for changes in attitude, emotions, and thoughts. For example, instead of a Sonny who is always menacing, add an apparent friendliness. He can smile, laugh. *Then* he can shift to a threatening attitude. The result is an enhanced dynamic life.

Playwrights, actors, and directors give characters action, individuality, and dimension by emphasizing the character's objectives and reactions to conflicts and obstacles; and they transform characters into believable and credible individuals by establishing a specific environment and social background with character biographies. The artist's intellect chooses how the pieces will fit together, and the artist's vision, theatrical experience, and eagerness to tell a story breathe final life into the characters.

One good place to start developing dimensionality is to identify the character's objective. What does the character most want? What is he or she is compelled to achieve at all costs?

THE CHARACTER'S OBJECTIVE

A character's objective is a total commitment to a present action that will lead to a desired future. In life you see that humans are hardwired to achieve goals, and we enjoy witnessing an individual's struggle to get to a particular destination because in those battles we recognize aspects of our own life struggles. Watch a batter in a major league baseball game, a boxer in a championship fight, or an Olympic ice skater in an international compe-tition: you can feel the raw energy of total dedication and concentration, the compelling absorption to achieve an objective, the complete concen-tration on *this moment* to achieve a future payoff.

The intensity is so powerful that you tense your muscles as the pitch comes to the batter, grunt in pain when the boxer takes a hard right to the chin, or wince sympathetically when the ice skater falls while attempting a difficult jump. You join the crowd roaring approval or groaning disap-pointment. We in the audience respond emotionally, intellectually, and physically to the character in action. No wonder athletic events are so popular: we admire the athlete's absolute focus and dedication, and we're pulled in to participate empathically with the person who is so clearly determined to succeed despite numerous obstacles.

Such dedication is not limited to sports arenas. You see the same focused energy all around you: a young child immersed in a game, a stu-dent taking an important exam, a politician in a vigorous television debate with determined opponents, a painter working on a canvas in the privacy of her studio. A compelling absorption to achieve an objective will create energy full of flashes of lightning.

As in life, so also in theatre we see the effects of that energy: a power-ful actor giving a gripping performance, a director leading a company to fulfill a vision, a designer capturing a new environment. Awareness of the importance of energy helps us strive to achieve it ourselves, just as mon-odramatist Eric Bogosian said he wanted his stage pieces to have the energy of objective-oriented rock-and-roll performers he admired.

Committed Characters

A successfully drawn dimensional theatrical character is as committed to an action as the athlete, painter, or politician. In theatre, however, the action is necessarily enlarged so it can be distilled into a short time span. We don't deal with an entire life but instead with a moment that encap-sulates the significant aspects of that life. For example, a novelist might tell virtually everything of Sonny's life, but theatre is more selective, seek-ing *action* instead of descriptions. Therefore, in *Nice Shoes* Bogosian shows a single selected moment—a moment of action—that encourages the audience to use its imagination to infer details of how and why Sonny became master of his turf.

As playwright Marsha Norman says, the essence of theatre is a character who desperately wants something: theatre is a story of a little boy propelled to action by a consuming passion that attracts the audience. Establishing a character's goal, so strong it actuates him or her to action despite opposition, is one of the most important creative challenges facing playwrights, actors, and directors. It helps make the difference between a stick figure and a dimensional human.

Creating Dimensional Characters

Imagine a simple pencil drawing of a stick figure: head, arms, torso, legs. No color, no environmental surroundings. Bland, uninteresting, flat. Think of that crude drawing as your initial germinal idea of a character. Now imagine turning that figure into a richly dimensional theatrical character.

☐ The character's objective or goal—so strong it defines the internal person and is even a reason for existence—gives that simple figure a hungry purpose, thus adding heart and brain.

☐ An intense drive to achieve that major objective adds bones, sinews, muscles. The character now is animated into energetic actions.

☐ The way the character pursues the objective—especially if he or she has clever devices to overcome setbacks and obstacles—gives the person unique texture, color, vocal qualities, mannerisms. A distinct personality emerges.

☐ The character's reaction to opposition shows what the person is made of, the presence or lack of those inner qualities we might call resilience, persistence, backbone, chutzpah, or grit.

And if the character has no objective? Encounters no opposition? Is not actively engaged in conflict? Then he or she has no reason to change, no reason to use various tactics to overcome obstacles. Only a simple stick figure remains. That's not what you want.

Examples of a Character's Objective

A character's primary objective is the major unifying force in a play. All action stems from that single-minded, dedicated, active pursuit, as you've seen in well-known multicharacter plays. For example, Shakespeare's Hamlet *must* avenge the death of his father; in Tennessee Williams's *The Glass Menagerie*, Amanda Wingfield *must* find security for her fragile daughter, Laura; and in *Death of a Salesman* Arthur Miller's Willy Loman *must* gain respect and love from his son, Biff.

So, too, in monodramas you find that characterization is enhanced by objectives. The solo character's objective propels the action and gives the character life, dimensionality, and vitality. Anna Mae *must* get to McDonald's. April March *must* twirl so she can experience that religious ecstasy. Sonny *must* control Mike.

Secondary Objectives

Primary objectives often cause secondary objectives, which some actors call *intentions*, or a manner of dealing with a new obstacle that threatens the overall objective. Think of these as tactics to achieve the objective. Hamlet, for example, must first ascertain if the Ghost really is his father before pursuing his primary objective of revenging the murder of his father, and he therefore uses the tactic of a "play within the play." To achieve her objective of making secure her daughter Laura's future, Amanda first tries the tactic of getting Tom to accept responsibility for Laura, then she decides only a Gentleman Caller—we almost hear the capital letters in her voice when she speaks about a Husband for Sister—will be able to provide for Laura's future. In solo plays you find comparable intentions. Sonny, for example has a primary objective: to control his turf. To achieve that major goal Sonny has secondary objectives or intentions: to frighten Mike, to force Mike to kneel in homage, and to humiliate Mike by taking his shoes.

Playwrights, actors, and directors find that objectives—whether primary or secondary—are major forms of action because the character's quest for a goal creates a forward motion. These objectives also give the character dimensionality as the character's efforts to achieve the goal show additional aspects of the character.

Clarifying the Objective

In some plays the character knows his or her objective and therefore states it clearly. For example, Herbert Mitgang's Abraham Lincoln knows he *must* take action regarding the slavery issue, and Jane Martin's Anna Mae knows she *must* live at McDonald's. For them, it is a life destination.

In other plays the character may not state the objective specifically, but through action the destination is clear. Eric Bogosian's Sonny *must* prove he is master of his turf and focuses on Mike's shoes to prove the point.

But Sonny never directly states his objective. Does that mean we in the audience are unable to know what he wants? Or are Sonny's actions clear implications of his objective?

Questions that Identify the Character's Objective

Questions can help playwrights, actors, and directors discover and establish the character's objective. You might ask questions such as these:

- ☐ What does my character intensely *want*?
- ☐ Why? What motivational forces drive my character to seek that objective? What emotions move the character?
- ☐ What is my character's stake in the outcome? What will my character lose if he or she doesn't achieve that objective?
- ☐ What is my character willing to do to attain that objective?
- ☐ At what specific points in the play is my character actively working to achieve the objective?
- ☐ What contrary-minded forces stop my character from succeeding?
- ☐ How does my character react to those counterforces?
- ☐ What actions does my character take to overcome these obstacles?
- ☐ Does my character ultimately succeed or fail?

All the examples we've cited deal with a character strongly rooted in the present, deeply committed to a future. Drama is an art about this minute and the next, not yesterday; dramatic action is an avalanche roaring down a mountain toward a town, not a history of a decade of snowfall. Theatrical characters play their objective for the present and future, not the past.

Implicit in the idea of an objective is forward movement to a future, the opposite of looking backward. If the character must refer to the past, theatrical artists know they can't lose forward momentum, so they give those moments a vital sense of the present by making the past directly influence the character now, with implications for the future.

Playing the Objective

Playing the objective means keeping your attention on your character's action. The purpose is for the actor to concentrate on the character, the character's objective, the situation, the action, and the other characters. The playwright creates the character within the framework of that major objective. The director shapes the production around the character's objective.

Marsha Norman's little boy is totally committed to his future and has no interest in his past, Eric Bogosian's Sonny says nothing about his past (although audiences are given enough clues to imagine Sonny's background), and Jane Martin's Anna Mae is focused on moving into McDonald's as soon as possible.

Character Versus Narrator

Some beginning monodramatists make the mistake of thinking of a narrator instead of a character. Most often it isn't a wise choice. The distinction is vital. You want to create a character who cares deeply about his or her dilemma and situation and is now in action to achieve a solution, not a narrator who describes observed qualities. A character has an emotional stake in the story and participates in the events; a narrator remains a distant stickfigure, a dispassionate observer. A character is affected, evolves, and changes; the narrator remains the same throughout. A character lives the story; a narrator is an announcer who reports it.

The Character's Biography

Good characterization is like an iceberg: nine-tenths is hidden under the surface and what we see of a character in a play is only the top one-tenth. The artist's knowledge of the full iceberg, although not put into the monodrama, supports that small percentage that shows above water—the play itself. The analogy is especially pertinent when a playwright or an actor creates a character in a monodrama. Constructing a fully detailed biography will help you know the total person, not merely the stage character, and you'll be better able to create a dimensional and unique individual. The biography should connect with the character's present and future.

Questions can help you know the character better. Ask yourself questions about the character. Where was he or she born and reared? Educational background? Dreams fulfilled and those left hollow and empty? Parents alive or dead? Marriage? Occupations? Economic and social status? Favorite foods, books, colors, recreation, clothing? Politics? Hobbies? Loves? Hates? Vocal and physical mannerisms?

You also can ask yourself what the character does when not in your play. What was he or she doing just before entering? Where does the character go when he or she exits? Think, too, about the character's reactions to stimuli not in your play. For example, what would the character do if arrested for speeding? What would incite him or her to commit murder? Does the character have attractive and playful traits, such as feeding ducks in the park, sending anonymous good-job notes to strangers, or playing ball with neighborhood kids? Write your answers to these and other questions in your monodrama notebook where they can serve as stimuli for additional ideas about the character.

Audience Response to the Character's Objective

Your character's dynamic objective and reactions to conflict and obstacles will increase audience interest in your monodrama. Audiences become involved in the theatrical experience through the psychological phenomenon called *empathy*, intellectually and emotionally feeling in the character's situation. The process is similar to our physical reactions when we flinch as we see a boxer take a hard punch. Empathic responses are stronger when they deal with emotional involvement, such as our feelings while watching a sad love story or a delightful comedy. The character's driving desire to achieve an objective creates suspense that engages the audience's attention.

Empathic responses are most clear with young audiences at theatrical productions as the kids laugh, cry, cheer the hero, or boo the villain. One of theatre's classic moments comes in James M. Barrie's *Peter Pan* when Tinkerbell is dying and Peter asks the audience to applaud if they believe in fairies. The children's noise is almost deafening, a clear example of empathic response. For adults, empathic responses often are more subtle, but nonetheless equally significant, and they may be strongly emotional or intellectual.

DECIDING TO WHOM THE CHARACTER IS SPEAKING

Some monodramatists find that before they can write a monologue they must first answer the question, Why does he or she speak aloud? They try to invent motivation by giving the character a thing to which to talk, resulting in characters having friendly relationships with goldfish, parakeets, plants, or teddy bears. Other popular devices are the telephone or photographs, usually of a dead friend or spouse.

Such devices aren't interesting solutions for most monologues. There's a danger that dolls, teddy bears, parakeets, or comparable objects may appear contrived, distracting from the monologue's examination in depth of a human. Machines such as a telephone may remove some of the humanity from the play and create deadly pauses while the character listens to the other person on the line.

Compelling Characters to Speak

Jon Jory, director of many monodramas (including those written by Jane Martin) at the Actors Theatre of Louisville, believes the successful monodramatist starts with a character who faces an urgent emotion or situation that *forces* him or her to speak. "The monologue often takes place when the character is driven to speak," Jory says. "At the point where the character can no longer contain an emotion, the monologue is born, and the best monologues take place at a moment when the character can no longer remain silent. That gives them the high energy of a key moment in an ordinary play."

With such motivation, the question of why the character speaks becomes less significant. For illustration, audiences aren't apt to wonder why a Hamlet or Macbeth speaks inner thoughts in their soliloquies. Equally, audiences at musical comedies seldom ask why a character exposes personal secrets, illustrated by Adelaide in *Guys and Dolls* when she sings "Adelaide's Lament" or by Polly in *Crazy for You* when she sings "Someone to Watch Over Me." So, too, effective motivation in monodramas such as *Twirler* and *Fires in the Mirror* will eliminate the question.

Speaking to an Unseen Character

To answer the question, To whom does the character speak? you may want to assume that one or more other characters are on stage—of course, invisible and silent. For example, Lanford Wilson's A *Poster of the Cosmos* puts the character in an interrogation room, speaking to police. They aren't visible. They also are mostly silent: Wilson deftly avoids the trap of having the invisible police speak, which would require his character to pause frequently to listen, even restating the question for the audience. Wilson creates a character who is so earnest, so compelled to talk, that the police haven't a chance to interrupt.

Speaking to Self

Characters in monodramas most often speak to themselves. Anna Mae in *French Fries* seems self-reflective. Equally, the character in Beckett's *Krapp's*

Last Tape speaks to himself, although he uses a tape recorder. Each birthday he listens to tape recordings he made during previous birthday celebration and then makes a new one. It is a fascinating character study. In such instances the characters are driven to speak because their emotions have reached such a high pitch that silence is impossible.

Ignore the Question

The solutions given here can be helpful, but you may find that an effective solution is to ignore the question, To whom does the character speak? Simply write your monodrama. Spending too much time finding clever reasons for justifying why the character speaks is like trying to win the Indianapolis 500 by racing in cul-de-sacs: caught in explanatory circles, the playwright just doesn't get anywhere. If your character has strong emotional and mental involvement in his or her situation the To whom does the character speak? question is likely to disappear.

BRINGING OTHER CHARACTERS ON STAGE IMAGINATIVELY

How can I describe [Ruth Draper's] magic, even when she was elderly, alone on an empty stage convincing audiences that they saw not only a procession of characters, men, women, children, and their dogs, but also a variety of rooms, a church in Italy, the porch of a white clapboard house in Maine, a dressmaker's salon in Paris, a Court House in a poor part of New York, the waiting room of a hospital, and the inside of a large chauffeur-driven car in thick traffic, etc. See them is what we did. Producing these phenomena was surely a mammoth exercise in suggestion. . . . Ruth could make you see [invisible] objects as well as people and places. Miming is usually done in silence, as Marcel Marceau does it. Ruth was a hand-mine. She [pantomimed] hairnets, hats and combs; knives, forks and glasses; telephones, buttons and scissors, and so clear was she that there was no possibility of confusing a fork with a spoon. . . . When she cut the big pie to send out to the men on the snowplough in Railway Accident on the Western Plains she used a slicer to put the pieces on to a plate. I swear I saw it. Buzz [an unseen character], the boy who helped in the station buffet, had to carry it out. Before he went she scooped up the crumbs and popped them into his mouth, and when she told him to open wide the audience opened wide too. I remember the taste of those good brown crumbs. —Joyce Grenfell

Among the monodrama's strengths is its intense focus on a single character. But that focus can include others. Your solo character may be involved with one or more other characters, literally unseen but made visible in the audience's imagination, whose actions are powerful direct influences on his or her present and future. As Joyce Grenfell indicates, Ruth Draper's ability made real the imaginary props and characters. Grenfell, herself a solo performer, playwright, and actress, thought Draper's pantomimic skills made the pie crumbs so real she still remembers even tasting them.

To cite another example, Jane Martin's *Clear Glass Marbles* first focuses on a young girl who is attempting to cope with the death of her mother, but soon the invisible mother becomes a vital participant in the action through the girl's descriptions, and by the end of the play the audience members feel they know the mother at least as well as they know the girl. Wilson's *A Poster of the Cosmos* also has that double focus, stimulating the audience's imagination to know the absent friend. Even though only one character is visible, such monodramas take on some of the texture of multicharacter plays.

Adding Other Characters

English actress Joyce Grenfell, who wrote a number of monodrama programs for herself to perform on tour in the 1960s and 1970s, credits her success to Ruth Draper (described earlier as a major influence on the modern monodrama). Grenfell, like Draper, seemed to be able to fill her stage with other people. For example, her comic monodrama, *George—Don't Do That*, contains six short "Nursery School Sketches" that operate on the premise that the solo character is a teacher in a roomful of young—and hyperactive—children. In *Free Activity Period*, one selection from that collection, the teacher has an undying, cheerful, and quite desperate energy. The following passage starts with the beginning of the monodrama. Spelling and punctuation are Grenfell's. Italics indicate the teacher's speeches to a Mrs. Hingle, who has just entered. Note how Grenfell crafts the teacher's response to each child to encourage us to imagine what the youngsters are doing. As you read the script, see the production imaginatively in the theatre in your head. Actors may wish to read it aloud, performing the role of the desperate teacher.

FREE ACTIVITY PERIOD
FROM GEORGE—DON'T DO THAT
by Joyce Grenfell

Oh, hello, Mrs Hingle. I'm so glad you could come along. As you see, we're just having a Free Activity Period, and in our Free Activity Period each little individ-

ual chooses his or her own occupation. Some are painting, some are using plasticine, and some work at a sand-table. We feel that each little one must get to the bottom of his or her self and find out what he really wants of life.

Who is making that buzzing noise?

Well, stop it please, Neville.

Hazel, dear, come away from the door and get on with your plasticine.

I love to see them so happily occupied, each one expressing his little personality . . .

George—don't do that . . .

Now, children, I want you all to say 'Good morning' to Mrs Hingle. Good morning, Mrs Hingle.

No, Sidney, not good-bye. Mrs Hingle has only just come. You don't want her to go away yet?

No, she hasn't got a funny hat on, that's her hair.

So sorry, Mrs Hingle. Sometimes we ARE just a trifle outspoken. We try to encourage honesty, only sometimes it doesn't always . . .

And this is my friend Caroline, and Caroline is painting such a lovely red picture, aren't you, Caroline? I wonder what it is? Perhaps it's a lovely red sunset, is it? Or a big red orange?

It's a picture of Mummy! For a moment I thought it was a big red orange, but now you tell me, I can see it is a picture of Mummy. Aren't you going to give her any nose?

No nose.

It's so interesting the way they see things.

Sidney, don't blow at Edgar, please.

I know I said you could choose what you are going to do, but you cannot choose to blow at Edgar.

Because it isn't a good idea.

Yes, I know it makes his hair go up and down, but I don't want you to do it. Now get back to the sand table, there's a good boy.

Yes, there is room, Sue; there's heaps of room. Just move up a bit.

Susan! We *never* bite our friends.

Say you are sorry to Sidney. You needn't kiss him.

No, you needn't hug him, Susan, PUT HIM DOWN.

No fisticuffs, please.

She hasn't made any teeth marks, has she, Sidney?

Sometimes our little egos are on the big side, I'm afraid . . .

Hazel, dear, I don't want to have to say it again: please come away from the door.

Why can't you?

Well, you shouldn't have put your finger in the keyhole, and then it wouldn't have got stuck.[1]

The scene continues with Sidney also getting his finger stuck in the keyhole of the door. The teacher sends Mrs. Hingle off to call the fire brigade and returns to face the children with the same bright forced smile.

Performing Multiple (Unseen) Characters

Just as you can evoke the presence of other characters, so you can have other characters "speak." Instead of having the solo character report a conversation (which tends to tell instead of show), you may want to create dialogue, using the actor's talents to imitate other voices. For example, assume your character needs to report something such as a mother's lecture about sex and love. You could simply write:

JILLY: I remember how cold my mother was, how unromantic, how she told me there was no such thing as love.

Such direct statements may make clear Jilly's feelings about her mother, but revisions can make the effect stronger and less like a narrator. Imagine, for example, bringing the mother on stage through dialogue:

JILLY

(*Wryly; shaking her head.*)

Mother. Her monthly mother-daughter sessions.
  (*Her mother's voice; brisk, matter of fact.*)
Chemistry, Jilly. That's all. Hormonal chemistry. What you're thinking is "love" is merely the instinct of the species to perpetuate itself.
  (*Herself; much younger; to her mother.*)
But, Mom, when I'm with him I feel like—like he completes me, like without him I'm—only one half of a pair of scissors! Didn't you feel that way with Dad?

(*The mother.*)

Testosterone. Estrogen. Bulls and cows, Jilly. It is all simply pheromones. Humans must be more than animals in a state of rut. Rise up. Don't let hormonal chemistry dictate your life.

(*Herself; the present.*)

Thanks a helluva lot, Mom. Goodbye love/dove, moon/spoon. Hallmark would've loved your Valentine's Day cards. So with your words ringing in my ears, what am I going to do with Mark tonight? Tell him I'm bored because it all is just chemistry?

This sort of dialogue between the solo character and influential characters can spark your play. Note the advantages such dialogue offers. It changes the past tense reference ("Mother used to tell me . . .") to the present tense, introduces conflict, shows the mother-daughter relationship instead of telling, transforms the sound of the monodrama from a single voice to multiple voices (Jilly today, younger Jilly, the mother), lets the audience know the character's name (the mother calls her "Jilly"), and encourages the audience to imagine the mother's influence on Jilly's childhood. With dialogue, the mother becomes a character we can recognize; if merely described, however, there's less chance she'll come to life. Note that the dialogue also suggests Jilly's future complication with Mark. A monodramatist continuing the scene might bring in Mark's voice.

Example of Dialogue in a Monodrama

In *Einstein: A Stage Portrait*, a full-length solo play, playwright Willard Simms could have written a speech in which Einstein says, "No one believed my theories." Instead, Simms has the actor *become* the characters who are doubters.

FROM EINSTEIN: A STAGE PORTRAIT
by Willard Simms

(*He steps back and becomes an older man, asking Albert a question.*)

"What caused you to believe that light rays do not travel in a straight line, Herr Einstein, but are affected by the force of gravity?"

(*He becomes himself, modestly answering the question put to him.*)

Well, Herr Professor, I simply imagined that this must be so, and set out to prove it.

> (*Steps back, takes on a rigid posture, and a Prussian accent.*)
>
> "My dear Herr Einstein, is it not true that most of your theories are based on mere speculation? For instance, whatever led you to believe that photons exist in light rays?"
>
> (*He becomes himself, annoyed at the way the question was put to him.*)
>
> (*Mockingly*). My dear sir, whatever led you to believe that they do not?[2]

Simms *shows* the questions that Einstein faced, instead of *telling* the audience that many doubted his theories. The device also enlivens the script, gives the actor an interesting challenge, and reduces the effect of a single voice throughout the play.

THE MAGIC IF

Children constantly play the game of "What if . . . ?" *What if I were King Arthur . . . ?* or *What if I could talk with animals . . . ?* That What if? game can help you create theatre. For example, Stanislavsky describes the "magic if" as an act of *transformation* for the actor: "What if I were in Sonny's situation, would what I do?" (Note that the question is not "What if I were Sonny . . . ?" because that decreases characterization and reduces the sense of reality by focusing the actor more on self and less on character, objective, obstacles, and situation.) Such questions give insightful keys to the character's objective, make the situation more concrete and vivid, and guide playwrights, actors, and directors to find ways to bring the character to life.

One of the actor's major techniques, the magic-if approach is equally helpful for playwrights and directors. For instance, consider one basic question: "What if I were in Sonny's environment, feeling compelled to prove that I am master of my turf? How would I show that, what actions would I take, what would I say?"

For the playwright, responses to those questions make the monodrama almost write itself: *To show Sonny's need to be in control, I'll bring in an innocent stranger so Sonny has an opportunity to dominate an outsider invading his territory.* For the actor, the answers indicate variations in Sonny's attitude, voice, and physicalization. For the director, responses to these questions lead to a visualization of the environment, blocking, gestures, and costumes that show Sonny's character.

ENHANCING CHARACTERIZATION

(After writing several plays), I read Charles Dickens's Our Mutual Friend. *(Characters in my other plays) seemed pale and quaint compared to Dickens. I knew I had to goose my work. I knew I had to have characters who were more far-out. Your characters have to have some magic.* —Lanford Wilson

As playwright, actor, or director, you may want to think of developing characters who have distinctly unusual or even eccentric qualities that make them colorful and, therefore, appealing to the audience. The trick is to think of quirky characters—"more far-out," as Lanford Wilson says—who are nonetheless grounded in a basic life-like reality. That will help you ensure eccentric behavior that is part of a believable overall consistency, in contrast to characters who are simply so strange or weird that they have no connection with real humans and therefore lack credibility.

Avoiding "Typical" Characters

"The average coed." "The typical money-grubbing businessperson." "Your run-of-the-mill drug addict." Surely such characters lack vitality and freshness. Instead of stereotypical characters, think of distinctly individual humans who are *different*, with unusual personalities and dreams. In the monodramas you read in earlier chapters you saw the advantage of distinctive characters—an elderly lady who dreams of living in a fast food restaurant, a man who insists he is a normal "kinna guy" but has a unique reaction to his friend's illness and death—whose particular qualities make them memorable humans. They would be less effective if they were stereotypes.

Drawing Colorful and Eccentric Characters: Tracey Ullman

Actress, singer, dancer, and writer Tracey Ullman well illustrates the effect of creating vivid eccentric characterization. She is perhaps best known to television viewers through her *Tracey Ullman Show* and the *Tracey Takes On* series. For her TV work she has received five Emmy Awards from the Academy of Television Arts and Sciences. The multitalented performer also has appeared in movies, such as Woody Allen's *Bullets Over Broadway*; and on stage in productions, such as *Four in a Million*, for which she won the London Theatre Critics Award; and she has made record albums, including "Forever" and "You Broke My Heart in Five Places." In the New York Shakespeare Festival's production of *The Taming of the Shrew* Ullman starred opposite Morgan Freeman. On Broadway she was the solo performer in the one-woman show, *The Big Love*, by playwright Jay Presson Allen.

Ullman specializes in colorful characters, male or female, young or old, of various nationalities, and with differing economic and educational status. She is able to radically change her appearance as she plays the characters, easily adapting different voices and physical mannerisms. In her television shows some characters are instantly recognizable, such as Her Royal Highness, who bears an remarkable resemblance to British royalty and manages to insult everyone. Many are interesting in themselves but have added twists. For example, Chic is a male New York City cab driver who keeps a Thigh Master in the backseat for his clients, and Mrs. Noh Nang Ning owns a doughnut shop and manages to relate all aspects of life to doughnuts. Also in Ullman's repertoire are a right-wing housewife from North Carolina, a has-been actress in Los Angeles, an ever-so-innocent born-again Christian, and a 70-year-old former movie makeup artist whose shell-shocked son lives with her.

IMPROVISATIONS

Think of improvisations—improvs, in theatrical shorthand—as What if? questions that are transformed into physical activities to stimulate imagination, bring new insights into the character, and offer freedom to experiment and make choices. In this sense improvs are similar to the child's make-believe games, helping you remove inhibitions. An improv can consist of dialogue and pantomime, with no particular predetermined plan, that frees the actor's creative instincts. They are exercises to increase consciousness of the role, and they aren't intended for audiences (with the exception of Improvisational Theatre productions that call for interplay between actors and audience so they collaborate in creating characters and situations).

Improvisations may be private exercises designed to open one's mind to possible dramatic actions, complete in themselves without a planned use for a production. They also may be rehearsal techniques that the playwright, actor, and director use to enhance an existing script that will be produced. Typical improvisations start with a given scenario, to which are added invented actions and dialogue that are in keeping with the specific character, similar to the embellishments of *commedia dell'arte* performers of the sixteenth and seventeenth centuries.

Examples of Improvisational Exercises

Imagine you are acting in or directing Jane Martin's *French Fries*. Director and actress might find insight into Anna Mae by working improvs based on her activities before the play begins. One might put Anna Mae in conflict with selected friends or relatives not described in the script, seeking to discover her relationships with others. For example, perhaps you might invent an improv as a relative wants Anna Mae to move into a nursing home. A second improv might have her standing outside McDonald's, debating whether to enter. A third could show her reactions to people in a grocery or department store or perhaps show what happens when she asks people for help because she is lost and can't find McDonald's. Yet another might put her in conflict with Jimmy, who wants her to leave; and another could show her trying to get the man with "Cerebral Walrus" to come into the place despite his objections. Through such exercises, actor and director explore Anna Mae's personality, learning more about her so the script Anna Mae will have more texture and dimension.

THE W QUESTIONS:
GIVEN CIRCUMSTANCES AND MOTIVATIONAL DRIVES

Journalists are trained to ask who, what, where, when, why, and how. These questions lead to accurate and complete news stories. Playwrights, actors, and directors also seek answers to similar questions to develop dimensional characters. These questions connect directly to What if? questions and improvisations.

Dividing the W questions into two categories can help you see more aspects of the character. Questions about outer circumstances tend to be objective; driving motivation questions focus more on the inner character. Note the subjective answers to the questions: instead of saying "the character" thinks this or feels that, you put yourself into the character by responding "I."

Characterization Through W Questions

Part I: My Outer Circumstances

☐ *Who* am I? Think of a complete biography. How old am I? What is my history: education, employment, travel, physical aspects (height, weight, color hair, etc.), clothing preferences, and marital, economic, and social status? What are my inner aspects such as emotional qualities, self-image? What are my private fantasies and dreams, and how do I respond to the successes or failures of those dreams?

☐ *Where* am I? Am I in a small town or large? What region of the country? How do those environmental conditions influence my behavior? Do I own or rent this place? Did I decorate it? What do I see when I look around? What is my response to what I see? Do I enter the room confidently or shyly? What do I find when I leave this environment and go into the (offstage) world? How am I influenced by those surroundings?

☐ *When* is it? What year, season, month, time of day? How does the time influence me?

☐ *What* objects do I use (such as a cane, a hearing aid, an imaginary billiard cue, my vest or suspenders, etc.)?

☐ *Who* are the people who influence me? What are those influences? How do I feel about each of them?

Part II: *My Driving Motivations*

☐ *What* do I want? What do I *need*, must have all at costs? What is my general, abstract goal (such as to be happy)? What is my specific, concrete goal (i.e., I must marry Juliet immediately)?

☐ *When* do I want that goal?

☐ *Why* do I want it? Why is it important? How do I feel about what I want? What is my emotional investment?

☐ *What* do I lose if I don't achieve my goal? What's at stake?

☐ *What* obstacles prevent me from getting what I want? What are my intellectual and emotional responses to those obstacles?

☐ *What* am I going to do to achieve my goal?

☐ *What* are my specific mannerisms? What is my characteristic gesture (also called *psychologic gesture*)? What animal image applies to me? How do I use my body (quick movements or slow, graceful, still, awkward, etc.)?

☐ *Who* is the person most directly involved in what I want? What are my emotional and intellectual attitudes toward that person?

EXERCISES

1. Select two of characters described here and invent two different objectives for each (a total of four objectives). Phrase each objective with active verbs, using first-person singular (i.e., I want to. . . .), emphasizing the present and the future. Think of What if? questions to help you. Make a conscious choice between comic or dramatic treatment. Write your responses and keep them in your notebook.

   a. A college freshman. Forlorn, lonely, bewildered by all of the new experiences, baffled by professors, distrusts roommate.

   b. A high school nominee for a major social honor. The election is in two days.

   c. A young person. Virginal, facing heavy peer pressure to become sexually active. For many years has been dating the same person.

   d. A salesperson, office employee, or blue-collar worker. Late forties. Rumor is that the company soon will announce it must reduce its work force and identify those fired.

   e. An elderly person, seventies. All family members live in distant states. No friends nearby. It is Christmas Eve.

   f. A hiker. Inexperienced. Mid- to late twenties. At a campsite on a mountain or other remote trail. Expected to rendezvous here with a partner who is much more experienced and knows the area. The partner is late. It is dusk.

   If none of these awaken your interest, create your own brief exercise.

2. Describe in detail basic information about each of the four characters from the preceding exercise.

   a. What motivates each character?

   b. What is each character doing to achieve the objective?

   c. What conflict and obstacles does each character face?

3. Change the gender, age, and occupation of any one of the four characters, and shift your approach from comic to dramatic or dramatic to comic. Repeat Exercises 1 and 2 for this new character.

4. Select one of the characters and prepare a detailed character biography. Think of the W questions.

5. Do an improvisational exercise about that character facing *one* obstacle. Repeat the process, doing another improv about the character facing a second obstacle.

Actor Julie Harris describes her creation of Emily Dickinson in William Luce's full-length monodrama, *The Belle of Amherst*, for which she won a Tony Award:

I identified so strongly with that part. I read a lot of her biographies and when I read one of her poems at a benefit at the Booth Theatre in New York, director Charles Nelson Reilly said, "My God, that's exciting!" and we started that eight-year journey to bring Emily to life on the stage. . . . I had to learn seventy-five pages before rehearsals. I had someone come twice a week for about two months to test me. Studying for hours every day for eight weeks, raging, cueing, adjusting, digesting those words. You've got to chew them and chew them and chew them. I'd go to sleep not knowing them and miraculously wake up having them. You have to have the lines down pat to have freedom to rehearse the play. It's like being a musician, knowing the score. It frees you. Instead of me taking the play over I allow it to pull me along. I think acting should be discovery. You go through all those rehearsals then throw everything out the window and rediscover it all over again with an audience. Their energy gives you the answers. —Julie Harris

NOTES

1. Joyce Grenfell, *George—Don't Do That* (London: Macmillan, 1977), 39–43.
2. Willard Simms, *Einstein: A Stage Portrait* (Woodstock, IL, n.d.), 25.

7

CHAPTER

Constructing Plot with Character Objective

A play is an arrangement of the words of characters to tell a story. A play is nothing but characters in action. [*Emphasis mine.*] *There is nothing in a play but the characters. Every word that is uttered is uttered by a character. I labour this point because it's strikingly different in this respect from any other form of literature.* —Simon Callow

THE PLAYWRIGHT, ACTOR, AND DIRECTOR CONSTRUCT THE THEATRE experience with the *character in action*. For many of us, chararacters are an essence of a successful play because we have indelible memories of compelling characters we've met as a member of the audience. We treasure productions that allowed us to get to know intimately such classic characters as Shakespeare's Hamlet or Romeo and Juliet, Blanche DeBois from Tennessee Williams's A *Streetcar Named Desire*, or John and Elizabeth Proctor from Arthur Miller's The *Crucible*.

Undoubtedly you can add to this list your own favorite characters who, although fictional, have dimensions of real-life humans, so real that you'd not be surprised to meet them one day. You recognize their qualities, either in others or in yourself. Director Tyrone Guthrie took special delight in pointing out that in the British libraries one of the three most frequently requested biographies is of a *theatrical* character: Hamlet. (The other two, he reports, are Jesus Christ and Napoleon Bonaparte.) Real-life, indeed.

Such characters are as memorable as our parents or close friends. We readily identify with their needs and dreams, their emotions and thoughts, their responses to personal crises and dilemmas, and most especially their *actions* that define their inner beings. What makes Hamlet so intriguing is what we learn about him through his struggles, his reactions to the conflicts he faces, his changes—all through his actions. Therefore, we would agree with Simon Callow—whose experience with solo plays includes both acting and directing—who emphasizes, "A play is nothing but characters in action."

You saw examples of characters' actions in monodramas you read in previous chapters. You noticed that in those plays the theatrical action centers on a character mentally and emotionally committed to achieve an objective. Those monodramas showed you that because something vital is at stake, the character is motivated to action.

Those solo plays also showed that the character becomes dynamic when thrust into a *dramatic situation*, a tension built with the ever-present possibility of victory or defeat. The situation makes a razor's edge suspense: Will the character achieve or lose that important goal? Conflict—obstacles, reversals, discoveries, and complications—increases the tension. What will he or she do now? Conflict also stimulates the character to action, and he or she becomes more dimensional, interesting, thoughtful, and emotional in response to each new crisis. *The structure of the character's actions and of the tensions of the dramatic situation is plot.*

In this chapter we explore aspects of plot, looking at techniques that playwrights, directors, and actors can use to bring solo plays to life on stage. We marry plot to the character's motivated actions.

PLOT: THE STRUCTURE OF THE CHARACTER'S ACTIONS

. . . any character which a writer creates, or supposedly creates—puts down on paper, at any rate—is an amalgam of people and attitudes seen, a distortion of those people and attitudes, plus a certain amount of invention to put them into a situation. [*Emphasis mine.*]

—Edward Albee

One way to seek answers to just what is a play is to divide a play into components and examine each individually. One such division has remained with us for centuries: the traditional Aristotelian *six elements of a play*. In brief, the six elements are as follows:

☐ *Plot*, the structure of action. For Aristotle, plot ranks as the single most important element.

- [ ] *Character*, the people of the play.

- [ ] *Thought*, the play's meaning as shown by characters and action.

- [ ] *Dialogue*, what and how the character speaks. This category should also include subtext, the silent meanings beneath spoken dialogue.

- [ ] *Music*, musical instruments, sound effects, the actors' voices—all the sounds from the stage.

- [ ] *Spectacle*, all visual aspects of the production.

That standard approach is quite helpful for playwrights as they create and revise their plays, and it provides directors and actors a potent analytical tool to more effectively transform the play from page to stage.[1]

Instead of isolating plot to discuss it by itself like a solitary, lonely entity, however, here we unify all six elements with a basic organic concept: *a play is character in action*. Our premise is that a theatrical work shows the character's driving need to get something he or she must achieve at all costs while struggling against counterforces that would deny that goal. For multicharacter play or monodrama, comedy or tragedy, traditional or avant-garde, full-length or short-short script, *plot is the structure of the character's struggle to achieve an objective while confronting contrary-minded opposition, obstacles, and setbacks*. Whether you are playwright, actor, or director, that struggle unifies the major aspects of your monodrama—its meaning, characterization, situation, conflict, tensions, structure, language, sounds, and visual aspects on stage.

> Imagine a play is a human body. Plot is the skeleton on which all else is built; subject and theme make up the brain; emotional yearnings and dreams are the heart; and the character's action to achieve an objective is the sinew and muscle. Together the parts merge and interact to become a single living, active, vital theatrical work of art.

Plot: Action for the Theatre

Playwrights, actors, and directors share a significant common goal: to create action on the stage for an audience. For us in theatre, *action* doesn't mean *activity*, such as a movie's chase sequences (often so similar except for the vehicle: horse, car, or spaceship) or the actor's movements around the stage. In contrast to that sort of physical activity, *theatrical action* describes two compelling forms of dramatic energy which are closely married:

☐ The character's efforts to achieve an objective, which motivates psychological, emotional, intellectual, and attitudinal dynamic changes; and

☐ The designed movements of the plot, which put obstacles in the character's path, creating a pattern of increasing tensions and suspense.

These two forms of energy combine to make a vigorous organism for the stage, a river that carries us through rapids and whirlpools along a tightly controlled channel leading to an ultimate destination. Theatrical action is the "situation" that playwright Edward Albee mentions here, a growing torrent that threatens to ensnare the character. Without action, the character is static, simply a stationary boulder by the side of that river: no changes, no thought, no emotion, and therefore no drama and no theatrical experience.

Theatre as Action

Our vocabulary gives us clues to the significant essence of theatre. Three classical Greek words describe theatre as action: *drâ(n)*, "to do," *drâma*, a "deed" or "stage action of a play," and *the'âtron*, a "field of action" or a "seeing place," the root of our word theatre.

Plot: What Happens in a Play

One way to think of plot is the events in motion. For example, imagine you're telling a friend about a play or movie you saw. Possibly you'd say something like this: "Here's what happened. The character wanted this, so she started to do these things, but this guy stopped her, and therefore she decided to do this to outsmart him, but he got in her way again, and so she. . . ." This choice of a particular construction and ordering of significant events is plot. *But* indicates conflicts and opposition that interfere with the character's desires; *so* and *therefore* suggest a logically interconnected *building action*. For theatrical action we think of a rising crescendo, each new movement larger and more vital than preceding ones.

You construct your monodrama by organizing the order of what happens as the character tries to achieve an objective but encounters opposition. You design a situation to pit the character's desire against counterforce, building a series of stimuli and responses. These cause the character to change, to invent new tactics to overcome each new opposing force.

The idea of a play*wright* ("playwrite" is an incorrect spelling) is most relevant when we talk about structuring a play. "Wright" resonates with an old-world concern for impeccable crafting and pride in careful construction, like a clockwright, wheelwright, or a shipwright. The spelling reminds us that plays are *built*, brick upon brick of action.

> A plot's structure is your selection and arrangement of building actions that illustrate the character's hungers, move the character toward his or her objective, and create complications and obstacles that stimulate the character to respond.

The *wright* suffix is equally applicable for actor and director, who in this sense might be called "act-wrights" and "direct-wrights" because their artistic contributions to a play require careful construction of sequences of character action. The playwright constructs a framework of increasing tensions; the actor shows the character's objective and evolution while responding to conflicts; the director guides the actor to show that objective and uses the stage to display actions and conflicts. *Action* is the key in all instances.

For effective theatre, the character's objective is playable, action- and outer-directed, happening now, moving toward an achievable destination, and stated in active verbs. For example, a president is deeply committed to ending slavery, a young tough is determined to protect his turf, an elderly woman is convinced that her survival demands that she live in a fast-food restaurant, a famed scientist has convictions that help him overcome objections of other scientists, or a teacher in a chaotic classroom is desperately (and futilely) trying to control a gaggle of kids while pretending to be calmly in control.

As you've seen, the character's objective by itself is not enough to create dramatic action. The objective is one-half of a pair of scissors. The other half is built with *conflict*. Together they make theatrical action.

CONFLICT

The structure of a play is always the story of how the birds came home to roost.

—Arthur Miller

You'll recall that in the last chapter we quoted Marsha Norman, author of such plays as 'night, Mother, Getting Out, and The Traveler: "I am convinced that there are absolutely unbreakable rules in the theatre, and that it doesn't matter how good you are, you can't break them." Whether you write, act, or direct, one such rule is often stated baldly: *effective theatre follows the law of conflict.*

Although the phrase may sound dictatorial, it is based on sound understanding of the dramatic experience. Experienced playwrights, actors, and directors tell us that drama consists of force against force, one character's powerful need to achieve a goal while opposed by an equally strong counterforce. A play without conflict's clashes is nondramatic, static, and uninteresting, because a character who faces no opposition will simply achieve his or her goal. The character wouldn't have reason to adapt dynamically to changing circumstances.

Types of Conflict

Conflict is easiest to describe using analogies from sports. A boxing match. A football game. An Olympic contest. In such cases, our attention is excited by the clash of forces. The question of Who will win? captivates us. Necessarily, to be effective the conflict has to be *equal*—if one opponent is superior to the other, there's little clash or suspense.

In theatre, however, the conflict isn't likely to be physical. For us, conflict is psychological, human will and determination struggling against human will and determination. That struggle can take on various forms. Most often you'll use some variation of types of conflict listed below:

☐ One character against another. This structure is found in most plays.

☐ One character against many.

☐ A group of characters against another group.

☐ A character standing against an idea—say, a social, political, or religious view. The stand most often is implied by the action. A possible variation might show the character living that idea, encouraging the audience to supply the conflict by disagreeing with that stand.

☐ A character versus his or her environment, lifestyle, or condition.

☐ A character against self. Internalized conflict, a vital decision between two opposing choices, is found in many solo plays.

☐ Combinations of the above.

As you have seen from the examples you've read, the monodrama incorporates variations of these forms of conflict. For instance, Martin's *French Fries* pits Anna Mae against her situation and environment, and possibly we might find additional conflict between her and management at McDonald's. Her *Twirler* brings in a form of religion we in the audience find disturbing, encouraging us to supply much of the conflict as we worry about the influence of cults. Wilson's A *Poster of the Cosmos* has a surface conflict that pits Tom against the cops, which makes us sense the broader social conflict about society's view of AIDS victims. Smith's *Fires in the Mirror* focuses on individuals involved in major social conflict caused by forms of discrimination.

> Playwright, actor, and director create dynamic characterization with conflict. Questions help the creative process:
> ☐ What force stands in my character's way?
> ☐ Why?
> ☐ What actions will my character take to overcome that force?
> ☐ What are my character's emotional and mental responses to the stimuli from obstacles he or she encounters?

CONFLICT IN MONODRAMAS

Conflict may appear relatively easy to structure in multicharacter plays with one character's force of purpose clashing with another's. Clearly, for example, Hamlet's objective is opposed by Claudius, Romeo and Juliet must battle the Capulets and Montagues. Some monodramatists look at such plays and defeat themselves by concluding that conflict isn't possible in a one-person play because there is only one character, hence only one force. That negative conclusion is counterproductive if you want to create an active, dramatic monodrama.

Let the examples of conflict you've seen help you start with the belief that conflict *is* possible—and desirable—in the solo play. You can design conflict into your monodrama by showing your solo character facing diametrically opposed choices, struggling to achieve a goal that is denied by another person, or a group, or the character's own self.

Consider, for example, theatrical action in one of our generation's more significant solo plays: *Krapp's Last Tape* by Samuel Beckett. Its structure suggests one model you may wish to adapt in your monodrama.

You'll note that in many ways it resembles a soliloquy such as Hamlet's "To be or not to be" in that the play's basic conflict is internalized, based within the character facing choices.

This insightful monodrama about a human's personal goals and standards illustrates plot's *but* and *therefore* structure. Krapp is an aging male who once dreamed of being a successful writer and having a successful relationship with a woman he loved, or—we may not be quite sure—perhaps thought he loved. Those youthful dreams never were fulfilled. Krapp, like many Beckett characters, is deeply introspective; he records his thoughts and dreams. He does not simply talk about his past or write his thoughts and discoveries in a diary, which would not be effective theatre. Instead, Beckett cleverly has Krapp use a recorder to play tapes from previous years, in effect bringing a number of different Krapps to life.

The *but–so* action structure starts with the character's objective. Each birthday Krapp (a) is compelled to participate in an annual ritual of self-discovery, so (b) he listens to a tape from previous years' rituals, but (c) the tape forces him to face deeply distressing insights, and therefore (d) he turns off the tape and broods (in Beckett's plays, brooding and thinking are major actions), so (e) he returns to the tapes with new understandings, but (f) as he listens he discovers yet new insights. He repeats the process with increasing intensity.

The tape recordings give Beckett's solo play an effect of multiple characters. Beckett cagily crafts conflict into the play—younger Krapp versus the older man he is now, healthy youth versus growingly infirm present, past optimism versus present pessimism, idealized dreams he once had versus growing awareness of a hollow existence in the present.

Using Conflict to Generate a Dramatic Situation and Dimensional Characterization

Bogosian's *Nice Shoes* burns with a specific conflict that pits one man against another and implies a larger violence. To see the effect of that structure, imagine the play without conflict but with the same premise: Sonny's objective is to be master of his turf. In this imaginary version, however, no one challenges Sonny. Now there's no appearance of a Mike—a stranger who doesn't know he's invading Sonny's territory and doesn't know he is supposed to behave like a humble vassal to the Lord of the Street. All we would have is Sonny and his buddies on the street corner. Now what? What would they do? Talk? That's hardly action. Because he's not challenged, there'd be no motivations for Sonny to change. Bogosian's monodrama would be dully bland, perhaps consisting merely of long, didactic speeches that would talk about violence instead of showing it. So let's throw away the imaginary version and return to the play as Bogosian wrote it: conflict between Sonny and Mike shows Sonny's fascinating menace, a cobra weaving back and forth hypnotically to capture his victim.

Conflict and Characterization. For the playwright, actor, and director, conflict gives the solo character active, forward-moving qualities. A character who struggles against opposing forces will have to change as he or she reacts to obstacles, problems, and opposition. Those dynamic changes make the character more dimensional by showing the character's strength of purpose or weakness of will.

Conflict and the Play's Meaning. Conflict also makes clear the play's thought, its intellectual meaning. What Sonny does is a statement about street violence. For theatre, meaning is more inherent in the ebb and flow of action than in specific or even didactic speeches. Playwright, actor, and director use conflict in *Nice Shoes* to lead the audience to think about significant social problems.

Conflict for Comic Monodramas

Conflict is a vital aspect of comedy. Often the basic situation is exaggerated—extravagantly, for farces; more logically, for subtle comedies. For example, *The Break-Up Diet*, a delightful comic monodrama by Sherry Adams, is structured around a girl's conflicts as she tries to decide what action to take to restore her love life. The previous night while at a fancy restaurant she had broken up with her boyfriend (the play's *inciting incident*, a major event that happens before the play begins) over what she now admits was merely an inconsequential misunderstanding. She had capped the fight by dumping a plate of food over his head.

Now, the next morning, she is weepy-eyed as she wanders in her night-clothes, trying to cope with the problem. Will he phone her? If he does, should she coldly reject him or invite him to come over immediately so she can forgive him? Should she call him? If so, will she have to ask his forgiveness? What if she's convinced that he caused the problem? Should she decide he's not Mr. Right? But what can she do without him? If he doesn't phone, should she call him? For relief, she turns on the radio but—Oh, no!—it plays a Barry Manilow love song.

The phone rings and she runs to it with delight, ready to tell Mr. Right she will accept his apology. The calls—as of course you can guess—aren't from him. They are from friends, her mother, and so forth. Each call is a *complication*, a structural element that changes the course of the action, making the character respond, first full of hope when she thinks it is him, then despondently when she finds out it is someone else.

During the monodrama the girl comforts herself by eating amazing quantities of chocolates, chips, twinkies, pastries, and gooey junk foods, hence the play's title. The play's conflict gives the character interesting dimensions; exaggerated conflict makes the play a delightful comedy. For actress and director, the conflict invites numerous opportunities for rich characterization and stage movement.

Conflict in Dramatic Monodramas

Conflict makes Bonnie McDonald's *Help*! an intensely dramatic monodrama. The play examines the plight of a young boy who has been sexually abused by his older brother. When the monodrama begins, the young boy is holding a bottle of pills, trying to decide if he'll take them or not. He is facing unacceptable choices—between living a life with continued abuse he can't endure versus committing suicide. If he does nothing, his older brother will again abuse him.

During the play he experiences a number of related choices (each a *complication*). Shall he tell his parents? No, they won't believe him. Worse, if they believe him, that will destroy their love for the older son and he can't bear that. Can he seek help from a school counselor? No, he can't trust others. Perhaps he can confide in a friend? No, he is frightened that his friends at school somehow recognize what is happening with his brother. Do they conclude that he is an unacceptable human? Probably they do: that's why they've teased him in the gym. So he can't go back to school.

The young boy's major internal conflict is assignment of guilt: His brother is such an outstanding guy that the boy can't condemn him, which makes him conclude he must be at fault himself. He cannot escape the question of who is actually responsible for the sexual molestation, his brother or himself? The play ends as it began, with the boy holding the bottle of pills, trying to decide. The conflict creates a moving, insightful, intensely emotional dramatic monodrama. For actor and director, the internal conflict allows an intense portrayal of the young boy's dilemma.

Monodramas with Little or No Conflict

Conflict is essential for effective multicharacter one-act and full-length plays, but some monodramas make their own rules, succeeding with little or no visible direct conflict and instead depending on enhanced characterization, language, and theme. The short-short *character sketch*, for example, may sometimes succeed without conflict, providing it has quite rich characterization and powerful language.

Even so, an implied conflict is often present in most such plays. For example, Martin's *French Fries* depends more on its rich characterization and ironic statement than on visible conflict, but nonetheless there is also an implied indirect conflict of the old woman's desires versus contemporary social values. Certainly there is a conflict between the old woman's goal versus the implied standards of the McDonald's management. Will they let her live there? Not likely. The conflict is real, although not expressed directly.

You may want to think of conflict as a structure of component parts. Playwrights, actors, and directors designing conflict will use obstacles, complications, and action units.

OBSTACLES AND COMPLICATIONS

I love obstacles because on the simplest level you have to achieve those certain things as an actor because they're there, they're written in. But now you try to put everything in the way of achieving what you must achieve and you frustrate the character. The frustration does two things. It creates a higher level of energy and dramatic conflict within the scene, which therefore makes it more interesting and earns empathy. It gets empathy from the audience because they have frustrations and they tend to identify and so to understand and to care because of self-identification. . . . A good example of this . . . came in the introductory scene of [the movie] The Apartment. [Director Billy Wilder] had to show that he had all these different people using the apartment, and he had them on the phone trying to juggle time. It was a long scene, about five pages of calling to change appointments. . . . Billy did a beautiful thing. He gave the guy [Lemmon's character, who owns the apartment, which other men want to borrow for brief romantic liaisons] a cold, and the scene worked because the poor son of a bitch had a temperature and a cold and was perfectly miserable and the audience knew how goddamn lousy he felt and they loved the scene. —Jack Lemmon

The playwright calls them *complications*, major events that change the course of the action. The director thinks of them as *action units*, measurements of the play's active forward motion. Theatrical theorists describe them as *contrary objectives*, a conflict between two persons seeking opposing goals. Actors such as Jack Lemmon call them *obstacles*.

Despite the difference in terminology, all refer to basically the same thing: an obstruction the character absolutely must deal with, a frustrating wall in the character's path which he or she must try to go over, under, or around or even use dynamite to get it out of the way.

We can think of obstacles as potentially disastrous forces that run against the grain: the character would have progressed along fairly well, but the obstacle adds tension. Lemmon's character could have managed the number of telephone calls with at least some success, but the addition of a horrible cold—he sneezes, sniffles, holds the phone with one hand, and tries to write with the other while groping for a tissue—is an obstacle that sharply disrupts the character's comfort zone. As Lemmon points out, the result is a "a higher level of energy and dramatic conflict," which increases audience attention and empathy. Lemmon's character becomes more dimensional as he struggles to combat the obstacles. In the process, the character's difficulties awaken audience empathic responses.

Equally, Russian actor Vsevolod Meyerhold reports he had no vitality in rehearsals when Konstantin Stanislavsky helped correct the problem by giving him an unopened bottle of wine and a corkscrew, telling him to try to open the bottle while saying his lines. That obstacle, Meyerhold said, multiplied his vitality and gave his lines the ring of truth. Why? For the actor, the physical action externalized the character's inner turmoil.

Obstacles add interesting dimensions to the character. Without the obstacle the character will simply achieve the goal. That's hardly dynamic or dramatic. If Joyce Grenfell's teacher wants order in the classroom (her objective) and if she easily and immediately gets the kids under control, there are no obstacles, no need for her to try different strategies (her intentions or tactics), and thus no character changes and no action. It would be a pretty short and uninteresting play, wouldn't it? A struggle, however, captivates audiences with electrical tensions generated by *action*, the dynamic movement of objective versus counterforce and obstacles.

For playwrights, actors, and directors, obstacles show various aspects of the character's personality that would not otherwise be visible. For example, at each obstacle Sonny reacts by being charming, vicious, or clever. The character's *reactions* to those confrontations create dynamic changes and evolutions. Without reactions, the character remains static, a blank sheet of paper on which nothing ever is written, colorless, bland, uninteresting.

STIMULUS-RESPONSE MOVEMENTS

Whether you are playwright, actor, or director, you'll find that the stimulus-response cycle is a significant key to dramatic action. You probably encountered the S ➜ R concept in a psychology class. Often it is shown as a circle to indicate that a stimulus causes a response, which in turn is a stimulus that creates yet another response:

The stimulus-response circle is part of our everyday life. Each of us is like a sailboat, sometimes drifting aimlessly in calm waters until a sudden gust of wind—a stimulus—strikes the sails and causes a reaction, propelling the boat forward and changing its direction. Our lives are full of stimulus-response cycles: encountering a new person with whom we want to develop a relationship, planning a vacation but being struck by unexpected bills, discovering a fresh insight into an old idea. These are stimuli that cause us to react in life.

S ➜ R also is a vital aspect of theatrical characterization and action. Each stimulus goads the character to respond; often that response is itself a stimulus that provokes another response. Without stimuli, the character has no motivation to change, which results in flat characterization. That's the idea that Lanford Wilson expresses when he says "you have to goose the characters."

Most often—although not always—each stimulus and response is more or less equal in size. Otherwise the cycle might appear unreal. For example, a small stimulus that is followed by a large response or a large stimulus and a small response may appear artificial and contrived. For comedies, however, you may want to reverse that balance. You saw the effects of imbalance in the grimly cheerful teacher in Joyce Grenfell's *Free Activity Period*: she greatly underreacts to the children's large stimuli, giving the solo play a comic flair.

The motivational stimulus-response cycle is a major construction unit. Action A is a stimulus that provokes response B, itself a stimulus that triggers response C. Note the construction of cause-effect, stimulus-response process in, say, *Nice Shoes*. Sonny wants to be king of the jungle. Mike enters the jungle but doesn't show appropriate respect. Sonny challenges him. Mike retreats. Sonny forces him to return. Mike is reluctant. Sonny makes him kneel. Sonny's responses show he is playing with Mike, and the actor performing Sonny will show each step of the character's evolution.

The plan of stimulus-response cycles is a structure of action—plot. As it can be effective with exterior stimuli, so also it can be effective with interior stimuli.

Action in Monodramas Versus Multicharacter Plays

In multicharacter plays the dialogue is a major form of stimulus-response action: Character A speaks, forcing B to respond, which in turn makes A react, and therefore C retorts. In such instances, dramatic action is force against force in circular cause-effect movements: one character forces something on another.

Action in Soliloquies. We see cause-effect action with multiple characters, but is dramatic action possible with only one character? Certainly. For example, a soliloquy in a multicharacter play or a solo song in a musical carries the same sense of conflict we find in dialogue between characters. Hamlet's "To be or not to be," for instance, is a major encounter between Hamlet's two opposing sides, in effect "Hamlet A" actively pursuing the possibility of taking one action—"to sleep," or death—which causes "Hamlet B" to respond by denying that action for fear there will be "dreams," a possibly horrific afterlife. Equally, Billy Bigelow's "My Boy Bill" in *Carousel* is a major conflict as the character faces changing who he has been to who he must become, irresponsible "Billy A" versus "Billy B," who discovers that as a father he must become a responsible parent.

Dramatic Action in Solo Plays. As there can be dramatic action in "To be or not to be" and "My Boy Bill," so there can be in a play with a single character. Although the monodrama focuses on just one character, playwright, actor, and director can think of it structured with stimulus-response dialogue like the multicharacter play's speeches between two or more characters. Lanford Wilson's A *Poster of the Cosmos* insists that the character travel through a tortured journey of life against death; Samuel Beckett's *Krapp's Last Tape* goads an alienated man to struggle with the more idealistic dreamer he used to be; Jane Martin's *Twirler* forces the girl to encounter her religious self that is evolving from her secular self.

Playwright, actor, and director look for opportunities to create sparks of active characterization similar to dialogue of conflict in a multicharacter play. Your monodrama's character may be involved with action that forces self against self, self against one or more (unseen) individuals, or self against social forces. Action transforms your monodrama into a forward-moving play, not a long static speech delivered by a nonchanging character who appears to have little or no motivation to speak aloud.

Full-length plays are divided into *acts*, usually marked by an intermission, consisting of the development of a long major action. Full-length and shorter plays may have *scenes*, which are pauses in the forward motion, sometimes including a shift of scenery or lighting to change place or time. A play also includes smaller action units we can think of as *French scenes*, which provide an effective structural design.

FRENCH SCENES

A novel is a static thing that one moves through; a play is a dynamic thing that moves past one. —Kenneth Tynan

All writing is creating or spinning dreams for other people so they won't have to bother doing it themselves. —Beth Henley

When you read seventeenth-century French plays, such as Molière's *Tartuffe* or *The Miser*, you notice that the printed scripts indicate a series of numbered scenes, perhaps three to seven per act. Yet you know that the plays adhere to a strict unity of time, place, and action. Those scenes flow together without changes of scenery or lighting (unlike scene divisions in episodic plays, perhaps best illustrated by musical comedies with numerous shifts of time and place).

What, then, is the purpose of the "scene" divisions in seventeenth-century French plays? Quite likely you've already noted the answer: those scenes are marked by the entrance or exit of a major character, a stimulus that changes the action and situation but not the time or place.

The Logic of French Scenes: Construction of Changes

There's a neat structural and psychological logic to a French scene. The entrance or exit of a major character necessarily forces changes in the existing situation. It's a process of synthesis, like a lab chemist adding ingredients to a formula: each new addition creates a reaction that changes the existing compound.

For illustration, imagine a real-life situation. French scene 1: You (we'll say you are character A) and a close friend (B) are in her apartment. There's strong conflict as you argue about her involvement with a third person (C). Your objective is to get B immediately to break off her relationship with C. She has a contrary objective and wants to continue. There's strong conflict that continues for several minutes.

Imagine that C now enters the apartment. Of course, that entrance sharply changes the situation and dynamics, resulting in changes in character attitudes and intentions. In the logic of the French scene, that entrance creates Scene 2 because there are new factors, different stimuli. A and B must modify their behavior because C is a new ingredient. The emotional climate changes; quite likely the dialogue becomes heavily loaded with subtext.

The conflict grows increasingly intense and B has had enough. She leaves the apartment, perhaps yelling angrily or crying in frustration, leaving you and C. B's exit starts a new French scene: between A and C there is yet another different relationship, new intentions, a fresh conflict. A's objective remains the same—A continues to want to dissolve the B and C relationship—but the new situation calls for A to invent another tactic.

The French Scene in Multicharacter Plays

French scenes are an effective structural device for playwrights, actors, and directors. They are found in many plays, even if those scenes aren't given numbers. Think, for example, of Act One, Scene Three, of Shakespeare's *Macbeth*. Macbeth and Banquo enter alone on the "blasted heath" (French scene 1). Then the witches enter (FS 2), greatly changing the dynamics as the witches give Macbeth a number of prophesies, including a prediction he will become king. The witches exit (FS 3), leaving Macbeth and Banquo to puzzle over the witches. Soldiers enter (FS 4) to tell Macbeth that one portion of the witches' prophesies already has come true, giving credence to their other predictions. Although each French scene is brief, each has vital chemistry.

The French Scene in Monodramas

Creating French scenes appears easy in multicharacter plays, but do they have a place in the one-person play? Yes. In Bogosian's *Nice Shoes* you saw the French scene effect when Mike entered at the very beginning of the play and again when he exited close to the play's end. Protean monodramatists, such as Ruth Draper, Cornelia Otis Skinner, Hal Holbrook, Lily Tomlin, and Patrick Stewart, perform a number of characters who "enter" and "exit" during the play.

Expanding the French Scene Concept

The French scene is a remarkably convenient concept for playwrights, directors, and actors because it divides the play into units of motivated action. You can expand the entrance-exit concept to think of other stimuli that influence the character's pursuit of an objective. Instead of limiting a French scene to a character's entrance or exit, imagine a comparable stimulus "entering" the play.

Exterior stimuli. Perhaps the structure of your monodrama's French scenes might involve exterior stimuli such as a telephone call, a television announcement, or a letter. Each has the effect of a character's entrance or exit. In Adams' *Break-Up Diet* the phone rings several times; in McDonald's *Help!* the bottle of pills intrudes into the boy's consciousness; in *Krapp's Last Tape* each new tape is a new stimulus. Hal Holbrook's Mark Twain impersonates characters from his novels, and each time Huck, Tom, or others "enter," it is a structural element similar to a new

French scene. Spalding Gray's monodramas bring in a number of other characters and conversations, each making a change in action like a French scene.

Interior stimuli. Alternatively, and often more effectively, the new stimulus may be the character's discovery, a new insight, an awareness of personal changes, a decision to change direction. These discoveries are significant "entrances" that create the effect of a French scene. In *Krapp's Last Tape* Krapp slowly discovers personal changes, such as noticing today he doesn't know the meaning of a word he used when younger; in *Twirler* the character goes through an epiphany, discovering a major religious insight from the commonplace twirling activity.

The Action, or Motivational, Unit

A French scene is an excellent example of what directors call an *action unit*, or *motivational unit*. These are changes in the pattern of events, sometimes stimulated by a new idea or a complication, that influences the character's movement toward objective. That influence may conflict with the objective or encourage it, forcing the character to respond. A play is constructed with a number of such units, each related to the character's objective. Action units give the character and the play a lively sense of movement, in contrast to a play that appears static because there are no shifts. The longer the monodrama, the more action units are necessary to sustain dramatic tension, but short monodramas also require action units to maintain the tensions and stimulus-response cycles that enlarge the character.

Writing and Performing French Scenes

Building entrances, exits, and expanded French scenes. If an entrance, exit, or new discovery is a stimulus that marks a major new plot movement, it follows that it should be emphasized and sustained. Instead of thinking that only one line or speech begins or ends a French scene, playwrights, actors, and directors expand the theatrical effect by enlarging the moment. A character's entrance or exit (or a discovery) will be broadened to capitalize on the new event. For example, the writer uses foreshadowing to prepare for it, the actor uses pauses and other vocal emphases, and the director blocks the scene to emphasize the effect. These and other theatrical devices make the new plot stimulus an important event.

The Playwright's Role. The French scene concept can help you, as the, writer prepare a *scenario*, a step-by-step outline of the sequence of what happens in the play. The scenario briefly describes what takes place in each scene, how the character is moving toward an objective, the obstacles and complications the character is forced to encounter, the stimuli and responses, the scene's beginning, middle, and end, and the cause-effect actions. You may wish to number the scenes for your convenience. Although those numbers do not appear in your final script, you might want to use paragraphing techniques to organize them. While your monodrama is in scenario form you can easily shift the order of the scenes or add new ones to be sure the story has an appropriate building-block construction that is full of dynamic growth.

The Roles of the Actor and Director. Marking the play's individual French scenes can clarify the play's action pattern for actors and directors. Repeated rehearsals of each French scene permits actors and directors to be sure that character objectives are understood and shown. Because most French scenes have their own miniplay structure with conflict, beginning, middle, and end, rehearsing scenes individually can help ensure appropriate emphasis and rhythm. The director's play analysis includes giving each French scene or action unit a descriptive title to clarify the purpose of the unit; in rehearsals the director ensures that the meaning will be clear to the audience.

The director thinks of a play as a single major movement composed of smaller pieces, such as French scenes or action units, that indicate the rhythm of the play. In this sense a play is comparable to a symphony and the director has the conductor's role, establishing the appropriate rhythm. A play with a number of short units suggests a fast tempo; a play with longer units implies a less hectic pace. For example, *Krapp's Last Tape* has longer units than, say, *Nice Shoes* or *French Fries.*

THE MONODRAMA'S BEGINNING, MIDDLE, AND END

Artistic growth is, more than it is anything else, a refining of the sense of truthfulness. The stupid believe that to be truthful is easy; only the artist, the great artist, knows how difficult it is. —Willa Cather

A play is composed of three parts, according to Aristotle: a beginning, middle, and end. At first glance that statement may seem simplistic and self-evident, but the three parts need to be carefully designed for an effective, well-shaped monodrama. Monodramas lacking a beginning may confuse the audience because the situation and character's objective aren't clear; monodramas with inadequate middles are unsatisfying due to a lack of action and character development; and monodramas that seem merely to stop, rather than conclude, can be irritating and make the audience suspect the playwright simply did not finish the script.

We conclude this discussion of play structure by examining aspects of these three parts of a play. What follows is an illustration of a typical model of a play, certainly not a prescribed formula. We indicate the ingredients of a play's beginning, middle, and end that you find in most scripts, but variations are common.

Brief Descriptions of the Primary Functions of the Beginning, Middle, and End

Beginning: The introduction. Relatively brief.

Purpose: Bring the audience into the universe of the play. Whether you're playwright, actor, or director, think of yourself like a host who wants to introduce a stranger—the individual audience member—to the play. Give information in a way that makes the stranger become interested.

Structure: If possible, start *in medias res*, or in the middle of ongoing action.

Contents: Inciting incident, exposition, foreshadowing.

Middle: The struggle. The longest of the three.

Purpose: Show the character's attempts to achieve the objective while encountering opposition. Introduce the play's major dramatic question.

Structure: Rising action.

Contents: Point of attack. Complications and obstacles. French scenes. Action units. Beats.

End: The resolution. Relatively brief.

Purpose: Show the resolution of the struggle. Answer the play's major dramatic question.

Structure: Descending action.

Contents: Denouement, resolution.

THE BEGINNING:
INTRODUCTION AND PROMISE OF THINGS TO COME

Your monodrama's beginning introduces the character, implies the basic situation, establishes the play's tone, whether comic or dramatic, hints at actions to come, plants the motivational reasons the character will pursue an objective, and suggests directions the play may take. The beginning typically is relatively short in comparison to the play's overall length. Although we don't want to state a mandatory length, in general the beginning of a full-length monodrama such as *Mister Lincoln* may be perhaps three to five minutes long; in a short-short monodrama such as *French Fries*, the beginning often is less than one minute.

The Inciting Incident

The inciting incident is a significant event that happened *before* the play begins.* An inciting incident is a major action that is important to the character, and it will start the character's objective. The murder of Hamlet's father, for example, is a strong inciting incident that lit a fuse, which is smoldering dangerously when the play begins. The fuse will touch off an explosion when the plot's action begins at the *point of attack* (described shortly), and therefore the inciting incident directly influences the play's action, theme, character and objective, plot, conflict, and situation.

Examples of Inciting Incidents in Monodramas. You've noted inciting incidents in monodramas we've discussed:

☐ The inciting incident in A *Poster of the Cosmos* is the death of the solo character's friend.

☐ In *Krapp's Last Tape* the inciting incident is Krapp's ritual of making tapes each birthday.

☐ The inciting incident in *The Break-Up Diet* is the argument between the girl and her boyfriend.

☐ In *Help!* the inciting incident is the brother's sexual abuse of the solo character.

---

* You may find some people say the inciting incident refers to the first major action event in the play, not to an event prior to the play's beginning. Such an idea ignores the importance of the action that "lit the fuse." As you'll see in the following discussion, here we say that first event in the play itself is the "point of attack."

In all these illustrations the inciting incident happened before the play itself began. That incident gives the character motivation to pursue an objective and it influences the play's structural action from beginning to end.

Often the inciting incident took place mere moments before the play begins. The inciting incident in Nice Shoes is Michael's appearance on the street, only a second or two before Sonny begins to talk to him. In other plays the inciting incident was some time before the play begins. In A Poster of the Cosmos the death of Tom's friend happened a relatively long time ago.

Advantages of the Inciting Incident. A dynamic inciting incident is a strong foundation on which the monodrama builds. It establishes what will become the play's conflict and the character's objective, both of which start at the point of attack. For the playwright, the inciting incident helps you write the play and structure the events of the play because it begins the plot, gives the character a vitally important objective, and introduces conflict. For the actor, the inciting incident helps identify the character's motivations, compels the character to speak, and motivates the character to take action. For the director, the inciting incident is an important clue to the play analysis and the desired tone to achieve in production.

Exposition and Foreshadowing

A play's beginning often contains *exposition*, which subtly and briefly introduces the character and situation, explains the inciting incident, and describes other essential background information the audience needs to know to understand the character's environment and given circumstances that motivate him or her to action. Often present, too, is *foreshadowing*, which hints at forthcoming action and events. Exposition and foreshadowing aren't limited to the beginning; they can appear later in play.

Exposition and foreshadowing may not be necessary in all plays. Short-short monodramas usually are more effective when they plunge directly into the action without exposition. For example, Nice Shoes has no exposition about Sonny's history, age, his partners, or the given circumstances or environment. Nice Shoes does use foreshadowing deftly and economically in the first moments: Sonny's apparent cordiality to Mike, "Come here for a second," has a hidden menace, and foreshadowing becomes more obvious with the entrance of the knife.

Longer monodramas, such as Mister Lincoln, tend to use more exposition and foreshadowing to establish a large framework on which the action will build. Lincoln's description of a slavery auction he witnessed is both exposition and implied foreshadowing of his objective and the play's thematic content.

Beginning Your Monodrama in Medias Res

Playwrights, directors, and play publishers recommend that playwrights begin their plays *in medias res*, Latin for "in the midst of things," or in the middle of action in progress. Starting *in medias res* means your monodrama begins *in the middle of ongoing action*, instead of starting with lengthy nonactive preliminary elements such as exposition, lead-ins, and general mood-setting descriptions. Whether writing a short-short, one-act, or full-length monodrama or multicharacter play, starting with action hooks the audience's attention immediately.

You can apply *in medias res* by envisioning a character *already involved in the situation or dilemma*, facing the situation from the beginning moments. For example, Wilson could have started A *Poster of the Cosmos* with a number of short episodes containing detailed exposition and introductory material: the character is arrested over his protests, is taken to the police station, refuses to talk and demands a lawyer, is taken to an interrogation room, meets the policemen, and the like. Wilson instead plunges into the story immediately, making the opening of A *Poster of the Cosmos* intense and dynamic. Equally, McDonald uses *in medias res* in *Help!* by starting her monodrama with the boy holding pills, wondering whether to take them, instead of placing that crucial action after lengthy exposition and other preliminaries. Bogosian's *Nice Shoes* uses *in medias res* to begin the conflict immediately when Sonny orders Mike to come to him.

Creating a Play's Beginning

Your English teacher taught you to write a term paper by starting with a *thesis sentence*. This expression of the core of the paper allows the reader to know your subject and how you intend to develop the paper. More importantly, a clear thesis sentence helps you write a formal paper and stay on track. Those advantages of a thesis sentence—carefully modified—can apply to your monodrama. Of course, a play isn't an essay, and any direct thesis statement is a poor idea, first because we expect theatre to show instead of tell, and secondly because it is hard to imagine a character who *needs* to say the play's thesis.

Those reservations made, however, you might want to consider starting your monodrama with an artistic expression of the play's basic thrust to give the director and actor clues to analyzing the play and to help the audience understand the play's basic thrust. The opening moments of the play also can establish the play's basic mood, comic or dramatic. For example, in the first scene of Shakespeare's *Macbeth* the witches say, "Fair is foul, and foul is fair," which neatly expresses the topsy-turvy world we'll see during the play while Macbeth violates legal and moral standards. So, too, the beginning moments of Wilson's A *Poster of the Cosmos* express an important thread that runs through the monodrama: Tom's statements about the "kinna guy" he is, in effect a thematic thesis sentence that is developed to make us in the audience wonder just what "kinna guys" we are and how our "kinna guys"—society at large—reacts to victims of AIDS.

For the actor and director, the beginning needs special attention. After lengthy rehearsals they know the play's details so well they may forget that the audience isn't aware of the situation. To be sure they properly introduce the audience to the play, actor and director think of themselves as storytellers who seek to pull the audience into the play. Often that may mean decreasing the pace to give the audience time to acclimate to the play.

The director may want to consider beginning the play with judicious use of *pantomimic dramatization*, telling a story with physical movements instead of dialogue, to show the situation before the dialogue begins. For example, *Krapp's Last Tape* starts with Krapp entering, fiddling irritably with the tape recorder, or looking for necessary props before he speaks his first lines. The director usually wants to establish the play's tone in the beginning, likely using quick and exaggerated physical movements to suggest a comedy or slower, more ponderous activities to suggest a drama.

THE MIDDLE: THE STRUGGLE

The middle, the largest portion of a monodrama, contains the dynamic action and characterization that make this the most interesting—and most important—part of the play. The middle is rich with conflict and complications; it is structured with scenes, French scenes, complications, obstacles, action units, and beats. Here the promise of the beginning comes to life, and the character begins to pursue his or her objective, fights for victory, reacts to opposition and setbacks, and formulates new strategies to overcome the counterforces. Think of the middle as the struggle that amplifies the character, the beginning and development of the conflict that was implied with exposition and foreshadowing, and the illustration of the play's thematic core.

In the typical short-short, ten-minute monodrama, the middle might be around, say, eight or nine minutes long. The action explores and illustrates the ramifications of the *major dramatic question* that is posed at the *point of attack*. The middle portion of plotted monodramas contains a number of *action units* and *complications* or *obstacles* to the character's goal, which change the course of the action and stimulate the character to evolve and change.

The Point of Attack

The play's middle is sparked by a *point of attack*, a major structural element that stimulates the character to start moving toward his or her objective. The point of attack starts the problem the character will face and initiates the through-line of action—the play's *spine*—for the entire play. The effect of the point of attack is like that of a large rock thrown in a pond: there is a large visible splash (the point of attack) and then a number of concentric rings (the play's actions) spread out in increasing circles. A monodrama without a point of attack is a play without action; the pond remains calm, undisturbed, motionless.

Inciting Incident and Point of Attack. In *Hamlet* the inciting incident (the murder of Hamlet's father) connects to the appearance of the Ghost to Hamlet, which is the play's point of attack and the beginning of the character's objective: Hamlet must avenge that death. The point of attack in *Help!* is the boy's major decision whether or not to commit suicide, which relates directly to the inciting incident, the pattern of sexual abuse. In *Nice Shoes* the inciting incident is Mike's presence in Sonny's neighborhood. The point of attack begins when Sonny calls to Mike, and it continues when he says, "Don't walk away from me when I'm talking with you," being reemphasized when Sonny again controls Mike by saying, "Don't walk away from me when I'm talkin' to you here now!" The point of attack shows Sonny's first action to achieve his objective: to dominate, to control.

Sustaining and Emphasizing the Point of Attack. The word *point* may be misleading. The point of attack isn't a brief moment or one short sentence or speech. It must be adequately sustained, strong enough to make the character begin movement toward the objective and clear to the audience so they will be able to sense the significant issue the character faces. To emphasize the point of attack the playwright restates the issue and enlarges the character's reactions; the director applies staging devices, such as placing the character full front center stage during the point of attack; and the actor uses pauses, vocal techniques, and gestures to increase the strength of the point of attack.

The Major Dramatic Question

The point of attack introduces the *major dramatic question* (MDQ), which is the essential thematic center the monodrama will illustrate by the character's pursuit of an objective. The MDQ is the play's meaning, its intellectual core. You've seen the MDQ in monodramas you've read: Will this girl be able to put together her love life? (*The Break-Up Diet*), Can the boy overcome the pain of the sexual abuse he's suffered or will he kill himself? (*Help!*), or Will the old woman achieve her goal to avoid death by living in a fast-food restaurant? (*French Fries*). The MDQ is prompted by the inciting incident and is sparked by the point of attack. The spine of the play's intellectual thrust, the major dramatic question, is illustrated by the character's struggles during the middle of the play and is answered at the end.

Complications, Obstacles, Reversals, and Discoveries

Complications, obstacles, reversals, and discoveries are forces that disrupt the character's movement toward the objective, stimuli that force the character to respond, or changes in the course of action. A play without such disruptions has little or no structural action. Complications, reversals, obstacles, and discoveries have separate distinguishing qualities, but all affect the character's desires.

Complications are plot movements that change existing dynamics and force the character to respond. The point of attack, which makes the character respond, is the play's first complication. The entrance of a major character or other force creates a complication, as in the French scenes we've discussed.

Reversals are surprising changes in situations and events that thwart the protagonist's progress toward the objective. In *Krapp's Last Tape* Krapp seems to start with a basic acceptance of self but is surprised by statements in the various tapes, and he ends increasingly alienated from himself and the world.

Obstacles usually are tangible or physical problems with which the character must deal while simultaneously working toward an objective. Obstacles often are created by the actor or director.

Discoveries differ from other disruptions that typically are exterior forces. Discoveries instead are personal, within the character. Most often they are significant insights the character experiences as a result of other actions. In *Twirler* April March discovers that the mundane activity of twirling can lead to a form of religious ecstasy. Such discoveries connect directly to the play's major dramatic question, and for us in the audience the character's discoveries can be ours as well.

Complications, obstacles, reversals, and discoveries threaten to stop the character's progress, in the process creating audience interest through suspense. What will the character do? Quit? Angrily overcome the problem? Cunningly step around it? The character's reactions are enlightening. Reversals in *Nice Shoes*, as when Mike tries to leave or curses Sonny, make Sonny become increasingly belligerent, more threatening, more frightening. In *Krapp's Last Tape* the discoveries include Krapp's new awareness about a past love and inability to define words he once knew (illustrating his changes over the years). Complications in *Help!* include the boy's internal struggle to kill himself or live as he searches for possible solutions to his problem, such as telling his parents or officials at school. That's the advantage of counterforces: they force the character to react, therefore becoming more dimensional and intriguing. The longer the monodrama, the more such complications are necessary to sustain the action and hold audience attention.

Creating a Middle Full of Action
Aware that a play needs action and movement, the *playwright's* process starts with creating a character with an all-consuming objective. The writer then crafts complications, obstacles, and reversals that force the character to react, responding emotionally and intellectually to successes and failures.

Starting with emphasizing the point of attack, the *director* designs special staging to draw attention to plot movements. In particular, the director carefully focuses audience attention on the character each time he or she actively pursues an objective or reacts to a disruption. The director's identification of the character's objective increases effective communications with the actor.

To create a unified through-line of action and changes, the *actor* uses the character's driving compulsion to signal the character's motivational drives. For the actor, each disruption is a new challenge the character must handle, and the way the character responds will show new aspects of the character's emotional and intellectual personal qualities. The actor is aware that each disruption changes the character.

THE END: THE ACTION CONCLUDES

Coda. The little boy is exuberant because he gets his marbles, or kills himself because he doesn't, or decides that marbles aren't worth the trouble after all. Anna Mae has no more to do and continues to be confident she'll move to the golden arches; Sonny proves he is king of the jungle and goes off with new shoes; Krapp gives up. The action runs to its logical finish; the character's objective has been achieved or denied; the building momentum has reached its peak; the major dramatic question is answered; there is nothing important to add. Any new material would be superfluous, perhaps even heavy-handed overkill.

End of play. Curtain.

Your monodrama's ending usually is brief. No set length can be dictated, but we can suggest something of the relative balance. In general the ending is perhaps a minute or so in a typical short-short monodrama, several minutes for the one-act-length monodrama, and three to five minutes in a full-length, two-hour play. The prime ingredient of the ending is the *climax*, which is the final action of the play that concludes the action and answers the major dramatic question that was posed at the point of attack. The ending of longer works generally contain the play's *resolution*, which completes the action.

Note that the ingredients do not include author's summation speeches to state or explain the theme. If the character's struggle in the middle hasn't adequately illuminated the theme, there's no relief in explaining it all at the end. We don't need the character in Wilson's *Poster of the Cosmos* to make an end-of-play speech that AIDS is a tragic disease because the action shows that concept.

Expect the ending to balance the play, neither overstating the conclusion nor leaving it hanging like an unfinished musical chord. Balance gives the play an artistic totality, a completion, even when it is designed to leave questions for the audience to answer. *French Fries*, for example, has an artistically balanced end, but the audience is left with questions about the character's goals and the importance of dreams. *Help!* has a "book-end" ending that leaves the character as he was in the beginning, facing the conflict about committing suicide. Each such monodrama has an ending that is appropriate for the playwright's purpose.

EXERCISES

1. Assume John is waiting on a street corner for his date to arrive. She's late; he's impatient. He doesn't know her—this is a blind date—but they've arranged a code so they'll recognize each other. Assume this is a comedy; therefore, you'll seek a fast pace.

   a. Create a scenario that uses French scenes, planning entrances and exits of characters. Be sure each is a stimulus that forces the character to respond.

   b. To that scenario include adaptations of the French scene concept, changing the action with interior or exterior stimuli but not characters entering or exiting.

   c. Give each French scene a descriptive title, like the title of a chapter in a novel.

   d. Divide the scenes into the play's beginning, middle, and end.

2. Take your favorite character and situation from your monodrama notebook and write a scenario that incorporates the points from the preceding exercise.

3. Return to the script of A *Poster of the Cosmos* (Chapter 6). In the margins label the beginning, middle, and end. Draw stars at the places you see the play's major dramatic question. Using colored marking pens, mark exposition with yellow, foreshadowing with orange, the point of attack with red, the beginning and end of action units or French scenes with black, and the climax with blue. When you have finished, read the play aloud, focusing on the character changes indicated by your marks.

What's the difference between a poor play and a good one? I think there's a very simple way of comparing them. A play in performance is a series of impressions; little dabs, one after another, fragments of information or feeling in a sequence which stirs the audience's perceptions. A good play sends many such messages, often several at a time, often crowding, jostling, overlapping one another. The intelligence, the feelings, the memory, the imagination are all stirred. —Peter Brook

NOTES

1. For detailed discussions of the individual Aristotelian six elements of drama for playwrights and directors, I invite you to examine my *Playwriting: Writing, Producing, and Selling Your Play* (Prospect Heights, IL: Waveland Press) or *The Director's Vision* (Mountain View, CA: Mayfield Press).

8

CHAPTER

Collaboration in Rehearsals

I've done three one-man performances now. It's wonderful and terrible for the same reason: everything depends on you. What's no fun at all, though, is that in rehearsal, all the notes are for you, too. After a run-through, one listens resentfully to the never-ending stream of criticisms thinking, absurdly, what about the others? Don't they get any notes? Oh well, if I'm as bad as all that, perhaps we'd better cancel the show—and so on. Directing a one-man show, contrary to popular imaginings, is not easy: a severe test of tact, humour and pacing. On the other hand, it's very cheap if you take the company out to lunch.

—Simon Callow

YOU'RE LIKELY TO HEAR DIRECTORS AND ACTORS WARN YOU THAT preparing, rehearsing, and presenting the solo play has sizable positive and negative peculiarities—but, then, can't we say that about every theatrical production? Or, indeed, about any collaborative or creative process? Surely all theatrical productions offer challenges and rewards. The one-person play is no exception.

Still, there's no question that certain aspects of rehearsing the monodrama do call attention to themselves, sometimes with sharp-edged growls and on other occasions with contented purrs. When the playwright is involved—and the director or actor may also wear the author's hat—the collaborative effort takes on yet additional dimensions. Whatever else you're told about the solo play, however, one point should be stressed: most of us who are involved in the monodrama find that it offers excellent opportunities to stretch creative muscles, work closely in a collaborative rehearsal environment, and enjoy an unusually intimate actor-audience relationship. These make the solo play distinctly rewarding.

We conclude this book with an examination of director, actor, and playwright collaboration during rehearsals. We then discuss how to find production opportunities.

Because space limitations prevent us from studying every aspect of rehearsals for actors and directors, we select only certain rehearsal techniques that will lead to the solo play's production. For more details, you may want to consult one of the many excellent texts for actors and directors. Necessarily, some of our points pertain to any theatrical production, but we focus in particular on special requirements of the monodrama.

POSSIBLE PROBLEMS REHEARSING THE SOLO PLAY

There is no such thing as a problem without a gift for you in its hands. We seek problems because we need their gifts.   —Richard Bach

On the premise that forewarned is forearmed, we start this discussion of rehearsing the solo play by looking at selected potential difficulties. Knowing what problems may arise can help you avoid them—or at least diminish their effect—and anticipating obstacles can prevent you from being unhappily surprised during rehearsals.

Both actor and director need to consider challenges that lie ahead, but the latter has special responsibilities for planning rehearsals and the production. Echoing director Tyrone Guthrie's statement that "the director is a chairman" who sets agendas and runs meetings, we who direct know that our responsibilities include establishing a vision of the play in performance, which involves setting rehearsal goals, establishing the schedule, and creating a positive working atmosphere that enhances creativity. As director, your awareness of special challenges will help you chart a course, from initial analysis, interpretation, and preplanning to final dress. That plan will guide you and the actor through fair and foul weather, evading dangerous shoals so you arrive safely at the destination of a successful performance.

Although we're looking at possible hurdles, we mustn't make too much of them. Experience indicates that actors and directors find that advantages of the solo play far outweigh any disadvantages. Better, we ought not even think of problems and instead see what Richard Bach calls a gift—unique circumstances, opportunities for new experiences and artistic growth, and a chance to make a personal statement for individualism that rebels against the group thinking, group behavior, and group living that permeates our society. After all, we all relish challenges—were it not so, we wouldn't venture into theatre—and certainly the solo play has enough to kindle our creativity.

The Solo Play: "Wonderful and Terrible for the Same Reason"

Actors and directors quickly notice differences between rehearsing the monodrama and multicharacter plays. Most conspicuous are the unique working arrangements. Unlike rehearsing large-cast shows, rehearsing the solo play is an intimate one-to-one actor-director experience. If you're a director, you'll agree with actor and director Simon Callow, who says in the quotation that begins this chapter that the director finds that solo play rehearsals are "a severe test of tact, humour and pacing." If you're an actor, you'll nod in recognition at Callow's comment that the solo play "is wonderful and terrible for the same reason: everything depends on you."

One symbol of the unique aspects of the one-person play is clearly visible to the actor during that anxious eternity before curtain. The normally boisterous backstage Green Room, usually bubbling with many excited actors laughing and talking, calls attention to itself as the solo actor, waiting in silent solitude, listens to the clock ticking down. When the play begins, however, the actor relishes the opportunity to be fully in charge, independent, free from distractions of other actors, personally responsible for the performance, and happy to tackle that solo Matterhorn with pride and self-assurance.

The Absence of the Supportive Group Process

One special circumstance of rehearsing the monodrama can strike a sneaky blow at morale. Actors and directors with experience in large-cast productions may feel vaguely disappointed that rehearsals for a solo play seem somehow less lively, and simply aren't as much fun as rehearsing for multicast shows. They may conclude that they are doing something wrong, feeling guilty for not making rehearsals more effective.

Quite likely that's an incorrect conclusion. More probably they unconsciously miss the supportive atmosphere, cheerful camaraderie, and bustling activities that so often characterize rehearsals for a multiple-character play. A larger cast has a positive enthusiasm that is infectious, and an actor who is tired or dejected will receive energy transfusions from colleagues.

For people trained in the bustle of large-cast rehearsals, preparing a solo play may seem uncomfortably sterile by comparison. To overcome this potential letdown, the director and actor might talk frankly about the new situation during an early rehearsal. A casual and good-humored discussion is preferrable to avoid the risk of making the situation worse. An optimistic stance is advisable. Try inventing jokes about the lack of a crowd and stressing positive aspects of the close working relationship you'll enjoy. Lead yourselves to remember the disadvantages of rehearsing a large-cast show, being merely one among many. Look forward to the disciplined privacy of quiet rehearsals and the challenges of the solo performance.

Rehearsal Warm-ups

Professional actors often conduct their own personal warm-ups, but in the amateur theatre the norm is group warm-ups at the beginning of each rehearsal. Often warm-ups for large-cast productions are playful, inventive, and pure fun, tending at times to be like recess in an elementary school's playground. Warm-ups typically include physical activities, vocal exercises, group games, and improvisations that seek to build energy and help the actors prepare body, voice, spirit, and creativity for rehearsals. Such warm-ups serve an important function as a transition from daily concerns of the workaday world to a focus on the play, and they are also bonding activities that help build an ensemble.

With only one actor, however, exercises and warm-up activities quite likely will seem less enjoyable and less effective. There's no bonding with other actors, no construction of an ensemble that helps each actor rise above personal limits, no frisky group games. Monodrama directors may seek to overcome this apparently dour situation by adding a bit of spice to warm-ups by playing up-tempo music or carefully planning warm-up exercises that challenge, stimulate, and charm the solitary actor. Improvisations can be effective warmups. Some improvs may range far afield from the character, used primarily as an exercise; others can be directly related to the character. By all means ask the actor to contribute warm-up exercises. The director's goal is to incorporate a spirit of playfulness that brings creativity into rehearsals, opening the actor to see new insights into the character's emotions, thoughts, and goals.

Increased Importance of Director-Actor Relationship

Our experience in rehearsals makes us aware that at times an actor may be sensitive or suffer hurt feelings. Likely we all remember sticky situations when an actor brought personal problems into the rehearsal hall. (Who of us can ever forget—much as wish we could—cast dynamics when an actor mournfully broadcast news about his or her "unrequited love" or "my partner just broke up our relationship"?) In a large cast, those sorts of individual crises tend to be relatively invisible in the crowd, and the group's supportive attitude can reduce or eliminate such awkwardness. Directors might be aware of that actor's problems but often they decide the best course of action is to pretend not to notice the situation, letting the actor find solutions. Other actors usually find ways to help the actor think more professionally about what belongs in rehearsals.

In the solo play, however, such problems are more visible, more difficult to ignore. They therefore test directorial tact and diplomacy. Furthermore, because there aren't other actors to deflect directorial critical comments and suggestions, the solo actor's feelings might be more easily bruised, again requiring directorial sensitivity.

Both actor and director approach solo play rehearsals aware that the closeness of the director-actor working arrangement can require conscientious attention to interpersonal relationships. Both carefully build an atmosphere of trust, based on mutual respect, to establish a professional attitude toward their primary goal of preparing the production. Such topics can be the subject of beneficial discussions at early rehearsals. Should aspects of that trust appear to be suffering, fence-mending is called for, best accomplished at lunch or over a cup of coffee outside the rehearsal hall.

The Lack of Actor-to-Actor Stimulation

During rehearsals of multicharacter plays, actors can feed each other ideas, techniques, and inspiration. If one actor hits a wall, other actors often can directly or by example contribute suggestions to make the wall go away or at least shrink it to a less intimidating size. The solo performer doesn't have the stimulation of other actors. That's obvious within the script and production—the one-person play has no interplay between various actors—and perhaps less obvious but equally applicable in working relationships during rehearsals.

Aware that the stimulation from other actors is markedly absent, the wise director therefore will seek ways to fill the void. For example, the director can make comments and suggestions to replace the stimulation other actors provide during rehearsals. To help the actor open doors to alternative concepts, the director asks leading questions about characterization, objectives, emotions, and thoughts. Well-selected exercises and improvisations are significant stimuli.

SPECIAL ADVANTAGES IN REHEARSING THE SOLO PLAY

As we've suggested, rehearsing the monodrama brings advantages that are more notable than are the problems. Directors and actors often report they are surprised to find how smoothly they work together and how easily the show can come together, given director-actor trust and respect along with careful advance planning. Those who have worked on large-cast productions, such as a musical or Shakespearean play, say they find that the one-person play is comparatively much less problem-prone and more enjoyable. To them, dire predictions about difficulties are overblown. The solo play opens doors to a collaborative atmosphere that enhances creativity, and you will want to take advantage of the experiences.

Directorial Focus on the Solo Actor

If you have directed multiple-character plays, you know that the larger the cast, the less opportunity the director has to work with individuals. In large-cast plays the director continually establishes priorities—this particular actor most needs attention now, then that one—and that means the director must spend more time working with actors who are having difficulties and less with others who are developing well enough but still need additional coaching. Because those troubling priorities often involve secondary or minor characters, an unhappy result is that the director regrets an inability to devote more attention to lead actors.

In contrast, there is a distinct freedom in rehearsing the one-person play. You likely will feel that directing a solo actor is remarkably easy, especially if prior experience has been directing large shows. You're free from the distractions of a crowd and therefore able to devote full attention to the lead—indeed, to accentuate the positives, to the entire cast. Without the pressure of handling a large cast, in the solo play's rehearsals there can be a comfortable give-and-take actor-director rapport that leads to neat progress toward a quality production.

For the actor, too, this close relationship can be a refreshing freedom. Most of us who've been in large-cast productions can remember times we rehearsed all evening and never received a single directorial comment, making us wonder wryly if the director even knew we were on stage. In contrast, while rehearsing a monodrama you can count on receiving comments, suggestions, criticism, and questions, all aimed at improving performance. During solo rehearsals you also are free to ask questions and to experiment with new approaches or techniques, knowing you will receive detailed directorial feedback.

Personal Relationships and Long-Term Friendships
For directors and actors, the solo play rehearsals are an opportunity to establish warm, close personal relationships. I have seen directors and actors form long-term friendships as a result of the intense experience during their work on the solo play. They often feel a union, the "two of us" becoming one unified force. With only two people involved, director-actor contact outside the rehearsal hall—lunch, a cup of coffee, a working meeting, a social event—is easy to arrange, increasing the bonding and mutual understanding.

Accumulating Experience for Other Productions
The one-person play needs no plea for its existence. It is as valid an artistic theatrical experience as any of its multicharacter relatives and is no less powerful. Indeed, some of its fervent supporters would argue that an effective solo performance can be a more powerful stage piece than other theatrical forms due to its ability to show the inner secrets of a human within an intimate actor-audience relationship.

That said, however, we can point out that the one-person play is also excellent experience for other productions. For example, an actor who learns to handle a solo performance is prepared for the demands of a classic play's soliloquy, and the intense study to bring to life the monodrama's character is excellent preparation for any other play. Equally, a director who develops interpersonal relationships with the solo actor, while learning techniques to help the performer enhance characterization, will find those lessons directly applicable to working with actors in multicharacter plays. For playwrights, actors, and directors, the one-person play allows a concentration in depth into the essences of the theatrical experience, clearly beneficial for future theatrical work.

Ultimately, the great advantage of the monodrama is, simply, the challenge. For playwright, director, and actor, the monodrama awakens creative energies and stimulates personal growth. Meeting the challenge is a reward that enriches the artistic spirit.

COLLABORATION: AN EXAMPLE

Because of [a] remarkable rapport between [director Arabella Pettit] and me, the rehearsals were the most relaxed, comfortable, and enjoyable I have ever known. . . . It was quite a change to be the only actor in a show on which the director is completely focused, after having performed in many multicharacter plays in which the director's attention is scattered among many actors. At times it could be difficult to endure so much responsibility for a show, unable to ever rest and just blend into the crowd. Yet it was also extraordinary to feel such responsibility and importance for a show. I knew that I could blame no one else for problems, and I had to reply on myself, and those thoughts served to keep me motivated and focused throughout rehearsals. The work may have been more difficult, but in the end it was also much more rewarding. . . . My compatibility with Arabella unburdened the rehearsal process. I have never experienced such an easy, pleasant rehearsal atmosphere. . . .

—Allison Boye

Aspects of preparing a solo performance take on added dimensions if the playwright also is involved. In some instances, the author may be either the actor or director; in others, the playwright may be present, revising as a result of observing rehearsals and receiving suggestions from director or actor. With but one actor, the monodrama allows the luxury of close collaboration between playwright, director, and actor. That can result in a distinctly enhanced script, enriched rehearsals, and improved performance.

Harper Lee, I Suppose, Was a Child Once

The growth of *Harper Lee, I Suppose, Was a Child Once* illustrates effective working relationships during solo play rehearsals. We'll cite certain aspects of that production to illustrate playwright, director, and actor collaboration. Although, necessarily, each individual production will have different qualities, the *Harper Lee* experience is typical of the collaborative process that exists during preparation for solo plays.

Allison Boye was both playwright and solo performer for the premiere of this one-woman show about the famed but reclusive author of the Pulitzer Prize winning novel *To Kill a Mockingbird*. Arabella Pettit directed. I served as consultant for script and performance and observed their work.

Prior to the beginning of rehearsals, while the script was in final revisions, Pettit and Boye met often away from the theatre to discuss the script, production, and working arrangements during rehearsals. Those early discussions, informal and relaxed, free of pressures of rehearsals, built a relationship of mutual trust and respect, highly important in establishing an open, candid, and friendly environment that would continue during rehearsals.

For both, a major priority was establishing a cooperative atmosphere. Boye planned to follow the objectivity of playwright Harold Pinter, who, when asked questions about a play he had written, would respond as if he weren't the author: "Well, it seems to me that the playwright must've intended . . . ." During rehearsals Boye the actress would seek to separate herself from Boye the playwright.

Pettit, also a playwright whose solo play had been performed, was able to bring to discussions a sense of perspective as writer, director, and actor. One significant determination was an agreement on a sensible division of authority while maintaining their collaborative spirit. Boye alone would be responsible for final decisions about the script, although always open to Pettit's suggestions; Pettit alone would be responsible for final decisions about rehearsal goals and production details, although always responsive to Boye's ideas. No doubt that arrangement prevented misunderstandings or arguments that could have damaged the collaboration.

Evolving Changes in Script and Production

Boye had a completed script just before they started rehearsals, but she still faced a major artistic choice that had to do with audience expectations versus her goals in writing the play. One question was simple to phrase but difficult to answer: Should her monodrama include quotes from *Mockingbird*? During her writing and revision process, some who read the script urged her to use extracts from the novel, arguing that audience affection for characters such as Scout, Atticus, and Boo made imperative inclusion of their dialogue.

Although Boye recognized the value of quotations to remind audiences of their favorite passages from *Mockingbird*, she did not want to lose her focus from the play's major thrust: her personal sense of identification with Ms. Lee. For Boye, it was a matter of her own credo. She saw her play as a journey for self-understanding, seeking her own artistic identity through Harper Lee's. Boye, like Lee, is a southern writer, and she identified with Lee as a female writer. Lee's characters were part of Boye; and when she first read *Mockingbird* as a youngster it stimulated her desire to become a creative writer. She was more interested in a play that was, in effect, more about her responses to Lee and the novel, a personal growth as an artist and human, not a compendium of *Mockingbird* quotations.

Associated with the playwright's artistic choice about quoting the novel was the director's search for unification. Pettit wanted to find visual metaphors to serve as a glue, a running thread throughout the production. Their collaborative work helped playwright and director find solutions they felt would both make the script more cohesive and unify the staging. First, they created images of *shoes*, deciding that the script's very first lines should refer to a quotation from *Mockingbird*:

> Atticus was right. One time he said you never really know a man until you stand in his shoes and walk around in them. . . . Harper Lee, where are *your* shoes? I want to fill them, I want to walk around in them, I want to know about you. . . .

The opening dialogue's reference to shoes was combined with staging. During the play, Pettit blocked the character to change shoes at appropriate times in the character's evolution. Boye found inspiration in the idea of walking about in someone's shoes; Pettit found changing shoes effective staging to show the character's evolution.

A second collaborative decision involved script, staging, and even promotion. Based on the idea that the play involves a girl's search, they decided that the play's visual image would be a picture of a little girl wearing overalls, shoeless to match the previous decision, her back to the viewer. That became the motif for the program and advertising. Pettit married that idea to blocking. During the play she had the character go to an easel at significant moments, "painting" a picture the audience cannot yet see. At the end of the play the character shows the audience that picture: the young girl in overalls, back to audience. Pettit decided that the character also should wear overalls. Pettit then blocked Boye's exit so it matched the painting: a tableau in which the character's final pose showed her back. The audience is left with the idea of Scout looking toward a mockingbird, Harper Lee contemplating her past, and the character looking toward Harper Lee. Pettit and Boye made comparable collaborative decisions during rehearsals.

The *Harper Lee* experience can be a model for collaborative work as you prepare your monodrama. Certain aspects of that production deserve attention. Significantly for our point here, playwright and director found that collaboration was easily accomplished because the solo play allowed such close playwright, director, and actor interactions. They concluded that the collaborative process was especially effective because early on they established positive working relationships based on mutual trust and respect. They report that as a result of their mutual work, the rehearsals were smooth, creativity was constantly enriched, and the production grew in strength.

Part of the collaborative process involves careful use of rehearsals to prepare for production. We therefore move to look at the importance of honing vocal skills and using the stage to tell the play's story.

VOCAL SKILLS

First I exercise my vocal cords and my cord muscles by shouting full out in the open air, probably to an audience of cows. I try to extend my vocal range and make sure I can manage eight or more lines without pausing for breath. Then I practice the role in detail to myself. It is a great mistake to take up rehearsal time with technical matters. [Before his first rehearsal as King Lear] I knew exactly where to take a breath, how to light and shade my voice, and how to tonalize it at certain moments in order to get the utmost variety. The actor must keep an audience engaged by constant changes in inflection. . . .

—Laurence Olivier

You aren't likely to want to use Sir Laurence Olivier's personal warm-up exercise system of shouting at cows in pastures. (Rather boggles the imagination, doesn't it? One wonders about the reactions of passing farmers to this strange fellow bellowing at their animals, and we're prompted to conjecture a chorus of curious cows mooing responses to the actor.) You also won't want to return to last century's era of "golden voice" actors who prized vocal skills over every other aspect of performance. We can imagine those actors' technique by remembering announcer Ted Knight on the *Mary Tyler Moore Show*, his hand cupped over his ear to better hear his rolling, sonorous tones he loved so absolutely. Melodious, yes; meaningful, no. We can be happy that hollow bombastic style is long gone, replaced by a greater concern for truthful depiction of characters.

Still, we ought not dismiss the *concepts* behind Olivier's work to improve his voice, nor should we forget the golden-voiced actors' concern for vocal techniques. They realized that vocal skills were powerful communicative stage tools. In contrast, however, today many theatre practitioners fear that the modern theatrical quest for a Stanislavky form of "truth" often leads actors to think only of characterization and motivation, even to the point of ignoring the voice. That's unfortunate. To overlook vocal skills is to neglect a significant aspect of the actor's craft, like a carpenter who can expertly handle saw and hammer but is unable to use the plane and sandpaper.

Just as the playwright strives to achieve active language, so the director and actor need to pay special attention to vocal skills to make the dialogue lively, appropriate to the character, and interesting for the audience. That's true for any play; but for the monodrama, with but one actor on stage, vocal techniques take on increased importance.

To overcome lackluster vocal qualities, the director of a monodrama is wise to schedule rehearsals that stress vocal dynamics. An important goal is to use vocal variations to overcome the effect of the single voice. Here we discuss ways the director and actor may seek to improve the vocal quality of the production.

Vocal Variations

In multicharacter plays the effect of many different voices gives the production the effect of vocal variety. That effect is markedly absent in one-person plays. The solo performer therefore will want to seek to overcome the sound of a single voice by using vocal dynamics. As Laurence Olivier says, "The actor must keep an audience engaged by constant changes in inflection," using variations that enhance meaning. One effective way to achieve the goal is through characterization. Instead of creating a vocally lethargic character, the actor wants to invent one who *needs* to speak with lively emphasis and is deeply involved with what he or she is saying.

Remembering that art consists of making choices, one important goal is to choose which words and phrases to emphasize and to select the appropriate vocal technique to clarify those emphases. The director can help the actor improve vocal dynamics by leading him or her to make choices about which words and phrases must be emphasized. You can ask questions and make suggestions such as these:

☐ Just what is the character feeling and thinking at this moment?

☐ Do the speech again, emphasizing those emotions and thoughts, making them richer and larger even if you suspect you are exaggerating.

☐ Exactly what is the single most important word (sometimes phrase) in this sentence? Exactly what is the one significant sentence in this paragraph?

☐ Do the lines again emphasizing those words, phrases, and sentences.

☐ Put down the script and rephrase these lines in your own words, capturing the character's hungers.

Some actors recommend exercises that require them to sing their lines, a warmup activity the director may wish to schedule. The musical exercise has another modification. Often the director can help the actor by listening to the speeches and placing words on a mental musical score. Does the actor use only a few notes in a limited range? Does the actor always hit the same note when ending a sentence? If the director hears such vocal limitations or mannerisms, it is time to discuss the problem and to design exercises to help the actor achieve greater vocal flexibility.

Director and actor will want to avoid the dull monotone and its weary companions, monovolume and monotempo. The actor can think of vocal variety, "coloring" the dialogue as if with numerous paints. During exercises focused on vocal work, the director can lead the actor to read lines while deliberately looking for variations in rate, pitch, volume, resonance, and timbre. Additional exercises focus on inflections, emphasis, pauses, and rhythms. Exercises may repeat a given set of speeches, each time using different techniques.

Yet other exercises may suggest that the actor think of performing a radio broadcast, where all communication is vocal with no physical assistance. Helpful is thinking of *oral interpretation*—a form of platform reading with a highly skilled actor reading from literary works—which places great value on vocal dynamics. Popular just a few decades ago, oral interpretation is now, sadly, beginning to disappear, although you can hear well-known actors performing oral interpretation on story-reading programs such as *Selected Shorts* on your PBS station. Technique also can emphasize the vocal hills and valleys that give variety, a viable rehearsal exercise to encourage the actor to use his or her full range, although its possible artificiality means it ought not extend to performances.

Dropping the Ends of Sentences

An unfortunately common vocal problem for performers is dribbling off at the end of a sentence, losing vocal energy so the final words lack emphasis and vigor, perhaps even becoming inaudible. A chart of such line readings would show that the energy and inflection indicators start high at the beginning of sentences but constantly descend to the last words. If the actor does that once, no harm is done; unfortunately, once started, it seems to grow into a vocal mannerism. The result isn't pleasant.

Fading away at the end is counterproductive in any play and it is especially to be avoided in the one-voice solo play, where there aren't other actors using better techniques and giving the production energy. When the last words fade off, the actor's—and therefore the character's—energy and apparent desire to communicate is sharply damaged. Continually fading out at the end of a sentence can be a red flag warning of an unfortunate monotonous mannerism, and there is a very real risk of inaudibility, so that the audience may not hear those final words.

The "dribble-off" syndrome also contradicts good writing practices. Professional writers know that a sentence has three parts: beginning, middle, and end. Each carries a relative emphasis. The beginning most often is second strongest, the middle is the weakest, and the end is the strongest. That writing style is directly relevant to the actor's method of handling lines. To fade away vocally on the last few words is to lose the emphasis the author deliberately placed in the ending.

Correcting the dribble-off effect may require a number of exercises. The director may wish to start by calling the actor's attention to the problem, perhaps tape-recording selected portions of rehearsal so the actor can hear the effect. The director also can help the actor find the rhythm of final emphases with exercises that use nonsense sentences, perhaps constructed of numbers (say, 1 through 10) or the alphabet, insisting that the end be emphasized. Work on breath control often is therapeutic.

Breath Control

In the quotation that begins this section, actor Laurence Olivier says that his training allows him to speak eight lines or more comfortably, without needing to pause for breath. Such excellent technique requires breath support based on correct breathing, an essential skill for singers, musicians, free divers, athletes—and actors. Proper breathing is necessary for all actors but more important for solo performers to help them get through long performances without suffering vocal fatigue. Pausing deliberately for effect can be excellent theatre; pausing because one simply runs out of air is not.

Diaphragmatic breathing. As experienced actors know, group or private warmup exercises emphasizing *diaphragmatic breathing*—sometimes called "belly breathing," or breathing from the abdomen—are valuable to improve vocal resonance, breath control, diction, and inflection. Proper breathing can help avoid the dribble-off problem, which often is simply a result of inadequate air. Proper breathing also allows the actor to undertake the vocal rigors of an entire solo play, just as it allows singers to handle challenges such as operas or musicals. Not unimportantly, proper breathing is healthy because it uses the lungs' full capacity and floods the body with oxygen.

One visible symptom of improper breathing is a heaving of the shoulders while inhaling. Diaphragmatic breathing is different. It uses the diaphragm, a muscle located under the lungs, between the lower part of the chest and the upper abdominal cavity. You can locate it by placing your hand just under your chest and feeling the movement when you cough or make explosive sounds, the "Huh! Huh!" exercises you often hear in rehearsal halls.

To understand the structure, think of a wide jar (the chest cavity and lungs) that has a somewhat narrow funnel on the top (the throat) and a flexible rubber membrane on the bottom (the diaphragm). Pulling down the diaphragm creates a partial vacuum by opening the size of the chest cavity, thus expanding and filling the lungs with air. That allows deep breathing, giving the actor more air than customary shallow breathing allows. Flattening the diaphragm—slowly pushing up on the rubber membrane of the jar—controls the amount of exhaled air. The combination of full lungs and control of exhaled air allows the actor to speak long sentences without breaking for a breath.

The analogy of the jar describes diaphragmatic breathing, but a cautionary word is necessary here. *No part of the process is forced.* We aren't sharply pulling or pushing the membrane. Instead, deep breathing should be relaxed, comfortable. With practice, breath control is smooth, easy, and second nature.

Helpful Exercises. One breathing exercise starts with you, the actor, lying comfortably on the floor, knees raised and feet flat on the floor. Yawn several times to relax your body and inhale a large amount of air. Now breathe deeply and focus on abdominal breathing. Place your hand on your chest just under the rib cage and feel the movement of your breathing. Repeat the process until you feel comfortable. You aren't gulping air rapidly, which might lead to hyperventilation, but instead you develop a slow, rhythmic deep breathing.

After you have discovered how the diaphragm feels while you are lying down, stand and repeat the exercise. Start by relaxing your body. Shake out your arms and legs, stretch your neck, and shrug your shoulders to make them comfortable. Start with a relaxed yet erect posture, raising your shoulders so the ribs are not pushing on the lungs. Yawn several times. Again place your hand on your chest just under your rib cage and breathe in deeply while remaining relaxed. Avoid strain—proper breathing is not forced but should come freely.

Inhale; then very slowly flatten the diaphragm while humming a single, soft "ah" sound, maintaining it as long as you comfortably can, keeping the volume the same throughout. Once you have mastered that, try "pah! pah!" exhalations or making an "ah" sound that slowly ascends and descends a musical scale. The director and actor will want to design other breath exercises, using them at every rehearsal.

AVOIDING THE TYRANNY OF PUNCTUATION

Vocal variety can be enhanced by understanding the difference between the writer and the actor. Playwrights, committed to professional writing, necessarily take pride in their writer's craft. One part of that expertise is carefully using correct punctuation. Yet while punctuation is an important clue to reading the play and understanding meanings, we're in the theatre; the actor isn't "a reader" but is the character.

Experienced performers learn that punctuation is a *writing technique*, not at all the same as an *acting guide*. For that reason, actors should free themselves from what I like to call "the tyranny of punctuation" so they instead will express the inherent meaning. That tyranny can have unfortunate results if actors allow themselves to be enslaved by punctuation. For example, most actors usually make a *vocal end stop* at the period ending a sentence: the voice drops in pitch, the tonal inflection expresses a finality, and the actor pauses before starting the next sentence, all saying "end of sentence." Overdone, that quickly becomes monotonous. Actors also may put a vocal pause at each comma and come to a full vocal stop at every dash, semicolon, or exclamation mark. The result can be a pedestrian, noninventive vocal mannerism, which too often is destructive of characterization and—the dreaded word—boring.

What should the actor do with punctuation? Start by paying attention to it during your first study-readings of the script, discovering the meanings in each sentence and paragraph. That accomplished, when you read the script aloud, *ignore the punctuation marks.* *

Overcoming self-imposed limits that come with slavishly following every punctuation mark has a parallel to verse plays. No actor will pause at the end of each typographical line but instead will continue nonstop to the next, expressing the flow of meaning. So, too, with sentences: The actor can elect to flow sentences together without pause, perhaps with only a small vocal inflection at the period. Equally, there may be times when the actor will put a pause where no period exists. The goal is to express the character's stream of emotion, thoughts, meaning, sense, intention, and subtext. During rehearsals the director and actor will experiment with various line readings. One effective experiment can focus on the flow of meaning, as if all punctuation marks are absent.

BLOCKING

Blocking is the director's assignment of meaningful movement about the stage area. It is one of the director's strongest storytelling techniques, no less expressive than the playwright's dialogue or plot, and we admire a director's sense of theatre as shown in use of the stage. For one example,

---

* The advantage of ignoring punctuation was driven home to us while rehearsing Peter Weiss's *The Investigation*, a powerful docu-drama taken from actual court records of a World War II trial that charged Germans with crimes in a concentration camp. Weiss's script has no punctuation. The lack of such guides was at first off-putting, but it forced the actors to find the sense of their dialogue. That search for meanings and emotions led the cast to greater participation in their characters' speeches. It was, we discovered, more effective than if the play had standard punctuation. One wouldn't want to conclude that plays should be written without punctuation, but. . . .

much about the character is revealed if he moves briskly and energetically, such as we'd expect of Sonny in *Nice Shoes*, or if she moves slowly, as could be appropriate for Anna Mae in *French Fries*—if, indeed, she moves at all.

Basic Rules of Blocking

Blocking is the director's visual storytelling techniques through specifically designed movement on the stage area. We think of blocking as *area movement* from one stage space to another, in contrast to gestures or shifts of bodily weight or position. Still, those smaller actions can be meaningful ways of showing the character's objectives.

Effective blocking speaks clearly the character's objectives, emotions, and thoughts. Blocking also speaks about the style of the play. For example, we often think of slow and deliberate angular movement patterns for dramas and more rapid curved movements for comedies. Equally, certain performance concepts will affect blocking. Bogosian's "rock and roll" concept of his performance, for instance, will call for more energetic blocking.

When blocking, the director is aware of basic rules. They can be expressed simply, although applying them requires careful thought during the director's private work outside of rehearsals as well as during run-throughs of the play.

☐ Movement is storytelling.

☐ Movement merely for its own sake isn't a wise artistic choice and should be avoided.

☐ Every movement must be motivated.

☐ Every non-movement must be motivated.

☐ The audience must be able to recognize the motivation.

☐ Movement should be plausible and probable, appropriate for the character and the play.

Blocking Used to Emphasize Significant Moments

As a director, you can use blocking to emphasize the character's objective or plot lines such as the point of attack or a new complication. One way, for instance, is to follow basic premises about movement. First, the proscenium stage has *weak* and *strong* areas. The center areas, logically, are the most dominant, with down center being the strongest; the upstage areas are weaker, and most directors believe up left is the weakest. To emphasize a particular moment—character objective or plot point such as the point of attack or a new complication—you may wish to have the character up left before the desired emphasis and then move to center to highlight the point. Secondly, movement before a line will emphasize the line, so the director may have the character stop speaking, move, complete the move, and then speak the line that deserves emphasis.

We can illustrate these premises with possible blocking of *French Fries*. You might consider having Anna Mae start the play silently, standing profile as if looking through an imaginary window up stage left (a weak area), then, still without dialogue, move to a rocker right center (a strong area), by which she stands, and when the movement is completed she says she's always wanted to live in a McDonald's (letting movement before the line stress her statement).

In many ways, blocking a monodrama is easier than blocking a large-cast play. With but one character, the director doesn't have to worry about moving several characters out of the way to clear a doorway for another character's entrance, has no concerns about placing characters to maintain a visual balance or to achieve compositional factors, won't have to insist that other actors apply the adage of "move only during your line," and doesn't fret about characters covering each other.

Certain aspects of blocking may appear relatively easy in multiple-cast plays because a character can be motivated to move toward one character or away from another, each movement a communication of a character's emotions and thoughts. Those aspects of motivated blocking are absent with the solo play when no other characters are on stage.

The Director's "Homework"

Directors think of blocking outside of rehearsals as a matter of conscientiously doing one's homework to prepare the production, and you will want to plan blocking carefully in advance of rehearsals. This private work, away from the stress of rehearsals, gives the director time to create and think about the effect. You'll want to investigate character motivations for movement, stemming from the character's *needs, emotions,* and *internal conflicts.* Planning blocking privately also allows you to determine movement patterns that reflect the play's needs and style.

For this blocking homework, use a scale model or sketch of the set and floor plan. Create a scale character, perhaps using a chess piece or a bent piece of cardboard. Read the play slowly and repeatedly, seeing in your mind the character in the stage environment. Ask yourself what the character *wants* to do. Ask yourself, too, what key plot points and character objectives need visual emphasis. For example, if blocking A *Poster of the Cosmos*, you'll want to ask yourself if Tom, at the end of the play, stands and moves away from the cops, perhaps toward center, to think of the death of his friend in a private moment. Write the blocking in your directorial prompt book, the "Bible" of the production.

Don't expect yourself to see the entire play's blocking. Directors don't. Instead, they more typically envision a number of isolated moments. Some call attention to themselves because the script directly indicates activity through dialogue—the character goes to answer the telephone or moves to look out a window. Sonny's actions with Mike in *Nice Shoes*, for example, are clearly indicated in dialogue. Other moments express an emotion or thought—the character jumps up at this point, sits down in frustration now, moves abruptly and then stops, struck by a sudden insight or new idea. Tom in *Poster of the Cosmos*, for example, could rise from his seat and pace away from the cops when angry at their questions or while confiding certain intimate secrets.

Stage directions also help us envision blocking, but although directors pay close attention to them, they don't always feel compelled to follow them. Although the playwright often writes character stage directions such as "pacing" or "moves away," some blocking notes may reflect the stage manager's notes from the play's premiere production. The former help us because they let us know what the original creator envisioned. Stage manager's notes are less helpful because they are for a particular theatrical facility, scene design, floor plan, director, and actor, all of which vary from our production.

Observing the actor carefully during early read-through rehearsals can help you find ideas for blocking. That's one reason directors prefer to have "on your feet" rehearsals versus "sit down" read-throughs. The actor may move, say, six or eight times during a given action unit, and you may discover that one or two of those are especially effective. Note them in your prompt book and plan to use them when you start blocking rehearsals.

Blocking Rehearsals

Once the homework is done, you're ready for blocking rehearsals. You can block a very short monodrama such as *Nice Shoes* in one rehearsal. The longer the play, however, the more rehearsals you'll want, dividing the play into units like the French scene we discussed in the previous chapter and doing a few each rehearsal. For example, two blocking rehearsals ought to suffice for a short-short monodrama such as *French Fries* or *Twirler*, and you might want to divide a play such as A *Poster of the Cosmos* into three blocking rehearsals.

There are various methods for scheduling blocking rehearsals, but in all cases it is important to include review sessions to help the actor know the blocking. For example, at blocking rehearsal 1, block unit one. At blocking rehearsal 2, review blocking of unit 1 and then block unit 2. At blocking rehearsal 3, review blocking of unit 2 and then block unit 3. Follow that with several stop-and-go working runs so you and the actor can make corrections while you observe how the pieces flow.

Start by giving the actor the preliminary blocking you worked out privately. That done, the two of you can collaborate to ensure the blocking is appropriate for the stage and the character. Expect to make changes during rehearsals, eliminating or adding blocking according to the character's dictates and the actor's suggestions. Don't be surprised if blocking that seemed effective in early rehearsals will appear ineffective in later stages, because as the character develops and changes, some blocking no longer is motivated or appropriate.

Visual Liveliness

Directors keep in mind that theatre is a visual art, evidenced by audiences' references about going to "see" a play. Therefore, as directors we should ask ourselves during rehearsals, "Is this play visually interesting and captivating?" For example, while blocking *French Fries* quite possibly you'd conclude that Anna Mae may stay on her chair for the entire play— she doesn't seem to *need* to move and we certainly don't want movement merely for its own sake. Even so, that doesn't exclude visual activities that express her thoughts and emotions. Surely while in her chair she is motivated at special moments to shift positions and change weight, moving from side to side, leaning forward at a particular thought, sitting back in her chair for another emotion. Props may help motivate such movement, too, and Anna Mae might turn to a chairside table to get a particular item.

MEMORIZATION

Theatrical lore is rich in stories about actors going up on their lines. One favorite story refers to *Waiting for Godot*, Samuel Beckett's classic story of two tramps waiting . . . and waiting . . . and waiting. Many of their lines throughout the play are markedly similar. For its premiere performance the actors apparently totally lost track of where they were in the script, and they jumped back and forth throughout the play, each waiting for the stage manager to give them their correct lines . . . waiting . . . and waiting . . . . and waiting. Jon Jory, artistic director of the Actors Theatre of Louisville, tells a story about an actress in one of Jane Martin's one-woman plays from her collection, *Talking With* . . . . During the New York production the actress froze, a traumatic experience that was larger than forgetting lines, and it quite shook her foundations.

Such stories take on mythic proportions in Green Room retellings, but the director and actor of a solo play would prefer to become famous for other reasons. Memorization of the solo play can present problems because the character has more lines than do major characters in multi-cast plays and there's no colleague on stage to offer helpful lines. Knowing that, the director and actor will take special pains to allow adequate time for memorization. One typical directorial admonition—"Memorize on your time, not on mine"—reminds the actor of personal responsibility to memorize out of rehearsals. That's especially relevant to the monodrama and the size of the memorization task.

Scheduling "Off Book" Rehearsals

The director's careful attention to scheduling off-book rehearsals is a necessary first step. Memorization is best accomplished in increments, not all at once. Actors tend to memorize more easily after they have been blocked, so the director blocks the play before calling for off book.

Memorization is easier if there is a pattern of working a section, going off book, and review. For example, assume a relatively short play that can be divided into three sections. On Monday, say, focus rehearsals on section 1. On Tuesday, call for off book for section 1, backing up and repeating as necessary. In the latter part of rehearsals, work section 2. On Wednesday, review section 1, go off book for section 2, then work section

3. On Thursday, review sections 1 and 2 and go off book for section 3. Friday's rehearsal focuses on the memorization of the entire play, with stop-and-go corrections as needed.

After the actor is off book, speed run-throughs can help memorization and also quicken the pace. They identify pauses where the actor is searching for the next line. "Speedies" are best approached with a certain amount of playfulness—but always an insistence that the actor go through lines faster and faster. Pauses indicate memorization gaps, and those lines can be repeated until memorization is complete.

BEAT: A SHIFT OF GEARS

Beat has a number of meanings. Directors and playwrights may use "beats" to refer to action or motivational units (such as those we called French scenes in an earlier chapter). Directors also use the word in another context, telling actors to "take a beat," meaning to make a significant pause. A third meaning describes an actor's measurement of a single unit—action and reaction—that involves the character's *intention*, the tactic the character uses to overcome an obstacle or objection that is a wall in the path of the character's major objective. For the actor, *beat* is, therefore, a subdivision of the character's overall superobjective that runs through the play. It is comparable to a beat in a measure of a musical work; just as a symphony has many beats, so also a character's units of action is composed of a large number of beats.

Beat, however, is vague and tricky to explain and more difficult to apply. Given the unfortunate confusion infecting the term (and, truth be told, many theatrical terms), here we instead suggest thinking of a *shift of emotional or intellectual gears*. Such shifts are the character's dynamic movements. They can result from many stimuli—a discovery of a new aspect of self or a new thought, a change of attitude, a fresh determination, a new decision to take or not take an action, a tactic to overcome an obstacle, and the like. Think, for example, of Hamlet's shifts during his reflective "To be or not to be." To select but one change, "perchance to dream" is a new major insight—death may bring a particularly grim horror—and therefore it is what we're calling *a shift*.

Such shifts may happen frequently, depending on the character's emotional and mental changes, and shifts may be of various sizes. Perhaps you'll find a shift after only a few sentences. At other times the character may stay in a given mood, without shifts, for many sentences. These shifts can be compared to the writer's device of paragraphing, underlinings, subheadings, major headings, and chapter divisions.

The shift of emotional or intellectual attitudes is an internal aspect of the character. *Significantly, the shifts are reflected vocally and physically* both because shifts are reflected in voice and body and because they need to be communicated to the audience. Think again of Hamlet's "Perchance to dream"—what vocal change do you hear? What physical movement? These shifts are essential to create a dynamic and vitally alive character; for the solo performance, where only one actor is making shifts, they take on increased importance.

Finding and playing these shifts has many advantages. The process helps ensure that the actor understands the character's emotions and thoughts. They also help the audience perceive the inner workings of the character, and the character becomes more dynamic, more interesting. Importantly, playing these shifts will help prevent monotone, monovolume, and monorate vocalization, and they will give clues to the character's physical changes.

Both director and actor need to search out such character movements and find ways to communicate them to the audience. Both searches can be time consuming, one reason we spend so much time studying the script and rehearsing. During rehearsals the director serves as "an audience of one," a mirror that reflects to the actor which shifts are clear and visible and which need enhancing.

We conclude this book with some suggestions that can help you find productions. Whether you are a playwright, director, or actor, you'll want to team up with others and search out opportunities to perform your solo play. Use the same creativity that characterizes your theatre work and think of a do-it-yourself approach.

PRODUCTIONS: A DO-IT-YOURSELF PROJECT

While playing *Star Trek's* Jean Luc-Picard, Patrick Stewart found he had to continue his stage work so he would not—his word—"shrivel." He describes how he turned to the solo performance at college campuses.

> I started [returning to the stage] about halfway through the second season [of *Star Trek*]. It was then that the penny had dropped for me, that

this series wasn't going to go away. So, I started right then developing a parallel career. And the one thing that I could do was the simplest thing because we had no little time. I couldn't do plays then because our down time, our hiatus was so brief. So, I started developing a series of solo shows, something that I could literally put in the trunk of my car at a weekend—'cause we worked Monday through Friday on *Star Trek*— put in my car on a Saturday morning, drive to some college campus, get up on a stage and do some acting.

It was in order to try to illustrate to anybody who was interested that I was still an actor and not just an icon. But it was also for myself. I was not only frightened that my career would shrivel as a result of *Star Trek*, I was frightened that I might shrivel.

Theatre people fantasize of performing in a major Manhattan theatre. Your name in bright lights on the marquee. Signing autographs. Reading glowing reviews. Playing to full houses and taking bows during standing ovations. Agents and producers leaving urgent messages, promises of more productions. For playwrights, actors, and directors, such daydreams come with the territory and are a natural part of being a theatre person. For a select few, the fantasies may come true.

Broadway, however, is not the entire theatre world, and although you'd relish a New York showing, your primary goal is "stage time"—performing your monodrama in front of audiences. There are numerous non-Broadway production possibilities that you will want to investigate, remembering one model that led to a successful solo play career: While a college student, long before he became a famous Tony Award winner and successful film and television actor, Hal Halbrook continually tested a number of short scenes at various local clubs, learning from audience responses how to write and act his solo play—*then* he had the New York experience with his *Mark Twain Tonight!*

Becoming Your Own Production Company

A popular misconception is that agents find production opportunities for playwrights, actors, and directors. That may be true for a very few theatre people at the top of their careers, but more often agents urge theatre artists to search out opportunities for themselves. Certainly those at the beginning of their careers need to gain experience and build résumés, and that requires you to look for do-it-yourself projects.

Think of yourself as your own self-contained production company, agent, and promotions manager. Although it is possible for you to handle all such details yourself, you may wish to recruit others to help with the production in such areas as stage manager, lighting designer and control, properties, and sound. Where do you find these people? Check your local theatres. (You *do* attend them, don't you?) Make contacts with those you see doing outstanding work.

Starting in your local community makes sense. As you gain experience and achieve good reviews, branch out into larger areas. Prepare an attractive professional-looking packet that describes you and your show, and include copies of programs, reviews, and the like, so you are prepared to give it to people you contact about performing. There are a number of possible avenues you can explore, such as those we mention next. No, you won't become wealthy, but you can charge a modest admission fee and meet expenses while gaining valuable production experience.

Possible Production Venues

Colleges and universities. A number of solo performers find that college and university audiences are receptive to a wide variety of monodramas, ranging from socially involved issues to protean performances of Shakespearean characters to pure entertainment. College students make excellent audiences, and Patrick Stewart said that he enjoyed visiting campuses with one-person shows to keep himself from withering artistically. Lynn Redgrave has also said she finds campus audiences receptive to her *Shakespeare for My Father: The Life and Times of an Actor's Daughter*. The college theatre department itself may be interested in supporting your solo play. That failing, colleges have a number of other spaces suitable for performances, and you can talk with the institution's scheduling offices to obtain necessary permission.

High school groups. Like college students, high school students can provide lively audiences. Your local high school may be interested in helping you perform, especially if your script is appealing to students or deals with contemporary issues important to high schoolers. Expect the principal to want to look over the play to be sure it doesn't run contrary to school policies about content and language.

Libraries. Modern libraries aren't your grandparents' places. Gone are stern librarians frowning severely at anyone whispering. Now libraries increasingly embrace numerous events for their patrons. That includes performances. Because librarians by profession are deeply interested in culture and writing, they look positively on solo plays. Your local library may have an attached performing arts wing, usually a relatively small theatre that is excellent for intimate solo plays. Even without such performance wings, libraries often have space that can be relatively easily set up for the minimalist solo performance.

Coffeehouses. Enjoying a burst of popularity, coffeehouses seem to be replacing the legendary old country store, where citizens would sit around the cracker barrel and discuss politics, people, and the weather. Today's coffeehouse is a social institution as much as a haven for caffeine mavens, and many often sponsor poets and novelists reading their works, musical soloists or groups, and other forms of entertainment. Visit your local coffeehouse and envision your solo play in a minimalist production; then chat with the manager about the possibility.

Churches. Concern for community involvement leads many churches to offer a variety of programs. For the monodramatist, this open-door policy is especially attractive. Approach the churches in your area that sponsor events and arrange for your production.

Civic organizations. Consider approaching local clubs and groups such as the Kiwanis or Lions. Offer them a short program that fits within their normal meeting time.

Community theatres. Even the most active community theatre has down time when there are no performances. Talk with its leaders about the possibility of performing your solo play when it is between productions. Once you have established your reputation, you and the community theatre can think about the possibility of scheduling you on their regular season.

Regional not-for-profit theatres. Major professional theatres exist in many regions of the country. They offer excellent theatrical productions and often are, unlike Broadway, interested in new plays. Indeed, many popular Broadway shows premiere in these theatres. Some theatres offer a "second season," usually in a small space, for experimental works. For monodramatists, these are excellent top-of-the-line targets. Allen Jeffrey Rein, for example, wrote initial drafts of his *First Star Blues*, a powerful comedy about five quite different men that he wrote for himself to perform, while an acting intern at Actors Theatre of Louisville. He then performed it at the Horizon Theatre Company in Atlanta while he was a member of various other Atlanta theatres.

OTHER SOURCES FOR FINDING PRODUCTIONS

Helpful publications for playwrights belong in the writer's personal library. For all theatre artists, the Internet can be a profitable research tool. We can describe some of the more significant aids.

Publications

Two helpful books for playwrights looking for performance are *The Playwright's Companion: A Submission Guide to Theatres and Contests in the* U.S.A., edited by Mollie Ann Meserve and published by Feedback Theatre books (305 Madison Avenue, Suite 1146, New York, NY 10165), and *Dramatists Sourcebook*, published by Theatre Communications Group (355 Lexington Avenue, New York, NY 10017). Both are annuals and are, therefore, likely to contain up-to-date information about list play contests and awards, agents, play publishers, producers seeking new plays, and other helpful information. Both are relatively inexpensive. The two are sufficiently different to warrant buying both, and they are published approximately six months apart so each will have new material.

Your local library also will have valuable information. Two monthly magazines, *The Writer* and *Writer's Digest*, can be inspirational and informational. *Writer's Market*, published by Writers Digest Books, is an annual listing of producers, theatres interested in new plays, agents, and more.[1]

The Internet

You may want to search the internet for information about auditions, contests, theatres searching for new plays, and the like. Although there are more theatre sites than space allows us to discuss here, we can list the more significant sites. As experienced searchers know, opening one site will lead to dozens of others.

Search engines. Recent studies have shown that even the most powerful search engines are unable to find all relevant materials on the Internet, apparently missing as many as one-third of the available sites. For that reason, expect to use several search engines. You'll want to develop a personal list of a number of engines you find effective. Among those you may want to consider are the following:

AltaVista *http://altavista.digital.com/*
Yahoo! *http://www.yahoo.com*
Inference Find! *http://inference.com/infind/*
Northern Light Search *http://www.nlsearch.com/*
Dogpile (no, that's not a joke!) *http://www.dogpile.com*

Several have a culled list, perhaps a "top 5 percent" or the like. Those generally are quite effective.

The following sites can be valuable for theatre people. Each will lead you to additional sites.

Playbill On-Line

http://wwww1.playbill.com/playbill/

One of the two primary theatrical sites (the other is "Theatre Central," which you can access through this site), Playbill On-Line is regularly updated. Of special interest is the Casting and Jobs folder. Other folders lead you to "Late News," "Theatrical Listings," and even New York hotels and seating charts of major theatres.

Theatre Central

http://wwww1.playbill.com/cgi-bin/plb/central?cmd=start

Theatre Central says it has "the largest compendium of links on the Internet" and surely no one can match its hundreds of theatre sites. Actors find "Audition Notices" here. You also can find e-mail addresses of theatrical professionals and news about productions and casting.

Luckman's "Best of the Web"

http://www.bofw.com

Luckman's winnows down some possible 150,000 sites to a selected 25,000 "four- and five-star" locations. The web master gives each site a rating for ease of use and thoroughness. The search is by *channels*. Click the Art channel for theatre and you'll find pages of eclectic sites. The Entertainment channel also yields some theatre sites.

ELAC Theatre

http://www.perspicacioty.com/elacttheatre/

The website of Theatre Arts Department of East Los Angeles College offers a Writers' Workshop for playwrights as well as other materials.

Scott's theatre-link.com

http://www.theatre-link.com

Search Scott's for casting and contract services. Here, too, you can find many other relevant theatrical subjects.

Playwrights Cafe

http:/wwwPlayCafe.org/

This Cafe uses real scripts being written by members. You also can participate in discussion groups focused on playwriting, including those led by guest speakers, and track down a certain number of resources.

Digital Stage

http://www.tjhsst.ed/Drama/digstage/digstage.html

On this Stage you'll find a rich collection of theatre sources, guide to contacts, a limited number of academic theatre programs, and a list of links.

Newsgroups. It seems there is a newsgroup for any topic you can imagine and many you'd never think could exist. Newsgroups spring up with amazing speed, and even those that fade often still have a presence on the net. If you're searching for subjects, the following directory is helpful.

The Internet Newsgroup Directory

www.internetdatabase.com/usenet.htm

"Deja News," a search engine, can take you to internet discussion groups. Most are not moderated, which means that with possibly useful information you'll also find flamers and weirdos with too much time on their hands. The "Deja News" search engine can lead you to entries. For example, in a recent search, "theatre" listed over 10,000 posts.

Deja News

www.dejanews.com/

Deja News can lead you to theatre newsgroups you might want to visit, such as the following.

> *rec.arts.theatre.misc*
> *rec.arts.theatre.musicals*
> *rec.arts.theatre.stagecraft*
> *alt.stagecraft*
> *phl.theatre*

As we stated at the beginning of this book, *The Power of One* seeks to encourage you to develop your own one-person play. I hope it achieves that purpose. Good luck!

NOTE

1. For a more detailed discussion of such matters as copyright, organizations for playwrights, agents, contests, royalties, publications, and more, I invite you to examine Chapter 10, "Resources for the Playwright," in *The Elements of Playwriting* (Macmillan).

APPENDIX

The Evolution of the Solo Play

Whether you're an actor, director, playwright, or a combination of the three, your interest in the solo play connects you to a remarkably long-running theatrical tradition that began well before recorded history, certainly prior to the formal birth of western theatre in early Greece. Indeed, the solo play directly contributed to those origins of theatre. Furthermore, as we discuss here, your legacy is a distinctive form of art that even kept theatre alive during the Middle Ages; one that in later centuries was vital to help theatre overcome various religious and political oppressions.

Although the solo play has a distinguished list of accomplishments, theatre scholars ignore the one-person play. Strangely, you won't find discussions of it in books on theatrical history, playwriting, acting, directing, or design. Most books don't even mention the monodrama.

Such omission is unfortunate. It also is difficult to understand, given the one-person play's illustrious history and artistic triumphs. As a monodramatist you should know that your art form is rich in traditions that influence your creative work and that you are part of a highly distinguished family.

To help you better understand and appreciate the solo play's contributions over centuries, this appendix looks briefly at particular highlights of the monodrama's development.

PREHISTORIC "ONE-PERSON THEATRE": THE SHAMAN

Ritualistic religious ceremonies were the core of prehistoric society when, as director Tyrone Guthrie says, "Our primitive ancestors, often wiser than we, sought to relate themselves to God, or the gods." Leading those rituals was the tribal *shaman*, the wise religious leader presumed to have extraordinary, even supernatural, powers. In our frame of reference, the shaman also is the great-great granddaddy of today's solo performer.

The shaman's rituals illuminated mysteries such as birth, life, and death, as well as what to early humans were baffling movements of the sun and moon, which had to be understood because they seemed to indicate the gods' instructions when to plant, reap, or conduct other tribal affairs. Especially important to the shaman and his or her people were celebrations of the cycle of the seasons, particularly the wonders of rebirth in the spring. Such ritualistic tribal ceremonies led to the development of early theatrical activities in diverse countries like Egypt, Africa, China, India, and Greece. Comparable rituals continue to be observed today in various religions that commemorate rebirth, such as the Christian celebration of Easter.

Although we do not have records of such prehistoric rituals, we safely assume that the shaman's ceremonial performances contained elements we think of as theatrical. Significantly for our discussion here, the shaman was a *solo performer*.

Imagine you are a member of a primitive tribe, circled around a flickering fire, surrounded by a universe full of unknowable forces that you often fear. You hear noises from the woods that surround you, and you wonder which of the god-forces are responsible. You know that you and your tribe face a major decision, perhaps whether to leave this area and go to another, or you may be concerned about a forthcoming hunt.

Then into the circle—in effect, onto the "stage"—comes the shaman. You watch, entranced, as he performs rituals to help you and your tribe understand a particular mystery, helping each of you understand your role in the tribe and guiding you to understand aspects of your world. He is an expert entertainer, using pantomime, gesture, magic, and dance, as well as costumes, fanciful makeup, and masks to impersonate the gods, animals, and mysterious forces that are a part of your daily concerns. His *enactment*—a core ingredient of theatre—evokes his audience's emotional and intellectual responses. It is educational, religious, and entertaining. You're comforted by the familiar ritual that helps you discover that answers to major puzzles *do* exist.

The shaman's ceremonies are designed to appease the gods or to show the tribe the gods' wishes. The image is extremely powerful, as if the god is actually present. Of course no spectator is quite convinced that actors actually are the characters they imitate, but yet. . . . There *is* a undeniable magic that lifts the audience into belief. Through ritual the impersonation takes on reality, then in prehistoric times and now on our stages.

Although we credit the Greek actor and playwright Thesbis as being the first actor because he was the first to introduce an actor to converse with the Chorus (c. 534 B.C.), we can argue that the earlier shaman deserves credit for that honor. Certainly the shaman's ritualistic "performance" later became important to the Greek theatre, and elements of it are seen today when a skilled performer takes on the form of a god or human, reproducing the essence of life so that the image comes to a vivid life through impersonation.

THE MONODRAMATIST'S CONTRIBUTIONS TO EARLY GREEK AND ROMAN THEATRE

I believe that the theatre makes its effect not by means of illusion, but by ritual. People do not believe that what they see or hear on stage is "really" happening. Action on the stage is a stylized reenactment of real action, which is then imagined by the audience. The reenactment is not merely an imitation but a symbol of the real thing. If I may quote this instance without irreverence, it expresses the point clearly: the priest in Holy Communion reenacts, with imitative but symbolic gestures and in a verbal ritual, the breaking of bread and the pouring of wine. He is at this moment an actor impersonating Christ in a very solemn drama. The congregation, or audience, is under no illusion that he really is Christ. It should, however, participate in the ritual with sufficient fervor to be rapt, literally "taken out of itself," to the extent that it shares the emotion which the priest or actor is suggesting. It completes the circle of action and reaction; its function is not passive but active. This, I think, is exactly what happens to an audience at a successful theatrical performance. —Tyrone Guthrie

From the prehistoric shaman's performances we move to the monodramatist's contributions to as-yet-unborn Greek and Roman theatre.

The Rhapsodist: *Precursor to Early Greek Theatre*

Greek theatrical celebrations grew out of tribal ritualistic ceremonies around the thirteenth century B.C., some seven hundred years before the beginning of the formal Greek drama that is the foundation of today's western theatre. Many leaders in those early ceremonies were solo performers, similar to today's monodramatists. One significant soloist was the *rhapsodist* (also called a *rhapsode*), or oral reader, who wrote and performed epic poetry about legends, history, and important individuals. The term comes from "rhapsody," or "stitch song," because part of the *rhapsodist's* material was memorized and another portion was improvised, making him a poet who "stitched together" old and new songs.

The *rhapsodists* served as a transitional bridge from primitive tribal rituals to the growth of formal Greek drama that started in ceremonies celebrating Dionysus, a god of fertility, wine, and revelry who illustrated the seasonal changes and birth, death, and resurrection that so intrigued earlier societies. Formal Greek drama then began to come to full flower around 534 B.C., led by playwrights such as Aeschylus, Sophocles, Euripides, and Aristophanes, who established forms and techniques still prevalent today.

The Histrione: *Precursor to Early Roman Theatre*

In ancient Rome, as in Greece, individual performers helped establish the formal theatre. Granted, Roman theatre initially borrowed from the Greek, but earlier Roman solo performers had helped create an audience. Roman monodramatists included *histriones* (compare that term with today's "histrionic," referring to acting), who used movement and gestures to enact a variety of characters. Their stories focused on historical figures and events, similar to modern biographical monodramas about presidents, artists, and writers. These Roman *histriones* were followed by playwrights such as Plautus, Terence, and Seneca.

SOLO PERFORMANCES DURING THEATRE'S HIATUS

Despite its artistic and social contributions, western theatrical activities virtually disappeared from around the beginnings of Christianity through the tenth century, finally struggling back to life in A.D. 925. Theatre's hiatus was caused by several factors—the decline of the Roman empire from within and the invasion of barbarian tribes from without, the decrease of state support of theatre, and theatre's own excesses which led to artistic decay—but a primary cause was the increasing strength of Christianity and the church's objections to theatre.

Greek and Roman religions found strength and meaning in theatre, using various forms of dramatic productions to celebrate their gods and special religious occasions, much as primitive tribes had found theatrical rituals were an effective means to connect human with god. Early Christianity, in contrast, took special exception to the theatre. The Christian church saw theatre as a continuation of unacceptable pagan festivals. Especially dismaying to church leaders was what they perceived as an earthy licentiousness that characterized both performances and audiences.

No doubt some theatrical excesses earned the church's disapproval. For example, Heliogabalus, emperor of Rome from A.D. 218 to 222, ordered that all theatrical sexual acts should be presented realistically (some became so graphic we'd rate them XXX today), which was offensive to the teachings of Christianity. Perhaps, too, the Church, like most institutional bodies, disliked being the butt of jokes and was offended by performances that satirized Christian rituals such as the sacrament of bread and wine.

The Church took various stands against theatre, but its decisive action came in A.D. 398 when the Council of Carthage issued a decree forbidding theatre. The ruling said anyone who went to the theatre on a holy day, instead of to church, would be excommunicated; and officials of the Christian church denied actors the sacraments of the church. Such actions were effective. Theatre became feeble, its once robust health dissipating, and it substantially disappeared—but not completely, thanks to the solo performance.

THEATRE IN THE MIDDLE AGES

With the advent of Christianity, harsh antitheatre attitudes virtually eliminated theatre in the Western world from around the beginning of the Christian era through the tenth century. That's not to say theatre died, however. On the contrary, the powerful human desire to communicate through creative enactment, plus the equally strong hunger to receive such communications, resulted in various "amusements" that were at least semitheatrical, such as pantomime, "rope dancing" (loose- or tight-rope walking), dancing, music, and animal acts. Importantly for our focus here, to that list we add the solo performer.

Despite antitheatre pressures, one-man shows were popular in the Middle Ages, the period in European history between classical antiquity and the Italian Renaissance. Medieval clerical scribes describe nomadic storytellers and solo entertainers such as *ministrales*, *mimi*, *lusores*, *histriones*, and *ioculatores*. Some appear similar to today's folk singers, storytellers, and monodramatists who bring legends and history to life, at times using historical records to comment on the present.

The Scôp
One early Middle Ages solo performer was the *scôp*, who preserved oral traditions of the time by reciting sagas. The title comes from the Old English word for "jester, or one who scoffs." Popular in northern Europe during the fifth through the twelfth centuries, the *scôp* was a singer and poetic storyteller, reminiscent of the Greek *rhapsodist* or Roman *histrione*. An Old English bard or poet who was honored for his tales about local history and heroes, the *scôp* brought to life epics and legends, often with musical accompaniment, and in that sense I tend to think of the *scôp* as similar to a modern folk singer (the song about railroad man "John Henry" comes to mind as one illustration). Occasionally the *scôp* was an important member of a royal household. Similar to the *scôp* was the *skald*, a Scandinavian bard.

The Gleeman
Another popular solo performer was known as a *gleeman*, a strolling singer who traveled the European countryside in search of audiences. The gleeman's period of activity roughly paralleled that of the *scôp*, from the fifth through the twelfth century. The term comes from "glee" or "glee-song," a part-song for three or more voices. Often the traveling solo gleeman would teach members of the audience the musical parts, a Medieval version of sing-along activities that are popular with modern audiences. The gleeman, like the *scôp*, was a historian who chronicled significant events, although apparently *scôps* tended to focus primarily on the past and gleemen more often told stories of their contemporary lords. We better understand the nature of these performances by noting that *glee* refers to exultation, mirth, and jollity.

The Goliard
Eleventh-, twelfth-, and thirteenth-century theatrical performers who wandered through England, France, and Germany, the *goliards* were scholars, students, and clerics who wrote and recited Latin verses celebrating life's sen-

sual pleasures. A collection of their works, the *Carmina Burana*, praised wine and women, and their verses are full of a love of life as well as an earthy hedonistic ribaldry. The goliard took special delight in attacking religious corruption and parodying sacred subjects. As Blodgett and Swanson point out in *The Love Songs of the Carmina Buran*: "the effects would be similar to that of changing 'Hail, Mary, full of grace' to 'Hail, sherry full of grapes.'"[1] The outcome of such hearty irreverence is easily predicted: in 1227 the Church prohibited goliard participation in religious ceremonies, and sixty-two years later clerics themselves were ordered not to participate in such antiestablishment activities. Such prohibitions help us infer the goliards' popularity.

The Jongleur

Jongleurs were traveling solo entertainers who were active in medieval France and Norman England around 1000, although they originated several centuries earlier. They sang, told stories, recited poetry, juggled, performed clown and acrobatic acts, and exhibited wild animals. Songs were those they composed or were written by *trouvères*. Chaucer refers to them as *tregetours* in his *Canterbury Tales*. In a departure from customary practice, *jongleurs* apparently included females as well as males. As time passed *jongleurs* sought employment with wealthy lords and became more broadly known as *minstrels*.

The Trouvère

Medieval poets and singers-musicians who flourished in northern France during the eleventh through thirteenth centuries, the solo *trouvères* (the word means "finder, inventor") presented poetic works focused on love. Popular were their *chansons de geste* ("songs of deeds"), which were epic poems dealing with legendary or historical personalities or events. Perhaps the best known example is *Chanson de Roland* or the *Song of Roland*, which probably was written around the latter part of the eleventh century. Wandering *trouvères* and *jongleurs* may have prompted the later Paris street theatres that, still later, contributed to the American variety shows called vaudeville, which flourished from around 1880 to the late 1920s.

The Troubadour

Active primarily in southern France from the eleventh to thirteenth centuries, troubadours were literate young aristocrats who were the contemporaries of the *trouvères* in the northern regions. Their songs and poems dealt with *courtly love*, a highly stylized code of behavior that prescribed rules of conduct between lovers, or at least love among the upper social classes. The troubadour was a major participant in their era's instructional *courts of love* that focused on concepts of an ideal relationship of men and women. In contrast to earlier beliefs that women were inferior to men, courtly love idealized women who, it was believed, ennobled their lovers.

The solo performers' focus on courtly love later elevated English literature, especially in sonnets by writers such as Sidney, Spenser, and Shakespeare. We can understand the nature of courtly love by reading novels such as Sir Walter Scott's *Ivanhoe*—a lofty idealized relationship quite different from the sort of love shown in modern romance novels!—and perhaps we can compare the troubadours' musical qualities with twentieth-century melodic ballad singers such as Maurice Chevalier, Frank Sinatra, or Michael Crawford.

The Guslari and Pevaci

The *guslari* were performers active in Slavic countries around the fourteenth century. Their musical nature is shown by the source of their name—the *gusle*, a one-stringed fiddle. The typical *guslar* composed, sang, and recited poetry honoring national events. You can find Christian *guslari* today in Bosnia, along with *pevaci*, Muslim chanters who accompany themselves with the lutelike *tambura*.

The Minstrel

Many of the preceding solo performers lost their specific identity to become known as minstrels, popular performers at courts throughout medieval Europe in the thirteenth and fourteenth centuries. These musicians or other entertainers usually were in the service of noblemen for whom they sang or recited poetry and stories, most often to instrumental musical accompaniment. As minstrels became less dependent on their lords, the word grew to refer to all traveling entertainers. By the fifteenth century "minstrel" came to mean "musician," and the performers had a special musician's gallery in medieval banquet halls. Quite possibly minstrel performers influenced musical aspects of Elizabethan dramas, and the musician's gallery in the upper story of Shakespeare's Globe Theatre may have derived from comparable facilities at the manor's banquet hall. Minstrels declined after the development of printing and book publishing, the solo performer's storytelling techniques replaced by the printed form.

The solo performer was a significant contributor to theatre from the shaman's prehistoric ceremonies through subsequent centuries. During the Middle Ages, soloists provided forms of theatre, keeping the art alive despite religious objections. Interestingly, history repeats itself. In the following centuries the soloist again overcame antitheatrical laws and oppression.

SIDESTEPPING ANTITHEATRICAL LAWS

English and American mideighteenth-century theatre faced restrictive laws prompted by religious and political concerns about deviations from "acceptable" content. Perhaps we can understand such laws by looking at comparable prohibitions in more recent times. For example, early- to midtwentieth-century Russia banned "dangerous deviations" from approved socialist realism. Nor is that prejudice limited to past times or foreign countries. Even in our times we see certain American politicians and religious leaders attacking what they perceive as immoral theatrical productions.

Antitheatre decrees in the eighteenth century forced theatre artists and managers to devise creative machinations to circumvent the regulations. The solo play rose to the battle with tactics as clever as a brainy military general who manages to outwit the enemy with far larger forces but lesser will and determination.

Walpole and the Licensing Act of 1737

One example of restrictive regulations is found in eighteenth-century England. Prime Minister Walpole, incensed by theatrical political satires—especially those directed at him or his interests—compelled Parliament to enact the Licensing Act of 1737, which prohibited performances at "unauthorized" theatres. Walpole's act further specified that plays had to be licensed by the Lord Chamberlain, a highly effective form of censorship because the license was given to only "approved" plays. You can easily guess what such governmental approval meant. As a result of Walpole's prohibition, Drury Lane and Covent Garden became the only legitimate theatres in all England, making theatre virtually inaccessible for many citizens and terminating jobs for hundreds of playwrights, actors, directors, and theatre personnel. Theatre was unavailable to the population outside London, thereby eliminating citizens' habit of attending plays. It sounded like a fatal blow to theatre.

Translating Walpole's law into more recent times, it would be as if President Lyndon Johnson had outlawed antiwar plays during the Vietnam era, forbidding theatrical satires such as MacBird or musicals like Hair. Equally, it would be as if contemporary politicians managed to pass legislation to stop television's political jabs and satires such as those presented on late night talk shows and Saturday Night Live.

Samuel Foote and the Diversions of the Morning

The enterprising Samuel Foote (1720–1777) was one victim of Walpole's new Licensing Act. The British actor-manager and playwright was known as "the English Aristophanes" for his sensational and libelous plays (called "scandal-chronicles") that satirized well-known people. An illustration of Foote's pugnacious plays is The Maid of Bath, which attacked the suitors of Elizabeth Linley, then engaged to marry playwright Richard Sheridan. One modern text helps us understand Foote's topical satire by comparing him with twentieth-century wits such as Monty Python and playwright-monodramatist Dario Fo.[2]

The new antitheatre law should have permanently prevented Foote from any further work in theatre. It didn't. Foote was undaunted. He noted that Walpole's regulations prohibited "acting for gain, hire, or reward." Foote the actor decided to become Foote the nonactor. He cleverly sidestepped the regulations by presenting what he called "free entertainment"—actually a one-person show—to those who paid to participate in his An Auction of Pictures. Of course it was a play, but it was cleverly disguised.

One announcement said that "Foote will exhibit some entire new lots (a lot refers to a group of materials for auction), consisting of a poet, a beau, a Frenchman, a miser, a tailor, a sot, two young gentlemen, and a ghost."[3] Of course you recognize that these "items for auction" really were part of the cast of characters. Foote also offered audiences invitations to A Dish of Chocolate or A Dish of Tea, using acceptable social labels for what were actually solo theatrical productions. Further, instead of using an outlawed theatre building, the ingenious Foote advertised the entertainment would take place at "the Auction Room, late the little Theatre in the Hay."

We can imagine this sharp-witted writer-actor gleefully saying, "My dear Lord Chamberlain, please note I am presenting 'lectures' and 'parties,' not 'plays.'" Foote's canny stratagems confused Walpole's censors. By 1747 he was presenting a "nonplay" called The Diversions of the Morning. It proved so successful that other solo performers used the same enterprising subterfuge of calling their productions something other than theatre. A primary example was George Alexander Stevens' popular monodrama, A Lecture on Heads.

GEORGE ALEXANDER STEVENS AND THE LECTURE ON HEADS

The author and performer of the eighteenth-century's most popular monodrama also avoided Walpole's Licensing Act by a clever trick with words. The Lecture on Heads (sometimes also called The Celebrated Lecture on Heads) was the invention of George Alexander Stevens (1710–1784), who introduced it at England's Little Haymarket Theatre in 1764. Because it was a "lecture," it was free from the antitheatrical restraints of England's Licensing Act. Later, when it was taken to colonial America, the solo play–"lecture" equally overcame powerful antitheatre forces led by the puritanical elements in northeastern states.

The Performance of The Celebrated Lecture On Heads

Imagine you're a member of an eighteenth-century audience in a large theatre. Because you're well educated you take special delight in the satirical wit that dominates literature and theatre. You enjoy plays such as John Gay's The Beggar's Opera (1728), Henry Fielding's Tom Thumb, or the Tragedy of Tragedies (1730), and Richard Brinsley Sheridan's The Critic (1781). You and your friends are fond of music by new composers such as Johann Sebastian Bach, including his St. Matthew Passion (1729), and George Frideric Handel, especially The Messiah (1742). You've read novels such as Daniel Defoe's Robinson Crusoe (1719), Jonathan Swift's Gulliver's Travels (1726), and Henry Fielding's Tom Jones (1749).

You look around the theatre. All seats are taken in the pit and boxes, and most of the upper four galleries are full. The place is smoky and smelly because of the candles in the chandeliers, and the melting wax drips unpleasantly on your clothing. The stage is lit with various colors from the silk screens placed in front of oil lights and reflectors, and its floor is raked, with the highest part furthest from you. You buy an orange from a vendor and wait for *The Celebrated Lecture on Heads* to begin.

Then the green drapes open and George Alexander Stevens appears. Although this is a one-person show, it looks like a large cast: The stage is filled with rows of heads—wooden heads, papier-mâché heads, frowning heads, smiling heads, male heads, female heads, heads of elderly people, heads of young people, even plain blocks roughly shaped like heads. Some are wonderfully bewigged or adorned with the latest fashion in ladies' hats.

Stevens handles the heads with a puppeteer's skill. He often holds a head in each hand while one "talks" to the other. Stevens does magic tricks such as making money disappear or changing the faces on a deck of cards, and at times he shows that he is a skilled pantomimist as he pretends to play a musical instrument. He easily impersonates characters, concluding the show by putting on a wig and satirizing a religious teacher.

Gerald Kahan's *George Alexander Stevens and "The Lecture on Heads"* points out that the *Lecture* enjoyed remarkable success: "Before the vogue had run out in the early decades of the nineteenth century, the *Lecture* had gone through some forty published editions and had received wholly, or in part, an uncounted number of performances which must have totaled close to a thousand."[4] One thousand performances? Even today, despite greatly increased opportunities due to the expanded population, any solo performer would be delighted with that many performances. For Stevens, an earnest actor who so far had played small roles, the *Lecture* was an economic life-ring and his solo play gave him success that he never received in standard multicharacter plays.

In theatre, then as now, success breeds copycats. The *Lecture* gave birth to numerous one-man imitations such as lectures on hearts, tails, and even no-heads. For example, James S. Dodd created A *Satyrical Lecture on Hearts*, later adding another on *Noses*; and John Palmer, who worked for Samuel Foote and David Garrick, toured with his version on *The Living and the Dead*.

The solo performance took on new dimensions in the nineteenth century. Through the work of respected authors, it developed definite literary strengths which made theatre "acceptable," even to people who had reservations about attending theatre.

THE MONODRAMA IN THE NINETEENTH CENTURY: NEWFOUND RESPECTABILITY

Nineteenth-century audiences grew fond of the monodrama and it responded enthusiastically, as if it were an impatient seed waiting its turn to receive the nourishing encouragement that had been given its multicharacter relative. Nineteenth-century cultural tastes expanded rapidly, especially in literature. Victorian families gathered by the fireplace to read aloud from the Bible or literary works such as plays by William Shakespeare and novels by contemporary authors such as Charles Dickens, Edgar Allan Poe, and Mark Twain. As public interest in literature grew, so did receptivity to literary theatrical events. Respected authors such as Dickens, Poe, and Twain became popular one-person performers and their world tours drew large audiences, prompting other novelists, essayists, and poets to create solo performances. Logically enough, they were followed by solo actors reading, then performing, such author's works.

Increased Opportunities for Platform Readings

Family reading sessions and interest in literature encouraged actors to present one-person shows that were primarily readings of poetry and literature. In the early nineteenth century these performances were easily arranged: The actor simply rented a hall, put together a program consisting of readings from poetry and literature, and advertised the production. Such events—often called *platform readings* because they took place on a platform—lacked the complexities of multi-character plays because they didn't require rehearsals with others and could be easily presented without elaborate staging, expensive preparations, or theatrical facilities. Those advantages continue today.

Actors found readings an economic life preserver in troubled waters. In *Retrospections of America: 1797–1811*, John Bernard says he discovered that an actor traveling through America could give readings to replenish a thin wallet:

> If an actor were unemployed, want and shame were not before him: he had merely to visit some town in the interior where no theatre existed, but "readings" were permitted; and giving a few recitations from Shakespeare and Sterne, his pockets in a night or two were amply replenished. This easy resource, in rendering the actor independent, compelled the [theatrical] manager to be generous, and put both on a footing which tended not a little to uphold their pursuit.[5]

Platform readings became increasingly popular with performers and audiences in the nineteenth and twentieth centuries, in part due to the popularity of Charles Dickens, whose solo platform performances we'll discuss shortly.

Perhaps we can better understand those past performers by comparing them to modern solo platform readers. For example, in the 1990s actress Claire Bloom traveled America with her one-person show titled *Then Let Men Know*, a program about Shakespeare's women, such as Juliet, Desdemona, and Portia. Ms. Bloom also presented performances based on women in novels by Virginia Woolf, Henry James, and Charlotte Bronte. A second illustration is Lynn Redgrave, who toured her one-person show, *Shakespeare for My Father: The Life and Times of an Actor's Daughter* in the 1990s and won a Tony Award nomination. In her performance, dedicated to her father, Sir Michael Redgrave, she performed some twenty of Shakespeare's men and women. Other modern solo platform readers include respected actors such as Charles Laughton, Alec Guinness, John Gielgud, Douglas Campbell, Christopher Plummer, Patrick Stewart, and Michael York. They are but a few of the twentieth-century actors who have brought literature and drama to life through solo performances, and no doubt they also found that their "pockets in a night or two were amply replenished."

Victorian audiences who distrusted the theatre because they suspected it was immoral could in good conscience attend monodramas that presented acceptable literature by respected writers such as Shakespeare, Dickens, Poe, and Twain. These solo performances overcame negative attitudes toward the theatre, thus helping build audiences for monodramas and multicharacter plays.

Of the nineteenth-century authors and platform performers, two in particular were remarkably successful, setting high artistic standards and winning large audiences. These two excellent solo performers helped establish elements of the modern monodrama and deserve our attention. We'll look briefly at them both: Charles Dickens and Mark Twain.

CHARLES DICKENS: ACTOR AND NOVELIST

The literary achievements of Charles Dickens (1812–1870), one of the great novelists of the nineteenth century, overshadow his theatrical work. Yet Dickens almost became a professional actor when he was twenty, and he once said that he thought "I should have been as successful on the boards as between them."[6]

Dickens was an enthusiastic actor who presented plays at his London home, the "Tavistock House Theatre." He attended theatrical productions often, and he was especially fond of English actor Charles Mathews (1776–1835), a protean actor who performed a number of characters in his series of solo plays called Mr. *Mathews at Home* from 1818 until his death. Influenced by Mathews, Dickens took on as many as twenty different characters during his extremely popular solo readings of his works in America, England, Scotland, and Ireland in the midnineteenth century.

Some Dickens scholars believe that insight gained from playing characters in public readings helped him create characters in his novels. Yet one has to wonder how Dickens found time to write novels, given his busy one-man international touring schedule. In the 1885 book *Charles Dickens as I Knew Him: The Story of the Reading Tours in Great Britain and America*, his friend and manager George Dolby says the Dickens readings can be counted in two categories: an unknown number of charitable readings during 1854–1858, and 423 readings from 1858 to 1870.[7]

Popularity of Dickens as a Performer

The Dickens solo performances were enormously popular—and profitable: In just one four-and-one-half-month period during 1867–68 he received around a quarter-million dollars, an impressive amount then and more remarkable if translated into today's dollars.[8] Dolby describes long lines of would-be ticket buyers and speculators in almost every city in which Dickens performed. In New York, for example, patrons from Philadelphia, Brooklyn, and Jersey City started lining up to buy tickets for a Wednesday performance before the Tuesday reading was over, staying in line all night in harsh December weather that brought sixteen to eighteen inches of snow.

Dickens' Acting Ability

Warmly praised for his ability to portray a large number of characters, Dickens evoked both tears and laughter with his one-man stage versions of The Christmas Carol, The Pickwick Papers, and others. Dickens was a careful actor who believed in through preparation, rehearsing every aspect of his performances from smallest gestures to skillful representation of various characters. In Charles Dickens: The Public Readings, Philip Collins details the novelist's careful notes for twenty-one of his readings—words to accent, changes in language for greater impact, even instructions for small effects such as sighs or pauses.[9]

The inherent drama in Dickens' novels and stories has led to modern stage adaptations of his works such as The Cricket on the Hearth, Great Expectations, The Pickwick Papers, A Tale of Two Cities, and the perennial favorite, The Christmas Carol, perhaps the most frequently adapted stories written. Many are highly acclaimed, such as Patrick Stewart's series of one-man shows of The Christmas Carol in New York during the 1990s, in which he played numerous characters. Musicals from Dickens' works include Oliver!, Nicolas Nickleby, and The Mystery of Edwin Drood. Dickens himself also leads to solo theatre. For example, audiences in the 1950s saw Dickens brought back to life by playwright-actor Emlyn Williams in a biographical monodrama called Emlyn Williams as Charles Dickens.

MARK TWAIN: THE TROUBLE BEGINS AT EIGHT

Mark Twain, pen name of Samuel Langhorne Clemens (1835–1910), was a popular journalist, raconteur, humorist, short story writer, novelist, and, in his latter years, an embittered satirist. He was also a highly successful solo performer, although he never seemed quite sure if he should think of himself as a lecturer, reader, actor, or some other sort of curiosity.

In October, 1866, I broke out as a lecturer, and from that day to this I have always been able to gain my living without doing any work. —Mark Twain

Twain, like some other performers before him, constructed his solo performance around personal travels. His advertisement for his "lecture" on his travels to the Sandwich Islands reflected the comic nature of Twain's one-person show:[10]

A SPLENDID ORCHESTRA
Is in town, but has not been engaged.

Also,

A DEN OF FEROCIOUS WILD BEASTS
Will be on exhibition in the next block.

MAGNIFICENT FIRE WORKS
were in contemplation for this occasion, but the
idea has been abandoned.

A GRAND TORCHLIGHT PROCESSION
May be expected; in fact, the public are privileged to expect whatever
they please.

Doors Open at 7 O'Clock

The Trouble Begins at 8 O'Clock

Twain's Performance Style

Readers of Twain's novels and short stories know that his materials were excellent. His performance style was equally powerful. Twain's one-person show was influenced by the comic techniques of Artemus Ward and the strikingly simple staging of Charles Dickens, whose performances he attended. He affected a particular character when he performed. His platform persona spoke slowly (some critics protested that he spoke too slowly) and had a carefully designed appearance with formal clothing, a mane of hair, and bushy eyebrows.

Instead of acting many characters, like Dickens, Twain developed a single basic character, insightful yet something of a bumpkin, with a distinctly colloquial speech pattern. Twain's character was bemused by the foibles of the human race. His style was carefully designed for comic value with a deliberate deadpan expression accompanied by a look of wonder when the audience laughed, a comic technique similar to that seen in later comedians such as Will Rogers, who assumed the persona of a drawling cowboy, or Jack Benny, who pretended to be a miser. Although his observations often were biting and sardonic, Twain created a likable character whose pungent comments were acceptable.

TWENTIETH-CENTURY CREATORS
OF THE MODERN MONODRAMA

The celebrated actor Otis Skinner to solo performer Ruth Draper: "Neither age nor custom can take away my amazement at you. . . . But I have one serious quarrel with you. You carry one of the largest supporting companies I have seen. In each of your sketches you have surrounded yourself with a group of actors whose art is perfect and whose presence is compelling and hypnotic. And yet you pay them *nothing*!! Do you think that is fair?"

The evolution of the monodrama owes much to its early predecessors, which we've already discussed, but monodramas you see today have fresh styles and techniques that were established by twentieth-century theatre artists who contributed new realism, truth, and artistic styles, making the one-person play an increasingly popular, respected theatrical form. Twentieth-century leaders include such notable solo performers and writers as Cissie Loftus, Dorothy Sands, Ruth Draper, Charles Laughton, Cornelia Otis Skinner, Hal Holbrook, Emlyn Williams, James Whitmore, Henry Fonda, George C. Scott, John Gielgud, Ian McKellen, William Luce, Alec McCowen, Ben Kingsley, Roy Dotrice, Samuel Beckett, Jane Wagner, Lily Tomlin, Spalding Gray, Eric Bogosian, Paul Linke, Shane McCabe, Jane Martin, and Anna Deavere Smith, although that list easily could be doubled or tripled to include other significant monodramatists.

Space limitations prevent discussing all this century's monodramatists—the form has become so popular that an examination of modern solo performers could fill a book—so we here select a few playwrights and actors who made significant contributions through their dedication to one-person performances. We look in particular at monodramatists who represent various artistic approaches and have advanced the form.

BEATRICE HERFORD:
SHOWING THE IMPORTANCE OF ORDINARY LIFE

English actress Beatrice Herford (1868–1952) started her career in London in 1895 and was active through the 1920s, receiving warm praise from such contemporaries as playwright Bernard Shaw, actress Ellen Terry, novelist Henry James, and critic-author Alexander Woollcott. Herford's monodramas reflected the transition from Victorian extravagance to modern theatre's realistic style with psychological insights into lifelike people in recognizable situations. Her performance technique was quiet and restrained, in contrast to the oratorical bombast that marked the elocutionary style of her predecessors, more dependent on truth than on purple stylization.

Unlike her predecessors who presented exaggerated characters and situations, Herford performed sketches of ordinary life such as *A Lady Packing*, *The Book Agent*, *Telephoning the Doctor*, and *A Sociable Seamstress*. Critics praised Herford's performance style for its "incomparable wit and finesse" and described it as sharp, impish, and even occasionally malicious.

Herford was a significant model for twentieth-century monodramas. Her decision to dramatize the lives of realistic people in contemporary situations, rather than the overblown comic monodramas of earlier centuries, was echoed by later monodramatists such as Ruth Draper, Cornelia Otis Skinner, Eugene O'Neill, Hal Holbrook, Lily Tomlin, Samuel Beckett, Lanford Wilson, Eric Bogosian, and Anna Deavere Smith. You can find two collections of Herford's works: *Monologues* (1908) and *Beatrice Herford's Monologues* (1927). After she retired she established an amateur theatre in Wayland, Massachusetts, one of her several adopted homes.

RUTH DRAPER: THE CHARACTER ACTRESS

It is the audience that must supply the imagination. All I can do myself is to make the audience give it to me. I suppose my work needs more of this than most acting does, for I give people no help in the way of scenery, lighting, or stage effects. Long ago a man who knew a great deal about the theatre told me that the old advice to actors "You must put it over" was wrong. What is really important is not to put anything "over," but to bring the audience up onto the stage and into the scene with you. It is they who must give you even more than you give them in the way of imagination and creative power. Once this was the great fact of the drama. It needed no artificial effects; it simply brought the actor and the audience together and fused their minds and feelings in an imagined reality. The great trouble today is that so much entertainment—cinema, radio, television—makes people passive, deadens their imagination. It gives them so much that it leaves them with nothing to give in return. In the older drama—Oriental, Greek, Medieval, Shakespearean—the audience had to supply what wasn't there. The poet or dramatist gave the cues, and of course his genius lay in giving the right ones; but it was from the audience that the experience of truth had to come. —Ruth Draper*

Perhaps the single most influential contributor to the modern monodrama, Ruth Draper (1884–1956) enjoyed a long, successful career, performing in such countries as Europe, Africa, India, Asia, New Zealand, Central and South America, as well as throughout the United States. She set standards for twentieth-century monodramatists who followed her. Numerous solo performers such as Cornelia Otis Skinner, Joyce Grenfell, Pat Carroll, Lily Tomlin, and Bettye Ackerman have acknowledged their debt to Draper's inspiring trailblazing innovations. In further homage to Draper's artistry, Patrizia Norcia has developed her own monodramas based on Draper's work.

Draper started with small one-person "recitals" at private social events in the early 1900s, and she began her professional career as a monodramatist in 1920. She was active until 1956, dying quietly at home shortly after she had, at age 72, successfully performed a young girl in her monodrama *In a Railway Station of the Western Plains*, in which she evoked almost twenty other characters, at the Playhouse in New York.

Draper as Playwright and Performer

Draper wrote her own scripts, designing them for her special ability as a protean actress to perform a number of widely different roles in one play. By evoking the presence of (unseen) others on stage, she stimulated the audience's imagination to see a stage full of lively characters as if she surrounded herself, as popular actor Otis Skinner said, "with a group of actors whose art is perfect and whose presence is compelling and hypnotic."

Draper's talents as playwright and actress earned the admiration of audiences, critics, and notable theatre artists such as playwrights Edward Sheldon and Thornton Wilder and actors John Gielgud and Laurence Olivier. She was awarded honorary degrees from Smith College and the universities of Cambridge and Edinburgh, and for her artistic achievements she was made a Commander of the British Empire.

Critic Kenneth Tynan said that Draper's solo performances were "the best and most modern group acting" he had seen because "her large supporting cast, which exists only at her fingertips, is so much more satisfactory than any which makes the vulgar mistake of being visible." In "The Art of Ruth Draper," Muriel McKenna describes a definitive tribute to Draper's skill: "Even the usually bored stagehands in the wings forgot their crap games for a while to watch this lone woman make a large audience see and feel a whole group of people on the stage and a full stage setting. Surely this was almost the ultimate in compliments to her artistry!"[11]

Draper's Theatrical Storytelling Techniques

Draper differed from her predecessors in significant theatrical storytelling techniques and techniques. Instead of melodramatic exaggeration, her plays had a quiet, almost homespun quality in depicting the apparently ordinary problems that become major events in human life; and instead of safer broad comedy, she preferred poignant drama of everyday life. Draper was especially noted for creating realistic, dimensional characters facing problems that members of her audience could easily recognize. Today's monodramatists such as Jane Martin, Lanford Wilson, Samuel Beckett, and Eric Bogosian show a similar focus on intimate, familiar life.

Influences on Draper's Art

Draper's scripts and performance techniques were influenced by three major forces. One was monodramatist Beatrice Herford, discussed previously. A second influence on Draper's decision to portray a number of characters in her one-person shows was Lotta Crabtree (1847–1924), a popular and colorful American star who performed as many as six different roles in a given play (and who also was an all-around entertainer who acted, danced, sang, and played the banjo). Third, Draper was influenced by the minimalist staging techniques of Oriental theatre, which awoke the audience's imagination by using only a few carefully selected props or scenic devices to imply the environment.

Draper performed against simple stage curtains, using perhaps a single chair or table. Her costumes were equally austere, and she cleverly used a single shawl to depict various characters' ages, ethnic backgrounds, and personalities. Her shawls became her trademark, and when she died her casket was adorned not by flowers but with a collection of shawls.

The Character Actress

Draper described herself as a *character actress*, writing challenging short and full-length monodramas for herself to perform. In them she sought to show insights through subtle events. Titles suggest content, such as *Opening a Bazaar*, *Showing the Garden*, *Three Generations*, *Mr. Clifford and Three Women*, and *An English House Party*. Her scripts often had a distinctive international favor as she played several characters in a single work, speaking various languages and capturing personalities associated with a number of different countries.

Three Breakfasts illustrates Draper's versatility. She played three breakfast scenes, starting as a happy, young, new bride, then becoming a bitter middle-aged woman who matches her husband's infidelity with an affair of her own, and ending as an old woman who is tolerant, patient, and loving in a restored marriage. Throughout each scene the audience is aware of the presence of others, especially children. The only staging requirement is a dining room table and a straight chair.

Three Generations is typical of Draper's interest in poignant human problems. In it she performed three Jewish women—an eighty-year-old grandmother, her forty-seven-year-old daughter, who suffers from health problems, and her nineteen-year-old granddaughter—in a New York court of domestic relations. Present, but invisible, are the judge and court reporter. Conflict is clearly established: The grandmother and mother want the judge to order the grand-daughter to stay home to provide for her two older relatives, but the young girl wants to put them in a home for the elderly so she can marry and move far away to the west. Draper played each character testifying to the judge. She used her trademark shawl to depict characters: The old woman wears a black shawl over her head, the mother places it around her shoulders, and the daughter discards the shawl. Scenery consisted of only a plain office chair without arms.

Stimulating the Audience's Imagination

What I had as a child I've never lost—the child's ability to pretend: to be what he imagines he is. If you give yourself completely to what you pretend you are, you will convince other people it exists, and only then. —Ruth Draper

In *The Art of Ruth Draper*, Zabel tabulates each of Draper's monodramas according to the number of characters she played, ranging from one to six, plus the number of unseen characters she evoked in the audience's imagination, as many as twenty-four in a single one-person performance.[12] Draper's ability to evoke a number of other characters with whom her diverse personalities interacted gave her solo performances the texture of multicharacter plays.

Perhaps most significantly, Draper made audience members become active participants by stimulating their imaginations to see and hear the rest of the characters. She also pantomimed props, again stimulating the audience's imagination as one critic pointed out: "Watch the way she stirs a phantom cup of coffee with a phantom spoon. It tells you things about the way human beings stir coffee which we never noticed before, and the discovery interests us and fascinates us."[13]

You can hear Draper on a series of record albums called *The Art of Ruth Draper*. She also is the subject of monodramas such as *Cast of Characters* and *The World of Ruth Draper*. Draper wrote her scripts for performance and varied them according to her perception of audience reaction. Although she did not seek publication, you can find a collection of her monodramas in Zabel's *The Art of Ruth Draper*.

CORNELIA OTIS SKINNER: ELABORATE, FULL-SCALE PRODUCTIONS OF MONODRAMAS

Singer, actress, author, and playwright, Cornelia Otis Skinner (1901–1979) was the daughter of the well-known actor Otis Skinner (1858–1942), who performed a number of romantic roles such as Hajj in *Kismet*. Trained by Jacques Copeau, an influential French actor and producer, Skinner started her acting career in her father's company in 1921 and later began her work as a solo performer.

Skinner's Interest in Full-Scale Productions of Monodramas

Skinner, like Draper, was a protean performer whose acting ability allowed her to create various distinctive and dimensional humans as well as other imaginary onstage characters, unseen but present in the audience's imagination. But where Draper combined small scenes to make holistic short monodramas with minimalist settings, Skinner developed full dramatic productions with elaborate staging and costuming. Skinner wrote her own monodramas in the 1930s, specializing in full-length historical scripts such as *The Wives of Henry VIII*, *The Empress Eugenie*, and *The Loves of Charles II*, playing various characters in well-developed scenes. She also adapted the novel, *Edna His Wife* (1937), into a full-length monodrama, using techniques similar to Draper's to play three generations of women.

Skinner's most ambitious monodrama was *Paris '90* in the early 1950s, a full-length, three-act monodrama in fourteen scenes that brought to life fictional and historical Parisian women at the turn of the century. *Paris '90* was a complex production with the full-scale costumes, scenery, music, and lighting typically associated with multicharacter plays.

Skinner did not limit herself to monodramas. She performed in Broadway multicharacter plays such as George Bernard Shaw's *Candida* and Oscar Wilde's *Lady Windermere's Fan*. She also wrote (with Samuel Taylor) and acted in a multicharacter comedy of manners, *The Pleasure of His Company*, which was typical of her literate and sophisticated wit. She is author of a number of delightfully entertaining books such as *Our Hearts Were Young and Gay*, which relates her adventures traveling abroad. In the 1960s, after forty years of performances, Skinner quit solo performing.

Skinner's Goals
Distressed by anemic solo "recitations" that diminished the artistic quality of the one-person show, Skinner wanted the monodrama to rise to high artistic standards. She especially deplored pretentious social gatherings to hear readings of poetry or literature. In an article in the *New York Times* (Dec. 27, 1931) called "Monologue to Theatre: An Exponent of a Solo Art Discusses Its Rise from the Ranks of the Amateurs," Skinner argued that the monodrama should not be considered the province of "an army of artistically inclined ladies" presenting recitations at "their local parish house" but that it should "approach more and more to theatre until it is recognized as the legitimate offspring and not a left branch of the concert stage." Her passionate argument allows us to infer some of the problems that dominated solo performances in the 1920s and 30s.

THE BIOGRAPHICAL MONODRAMA:
HAL HOLBROOK'S MARK TWAIN TONIGHT!
Undoubtedly the best-known monodrama of the 1950s and 1960s was Hal Holbrook's *Mark Twain Tonight!* Holbrook wrote it for himself to perform, and both script and performance reflect Holbrook's painstaking attention to detail, love of his subject, and commitment to perfection. Thousands of audience members saw Twain spring to life in a brilliant tour de force, and they forever after thought of the celebrated American humorist as Holbrook presented him. Holbrook made Twain a colorful figure with a fierce walrus mustache and flowing white hair, dressed in an immaculate creamy-white linen suit, holding a cigar, speaking in a raspy voice that often sounded like a rusty gate, with impeccable comic timing and mastery of the pause, and sharing insight into Tom Sawyer and Huck Finn while also making dryly sardonic comments on the state of the world and humanity's foibles.

The Creation of Mark Twain Tonight!
Holbrook started working on bringing Mark Twain to life when a college student in the late 1940s. Initially it was a two-person touring program called *Great Personalities* with his wife, Ruby, playing the role of an interviewer asking questions of the famous novelist. When she retired from theatre, Holbrook narrowed his vision to what was to became a major solo performance.

Holbrook carefully researched Mark Twain, avoiding secondary sources and instead relying on Twain's published materials, interviews with people who knew Twain or had seen him on the lecture circuit, and a rare film of the novelist. Holbrook then tried out small scenes in intimate clubs, using audience response to guide him through revising his script and honing performance techniques. He developed more than six hours' worth of materials, allowing him to vary his program according to audience reactions and giving his performance more spontaneity than if he kept to one basic script. Holbrook decided to recreate Twain when Twain was 70 years old to allow him to show the author's full career from successful humorist to a man dealing with new insight into truth as he contemplates lost dreams.

Productions and Honors

Show business veterans told Holbrook that his one-person Twain couldn't possibly succeed in New York—"An actor alone on stage for two hours? Nonsense!"—and recommended he add other actors, major production effects, costumes, and even songs and dances. Undaunted by such bleak predictions, Holbrook held to his vision and proved that the "experts" were wrong.

Holbrook had developed *Mark Twain Tonight!* into a full-evening one-person program by 1954 and it quickly became a success. In 1956 he presented *Twain* at the Cherry Lane Theatre in New York and then began taking it on tour. He was invited to appear on television programs such as the *Ed Sullivan Show*, and in 1959 he presented it at the 41st Street Theatre in New York, receiving what the *New York Herald Tribune* called "the most scintillating set of reviews since *My Fair Lady*."

Holbrook enjoyed successful American and international tours, then returned to Broadway in 1966 and again in 1977. CBS television presented *Mark Twain Tonight!* in 1967. It was made into record albums and published in book form, won the creator the coveted Tony Award for Best Actor in 1966, and was the actor's springboard into numerous major stage, motion picture, and television performances.

Holbrook's Preparations to Perform Twain

I was privileged to be Holbrook's host at a college performance. His painstaking preparation was a lesson in professionalism. Holbrook arrived at the theatre some four hours before curtain and spent the time carefully applying makeup, mustache, and wig and getting into costume, all clearly part of the actor's process of becoming the character. He was totally focused on the forthcoming production, and there was no small talk or idle social amenities. As he laid out his makeup and costume, one had the impression of an old-world master craftsperson at work putting his materials in order.

Holbrook's concentration was remarkably intense as he focused his energies on *becoming* Twain to the point that during his lengthy preparation one could hear his voice changing and watch him evolving from a quick-thinking, brisk, and erect young man into a more deliberate, reflective, and bent older man. At various times during his preshow preparation he left the dressing room to check the stage setting and lighting—each time giving instructions to the crews in an increasingly Twain-like manner—and his knowledge of theatrical production and his demand for perfection stretched the capabilities of the stage and lighting personnel.

One of the most memorable qualities of *Twain* was Holbrook's ability to perform—to *be*—a seventy-year-old man who played young Tom Sawyer, Huck Finn, or other characters. It was a triple play, Hal Holbrook to Mark Twain to Huck Finn and others. Holbrook says he started by creating the character, such as Huck, then doing him again while *thinking* Mark Twain. Equally unforgettable was Holbrook–Twain's apparent spontaneity, as if Twain were in a freewheeling memory mode, continually thinking of new ideas. Although Holbrook's performance was carefully scripted and rehearsed, it seemed freshly created that evening. Holbrook's performance had masterful comic timing, yet Twain's pauses were clearly motivated.

You can hear Holbrook's *Mark Twain Tonight!* on various Columbia recordings. One is taken from the CBS television special; others are from actual stage performances. You also can read a published version of the script in *Mark Twain Tonight!—An Actor's Portrait*, by Hal Holbrook.

WAVES OF BIOGRAPHICAL MONODRAMAS FOLLOW HOLBROOK'S MARK TWAIN TONIGHT!

The success of Holbrook's *Twain* prompted a surprisingly large number of biographical monodramas, more than we can list here. Most focus on well-known individuals, primarily politicians, writers, artists, and actors. One of the more prolific authors of biographical monodramas is William Luce, who has written *The Belle of Amherst* (Julie Harris playing the poet Emily Dickinson, winning a Tony in the process), *Currer Bell, Esq.* (Charlotte Brontë's pen name; a radio production starring Julie Harris; later revised as a stage play called *Brontë*); *Zelda* (wife of novelist F. Scott Fitzgerald, performed by Lane Yorke and later by Piper Laurie; revised as *The Last Flapper*), and *Lillian* (playwright Lillian Hellman, performed by Zoe Caldwell). With a clear sense of self-parody, Luce also wrote *Luce Women*, a multicharacter comedy about a playwright who creates one-person shows, in which Zelda Fitzgerald shows Emily Dickinson how to dance a racy Charleston and Lillian Hellman teaches Charlotte Brontë how to smoke. More recently, Luce wrote *Barrymore*, the life of the colorful and celebrated American actor John Barrymore, for which Christopher Plummer won a Tony Award as best actor.

Other representative biographical monodramas include *Mister Lincoln* (Roy Dotrice as the sixteenth American president), *The World of Ruth Draper* (Ruth Brinkman recreating the artistry of the famed monodramatist), *An Unpleasant*

Evening with H. L. *Mencken* (David Wayne playing the dour American writer), *Clarence Darrow* (Henry Fonda as the colorful trial lawyer), *My Gene* (Colleen Dewhurst playing Charlotta Monterey, wife of Eugene O'Neill), A *Lovely Light* (Dorothy Stickney as the poet Edna St. Vincent Millay), and *Diversions and Delights* (Vincent Price performing the playwright Oscar Wilde).

SPALDING GRAY: THE AUTOBIOGRAPHICAL PERSONA

Spalding Gray, a solo performer of and for the 1990s, opens new possibilities for the monodrama. Instead of dramatic enactments of fictional characters developed by monodramatists such as Herford, Draper, or Skinner, Gray's materials are directly autobiographical, or what he calls "creative confession." Gray is both author and performer of more than a dozen different solo shows, starting with *Sex and Death to the Age of* 14 (1979), that he has performed in New York, toured successfully in many cities in America and numerous other countries, and made into films you may see on television. His particular strength is a total revelation of self, both strengths and weaknesses, with an associative style he likens to Thomas Wolfe's novels such as *Look Homeward, Angel* that are written with carefully designed digressions from the basic storyline into other areas.

Gray doesn't limit himself to monodramas. He studied with Richard Schechner's Performance Group, was a cofounder of the Wooster Group, performed roles in professional multicharacter plays such as the stage manager in a Lincoln Center production of Thornton Wilder's *Our Town*, and appeared in various motion pictures such as *The Killing Fields*, *Clara's Heart*, and *Beaches*. His experiences in *Our Town* and *The Killing Fields* provide him materials for his monodramas such as *Swimming to Cambodia* and *Monster in a Box*. More personal experiences also are subjects for his solo creations. For example, *Gray's Anatomy* is his story of problems with his left eye, and *It's A Slippery Slope* has an exterior shell about his desire to master downhill skiing, but it frames more intimate details such as holding his infant son.

An Earlier Autobiographical Monodramatist:
An Evening with Quentin Crisp

Gray popularized the autobiographical monodrama as he developed and honed his one-person shows, but perhaps an earlier monodramatist deserves credit for initiating the self-examination form. Quentin Crisp's *An Evening with Quentin Crisp* started in 1975 as impromptu, unscripted talks and over a period of years grew into a more formalized pattern, although always constructed with apparently randomly selected anecdotes. His material stems from his self-proclaimed unconventional lifestyle, and he urges audience members to develop a personal style that fits their own needs. His opening sentences reflect his *Evening* approach:

I've been forbidden to describe this occasion as straight talk from a bent speaker. Let's call it a consultation with a doctor who is more ill than you are.

Crisp's popular book *The Naked Civil Servant* contributed to his stage success by making him known, but Gray entered the one-person arena with no comparable support.

Spalding Gray's Monster in a Box

Illustrative of Gray's particular innovative autoperformances is his solo show *Monster in a Box* (1990). The dominant stage property is the "monster," a 1,900-page manuscript for his novel, *The Impossible Vacation*. His one-person script is based to some degree on his novel, which in turn focuses on his experiences, including performing the Stage Manager in Wilder's *Our Town*. In his solo performance Gray reenacts that role, showing the tension he felt between enjoying Wilder's character contrasted with his desire not to lose his actor's concentration in the face of theatrical misfortunes. Gray's monodrama includes a reenactment of one particular performance of *Our Town*: while Gray's stage manager character was talking about the townspeople, a young boy in the cast vomited violently, leaving Gray with the actor's no-win nightmare whether to continue his lines as if he hadn't noticed or to ad lib a response.

Gray's Monodramatic Technique

Spalding Gray's solo performances are curiously circular, mirror image reflecting mirror image. At first they appear autobiographical: as you watch you are aware of Gray, but as he brings you into his movie or stage roles, you see a double image, Gray the actor in other plays shown by Gray. Then you perceive the artist's stage persona, who is fashioned to reveal insight into the artist's inner self—or is the insight into the theatrical persona? At what point does the development of a stage persona inhibit the disclosure of the inner self? It is a hypnotic series of movements.

Gray explains his technique in the author's note of the published version of *Swimming to Cambodia*, a monodrama based on his experiences playing an aide to the American ambassador in Roland Joffe's movie *The Killing Fields*, which was set in Cambodia during the Vietnam war:

> *Swimming to Cambodia* evolved over two years and almost two hundred performances. It was constructed by recalling the first image in my memory of each previous performance, so it evolved almost like a children's "Round Robin" game in which a phrase is whispered around and around a circle until the new phrase is stated aloud and compared with the original. The finished product is a result of a series of organic, creative mistakes—perception itself becoming the editor of the final report.[14]

OTHER AUTOBIOGRAPHICAL MONODRAMATISTS

Gray's innovation prompted other monodramatists to create personalized one-person shows. We mention three here who acknowledge their indebtedness to Gray's candid self-examination of personal secrets. All deal with sensitive subjects that had deep emotional impact on their author-actors. Paul Linke fought to come to grips with the death of his wife, who died of cancer when she was 37, and his *Time Flies When You're Alive* (1987) is both an intimate revelation about her death and an affirmation of life. Shane McCabe's *No Place Like Home* (1988) is a journey through childhood by a survivor of incredible child abuse. Chazz Palminteri's *A Bronx Tale* (1989) is a protean performance involving the author-actor's difficult life in what he calls the school of the streets. New autobiographical solo plays continue to find their way on stage.

This quick trip through monodramatic history, with apologies for those not discussed, suggests that the solo play may have been the first form of theatre when part of prehistoric society. Certainly it has made significant contributions to theatrical art through its artistic accomplishments and innovations, and all theatre participants and fans must relish its victories over those who sought to limit or even outlaw our art.

NOTES

1. E. D. Blodgett and Roy Arthur Swanson, trans., *The Love Songs of the Carmina Burana* (New York, NY: Garland Publishing, Inc., 1987), xiv.

2. George Taylor, ed., *Plays by Samuel Foote and Arthur Murphy* (Cambridge: Cambridge University Press, 1984), 16.

3. Percy Fitzgerald, *Samuel Foote: A Biography* (New York, NY: Benjamin Blom, Inc., 1972), 65.

4. Gerald Kahan, *George Alexander Stevens and The Lecture on Heads* (Athens, Georgia: The University of Georgia Press, 1984), 1.

5. John Bernard, *Retrospections of America: 1797–1811* (New York, NY: Benjamin Blom, Inc., 1969), 263.

6. John Forster, *The Life of Charles Dickens* (Philadelphia, Lippincott, 1873), 380.

7. George Dolby, *Charles Dickens as I Knew Him: The Story of the Reading Tours in Great Britain and America* (1866–1870) (New York: Haskell House Publishers, Ltd., 1970), 450–451.

8. Alexander Woollcott, *Mr. Dickens Goes to the Play* (Port Washington, NY: Kennikat Press, 1922), 23.

9. Philip Collins, ed., *Charles Dickens: The Public Readings* (London: Clarendon Press, Oxford, 1975).

10. Fred W. Lorch, *The Trouble Begins at Eight: Mark Twain's Lecture Tours* (Ames, Iowa: Iowa State University Press, 1968), 27-28.

11. Muriel McKenna, "The Art of Ruth Draper," in *Women in American Theatre*, eds. Helen Krich Chinoy and Linda Walsh Jenkins., (New York: Theatre Communications Group, 1987), 116.

12. Morton Dauwen Zabel, *The Art of Ruth Draper* (London: Oxford University Press, 1960), 390–391.

13. Ibid., p. 100.

14. Spalding Gray, *Swimming to Cambodia* (New York: Theatre Communications Group, 1985), xv–xvi.